*The Comic Genius of
Dr. Alexander Hamilton*

The Comic Genius of Dr. Alexander Hamilton

Robert Micklus

The University of Tennessee Press

KNOXVILLE

Copyright © 1990 by The University of Tennessee Press / Knoxville.
All Rights Reserved. Manufactured in the United States of America.
First Edition.

Chapter 2 is based on an article, "The Delightful Instruction of
Dr. Alexander Hamilton's *Itinerarium,*" that first appeared in
American Literature, 60 (1988), 359–84. It is used by permission.

The paper in this book meets the minimum requirements of the
American National Standard for Permanence of Paper for Printed
Library Materials. ⊚ The binding materials have been chosen for
strength and durability.

Library of Congress Cataloging in Publication Data

Micklus, Robert.
   The comic genius of Dr. Alexander Hamilton / Robert Micklus.—
1st ed.
    p.   cm.
   Includes bibliographical references.
   ISBN 0-87049-633-6 (cloth: alk. paper)
   1. Hamilton, Alexander, 1712–1756. 2. Hamilton, Alexander,
1712–1756—Humor. 3. Authors, American—Colonial period, ca.
1600–1775—Biography. 4. Annapolis (Md.)—History—Colonial period,
ca. 1600–1775—Biography. 5. Physicians—United States—Biography.
I. Title. II. Title: Comic genius of Doctor Alexander Hamilton.
PS763.H35Z78   1990
818′.109—dc20   89-22468   CIP

For Loquacious Scribble

My thanks to Leo Lemay, Norman Grabo, and Lee Campbell Sioles for their time and advice, and to Carol Orr and the staff at the University of Tennessee Press for publishing this book the old-fashioned way.

Contents

	Introduction	[1]
ONE	A Life of Liberality	[19]
TWO	Delightful Instruction: The *Itinerarium*	[75]
THREE	"A Few Crude Thoughts": Periodical Pieces	[113]
FOUR	"The Sempiternal Comedy": *The History of the Tuesday Club*	[141]
	Epilogue	[199]
	Bibliography	[203]
	Index	[217]

Illustrations

Mr Neilson's Anger Restrained
by Philosophy [35]

Loquacious Scribble Esqr, Secretary
and Orator of the Ancient and
Honorable Tuesday Club [44]

Jonathan Grog Esqr, Poet Laureat
and Master of Ceremonies of the
Tuesday Club [50]

The Phrensy of a Baltimore Bard [117]

Mr Secretary Scribble Delivering
a Speech in Club [169]

The Second Grand Anniversary
Procession [189]

The Honorable Nasifer Jole Esqr
Wears the Cap of State [190]

Introduction

From the 1950s well into the 1970s, the primary objective in American studies was to reconstruct our past to help explain our present identity as a nation. Anyone who makes a living teaching American literature today owes a real debt to, among others, Henry Nash Smith, Perry Miller, R. W. B. Lewis, Richard Slotkin, and Sacvan Bercovitch, whose works have helped to make American literature a legitimate field of literary study. But because it tends to foster a nationalistic—or, as some prefer to say, exceptionalistic—bias, the reconstructionist approach has never been particularly congenial or appropriate to the study of colonial authors such as Dr. Alexander Hamilton, who clearly thought of themselves as British writers and whose works can be best appreciated against the backdrop of eighteenth-century British culture, not by placing them into one American strain or another. As Carl R. Kropf asserts, the nationalistic emphasis in American studies has affected the study of American literature to such a degree that "our view of early American literature is seriously incomplete and distorted."[1] To this day we continue to have little use for many

---

1. "The Nationalistic Criticism of Early American Literature," *Early American Literature*, 18 (1983), 20.

colonial authors unless we can prove that they were the first American authors to do this or that or unless we can somehow plant them firmly upon the virgin, adamic, or regeneratively violent land that lay before them to discover the origins of ourselves through them. The most unfortunate consequence of this approach has been that the literary effusions of many lesser authors who can be mainstreamed into one American studies theory or another have often been overestimated while the achievements of more proficient though solidly British colonial authors such as Hamilton have been only passingly mentioned and sometimes completely ignored in studies of colonial literature and culture.[2]

Over the past decade, however, scholars have increasingly called for a more inclusive approach to the study of American literature in general and colonial literature in particular. In a review of Bercovitch's *Puritan Origins of the American Self,* Alan Trachtenberg was among the first to state that the practice of interpreting American literature according to "an inherited mode of thought seems to foreclose investigation into the precise social and cultural tensions that figure in the making of specific texts... [and] to risk diminishing the writing to cultural pathology."[3] Michael J. Colacurcio has argued that the reconstructionist approach makes the study of literary history "less a function of that endlessly com-

---

2. As general editor of the new *Cambridge History of American Literature,* Bercovitch has tried to counteract this tendency by founding those volumes upon a principle of "dissensus" (see his essays, "America as Canon and Context: Literary History in a Time of Dissensus," *American Literature,* 58 [1986], 99–107, and "The Problem of Ideology in American Literary History," *Critical Inquiry,* 12 [1986], 631–53). Annette Kolodny has also stressed the need for pluralism in redefining the American literary canon in "The Integrity of Memory: Creating a New Literary History of the United States," *American Literature,* 57 (1985), 291–307.

3. "The Writer as America," *Partisan Review,* 44 (1977), 474.

Introduction

plicated process by which reality... generates texts by encounters of consciousness and intention and more a matter of that simpler procedure of creating some putative whole by reading texts in sequence.... The trick," Colacurcio concludes, "is to continue to believe in the historical significance... of American literature without positing the existence of America as a metaphysical entity, with so many abstract possibilities, each somewhere filled up, and all mutually relational."[4] And the most outspoken critic of the nationalistic bias in American studies over the past decade, William C. Spengemann, has persuasively argued in a series of articles that "the history of what we call American literature... is inseparable from the history of literature in English as a whole."[5] Spengemann has argued particularly well for a complete reappraisal of colonial literature, stating that we need to begin by replacing the nationalistic titles "colonial American" or "early American" literature with a more accurate title—he suggests "the literature of British America"—and that we need most of all to accept and appreciate "the extension of British culture into the New World and the resulting impact of this extension on that culture."[6]

---

4. "Does American Literature Have a History?" *Early American Literature*, 13 (1978), 130.

5. "American Things/Literary Things: The Problem of American Literary History," *American Literature*, 57 (1985), 477. Spengemann has developed his argument in various essays, but see esp. "What is American Literature?" *The Centennial Review*, 22 (1978), 119–38; "Discovering the Literature of British America," *Early American Literature*, 18 (1983), 3–16; "American Writers and English Literature," *English Literary History*, 52 (1985), 209–38; and "American Literary History: Some Still Unanswered Questions," *Early American Literature*, 23 (1988), 90–100.

6. "Discovering the Literature of British America," 7–8. Spengemann makes a good case for deleting "American" from the title of colonial studies, but the title he has chosen in its place is unnecessarily cumbersome. I use "colonial literature" throughout this study, which implies the same thing to anyone reading a book on a colonial writer of British America.

As Philip F. Gura observes, however, most studies of colonial literature continue to view it as a prologue to nineteenth-century literature, to stress exceptionalism, to focus predominantly upon the literature of New England, and to concentrate upon religious language and symbol to the exclusion of other forms of discourse.7 Scholars such as Spengemann and Colacurcio, Gura asserts, have remained

> prophets without honor in the field. Because of the intellectual glamor that attaches to studies of the connections between colonial American literature and the American Renaissance (and beyond), and, similarly, to those that continue to insist on the exceptionalism of American culture from the days of settlement on, there is little chance to stem the tide of books and essays that derive from what many historians would consider highly problematic assumptions.8

As Gura suggests, we need to examine more fully the influence of British culture upon colonial literature, north and south, and to study more closely the works of authors outside of what has been perceived as the Puritan New England roots of American literature. Studies such as Richard Beale Davis's *Intellectual Life in the Colonial South* and J. A. Leo Lemay's *Men of Letters in Colonial Maryland* have pointed the way toward a mine of literature that

---

7. "The Study of Colonial American Literature, 1966–1987: A Vade Mecum," *William and Mary Quarterly*, 3rd Ser., 45 (1988), 308. A good review of the various strains in colonial literary criticism appears in Michael Clark, "The Subject of the Text in Early American Literature," *Early American Literature*, 20 (1985), 120–30.

8. "The Study of Colonial American Literature," 317. For the problematic nature of this approach to cultural historians, see Gene Wise, "'Paradigm Dramas' in American Studies," *American Quarterly*, 31 (1979), 293–337, and Laurence Vesey, "The Autonomy of American History Reconsidered," *American Quarterly*, 31 (1979), 455–77.

Introduction

deserves further research. In the Chesapeake area alone, Gura points out, writers such as Richard Lewis, James Sterling, and particularly Dr. Alexander Hamilton "epitomize the need for scholars of colonial American literature to consider in depth the transfer of culture from England to America."[9]

Like most colonial writers of his generation, Hamilton had little wish to think of himself as anything but British. He lived in Annapolis, Maryland, from 1738 to 1756, at a time when, according to Richard L. Merritt, most colonists were

> viewing their land more and more as a part of [the] British community. Viewed in terms of integrative and disintegrative processes, the British image during the twenty years from 1735 to 1754 reflected a slight weakening of Anglo-American ties of community, while at the same time the colonial image reflected substantial decreases in sentiments of separate identity and, by implication, an increased readiness to accept symbolic ties to the mother country.[10]

Merritt's point is well substantiated by a lengthy dispute carried in the *Maryland Gazette* during the spring of 1748 between a "Native Marylander" and "Americano-Britannus." Even the Native Marylander states that, although proud of his native status, "he

---

9. "The Study of Colonial American Literature," 320. Lemay provides excellent introductory chapters to the lives and works of these authors in *Men of Letters in Colonial Maryland* (Knoxville, 1972). A good essay concerning the opportunities for study in southern colonial literature is Robert D. Arner, "Literature in the Eighteenth-Century Colonial South," *The History of Southern Literature*, ed. Louis D. Rubin, Jr. (Baton Rouge, 1985), 34–47.

10. *Symbols of American Community, 1735–1775* (New Haven, 1966), 123. Jack P. Greene and J. R. Pole further develop this point in their introduction to *Colonial British America: Essays in the New History of the Early Modern Era* (Baltimore, 1984), 15; see also Gura, "The Study of Colonial American Literature," 338.

[5]

prides himself more in being descended from British Ancestors."[11] Like Americano-Britannus, Hamilton identified himself as an inhabitant of "British America"[12] and as a British author who wrote according to British standards. Although several well-meaning colonialists, including myself, have given him the honor of being the first American author to do one thing or another, that is not a distinction that he would have found particularly ingratiating.[13]

The things Hamilton appreciated most about colonial life were the things that reminded him of British culture. He concluded his travel diary, the *Itinerarium,* by stating that "as to politeness and humanity" he found colonial life equally crude wherever he went, "except in the great towns where the inhabitants are more civilized, especially at Boston."[14] After five years of living in Maryland, he was pleased that he could still tell a friend in Edinburgh that he had managed to "retain alittle of [his] native honesty" and had not "quite lost [him]self in the American Subtilty and selfishness."[15] Rather than embrace the ways of his adopted land,

---

11. *Maryland Gazette,* Apr. 13, 1748. In the June 29 issue of the *Gazette,* Hamilton published a dream vision concerning its contributors, in which he sided with Americano-Britannus (see Lemay, "Hamilton's Literary History of the *Maryland Gazette," William and Mary Quarterly,* 3rd Ser., 23 [1966], 282–84).

12. *The History of the Tuesday Club,* ed. Robert Micklus (Chapel Hill, 1990), 1:453. All subsequent page references to this edition (abbreviated *HTC* in citations) are provided in the text. (References are to Hamilton's manuscript pages, included in the margins of this edition.)

13. I attributed to Hamilton his share of American "firsts" in my first essay on him, "Dr. Alexander Hamilton's 'Modest Proposal,'" *Early American Literature,* 16 (1981), 107–32.

14. *Gentleman's Progress: The Itinerarium of Dr. Alexander Hamilton, 1744,* ed. Carl Bridenbaugh (Chapel Hill, 1948), 199. All subsequent page references to this edition (abbreviated *Itin.* in citations) are provided in the text.

15. AH to John B——r, Nov. 6, 1743, Hamilton Letter Book, Maryland Historical Society, Dulany Papers, MS 1265. Unless otherwise noted, all sub-

Introduction

he sought to imitate British culture by establishing the Tuesday Club of Annapolis, which met from 1745 to 1756. His narrative of the club's misadventures, *The History of the Tuesday Club,* "the finest humorous work of colonial America,"[16] is an original and innovative narrative that at the same time splendidly imitates British prose models. As Kropf points out, colonial scholars need "to bear in mind that originality was not a particularly prized quality" during the eighteenth-century: "imitation not only of the classics of the distant past but also of more recent acknowledged masters, was admirable and desirable."[17] And especially desirable to the many colonial authors who, like Hamilton, sought not to escape but to preserve British culture.

Hamilton would surely have exercised his "gelastic humor"[18] had he known that he might someday be identified as an early American author or even as a southern colonial author. Five years after his arrival, he still referred to Maryland—albeit half jokingly—as a "Barbarous and desolate corner of the world" (AH to Robert Hamilton, Sept. 29, 1743).[19] Numerous passages in the *Itinerarium* echo that sentiment, yet Hamilton is usually placed at the center of the "Golden Age of Chesapeake Culture." That

---

sequent letters to or from Hamilton appear in the Hamilton Letter Book and are cited parenthetically in the text.

16. Lemay, *Men of Letters in Colonial Maryland,* 213.
17. "The Nationalistic Criticism of Early American Literature," 24.
18. Hamilton frequently indulges what he calls his "gelastic humor" (from the Greek "to laugh") in *The History of the Tuesday Club.*
19. Hamilton's letter is addressed to his cousin Robert (not to his brother Robert), physician and professor of anatomy and botany at the University of Glasgow. As Kerry A. Trask has shown, Hamilton's perception of life in the colonial South was fairly typical during the eighteenth century ("Double Exposure: A Look at Southern Identity in the Eighteenth Century," *Southern Studies,* 22 [1983], 146–67).

phrase has been equally useful and misleading in studies of southern colonial literature. It has usefully suggested that from 1740 to 1770 there were many talented writers in the Chesapeake area, in many ways as proficient as the writers in colonial New England during the same period. But it has misleadingly created a sense of regionalism that did not exist at that time for writers such as Hamilton. Hamilton chose to settle in Annapolis because it was there that he could count on establishing a profitable medical practice; like many of his circle, he would have been just as happy—if not happier—living in the "more civilized" world of colonial Boston or Philadelphia.

Like many colonial authors of his generation, Hamilton fits into neither a national nor a regional strain. As Richard L. Bushman observes, however, we no longer "need to isolate a native strain or to prove that the colonies were capable of bearing civilization";[20] neither, one might add, do we need any longer to isolate a southern strain or to prove that the colonial South was capable of competing with colonial New England. That has been done, and done admirably well. Hamilton, to be sure, was a keen observer of colonial life, and this study looks closely at his observations. But he observed colonial life as a British gentleman, so rather than place him at the center of one American or southern strain, this study seeks to place him at the center of eighteenth-century British culture, to demonstrate the influence of that culture upon the variety of genres he employed, and especially to reveal the rich comic strains in his literature.

Hamilton was a comic writer, not a writer of comedy. Comedy is and always has been a form of drama; the comic is that which

---

20. "American High-Style and Vernacular Cultures," *Colonial British America: Essays in the New History of the Early Modern Era*, 348.

Introduction

provokes laughter, and a comic author is one who provokes laughter through satire, burlesque, irony, farce, humor, wit—sometimes, as in Hamilton's case, all of these and more in one comic work. That distinction has unfortunately become blurred by most studies of eighteenth-century satire, which have generally defined satire in opposition to what has been inappropriately referred to as "comedy." James Sutherland's position concerning satire and "comedy" remains the standard one: "The writer of comedy," Sutherland argues,

> accepts the natural and acquired folly and extravagance and impudence which a bountiful world provides for his enjoyment; he is a sort of human bird-watcher, detached and attentive.... This does not mean that [he] has no standards or norms... [but that] his attitude to those who fall short of them appears to vary from an amused tolerance to a cheerful or even delighted acceptance.

The satirist, however, is a sort of human bird basher: "confronted with the same human shortcomings as the writer of comedy," Sutherland states,

> he is driven to protest. For him those are not matters for pure contemplation; they must be exposed, held up to derision or made to look as hideous as he believes them to be.... Just as some people feel a sort of compulsion, when they see a picture hanging crooked, to walk up and straighten it, so the satirist feels driven to draw attention to any departure from what he believes to be the truth, or honesty, or justice. He wishes to restore the balance, to correct the error; and often, it must be admitted, to correct or punish the wrongdoer.[21]

This opposition between the harsh, judgmental nature of satire versus the good-humored, nonjudgmental nature of comedy has,

---

21. *English Satire* (1958; rpt. Cambridge, 1967), 3–4.

with few variations, been maintained in eighteenth-century criticism for the past thirty years.[22]

Most studies of eighteenth-century satire further stress that a break between comedy and satire—and a movement from satire to comedy—occurred by mid century. According to Ronald Paulson, "almost all theories of comedy before the eighteenth century equate comedy and satire, and most theories since then rigorously distinguish... ridicule (satiric laughter) from the risible or ludicrous (comic laughter)."[23] "The movement away from satire [to comedy]," Thomas Lockwood explains, "appears as a gradual change from the moral definition of the author-audience relationship to a social one; the writer comes increasingly to identify with the audience on the basis of social likenesses... rather than moral principles."[24] Other studies emphasize other factors that contributed to this change, but most point to the same general conclusion that a shift from satire to comedy occurred by mid century.

Critics have placed themselves in the awkward position of emphasizing, on the one hand, this shift from satire to comedy while admitting, on the other hand, that the two continued to be joined

---

22. Ronald Paulson, e.g., argues that when one set of values in a literary work "becomes normative and so causes a judgment to be made of the other, it tends toward satire"; "comedy," however, "makes no judgment, merely balancing the two orders of experience as equally acceptable" (*Satire and the Novel in Eighteenth-Century England* [New Haven, 1967], 16); in *The Fictions of Satire* (Baltimore, 1967), Paulson similarly states that "by the comparative intensity of [its moral stance] satire is distinguishable from the freer, more careless and permissive world of comedy" (p. 4). Leon Guilhamet has more recently provided much the same distinction in *Satire and the Transformation of Genre* (Philadelphia, 1987), 7–8.

23. *Satire and the Novel in Eighteenth-Century England*, 16.

24. "The Augustan Author-Audience Relationship: Satiric vs. Comic Forms," *English Literary History*, 36 (1969), 649.

Introduction

together during the eighteenth century. Paulson, for instance, observes that "the antithetical theories of comedy and satire... continued to flourish side-by-side after the middle years of the century, causing a fearful confusion in the statements of intention among novelists."[25] The eighteenth-century practice of using "comedy" and "satire" in much the same sense, P. K. Elkin observes, is "confusing to modern readers" because "we are inclined to assume that there is a radical distinction between the two modes, even while admitting that they are sometimes so closely interwoven in one work... that it is difficult to say where one ends and the other begins." Elkin then argues, however, that satire was generally perceived as being "more severe" than comedy during the eighteenth century and as "fundamentally [more] judicial." To substantiate his argument he points out that "satirical" is defined in eighteenth-century dictionaries as "severe, sharp, biting" and "comical" as "jocose, merry, diverting."[26]

The real source of confusion here is the tendency of modern critics to equate "comical" with "comedy." If we look at the way *comedy* was normally used during the eighteenth century (to indicate a form drama), it becomes apparent that satire, or severe wit, was perceived as central to comedy and that no such line of demarcation existed between satire and comedy by mid century.[27]

---

25. *Satire and the Novel in Eighteenth-Century England*, 69–70.
26. *The Augustan Defence of Satire* (Oxford, 1973), 13–14.
27. Countless eighteenth-century definitions indicate that satire was equated with severe wit. John Tillotson, e.g., wrote that "a little wit, and a great deal of ill nature will furnish a man for Satyr" ("The Folly of Scoffing at Religion," *Works* [London, 1696], 41); Addison called satire a "barbarous and inhuman Wit" (*Spectator*, No. 23; *The Spectator*, ed. Donald F. Bond [Oxford, 1965], is the source of this and subsequent quotations from the *Spectator)*; "Wit, cohabiting with Malice," Samuel Johnson wrote, "had a Son named *Satyr*" (*Rambler*, No. 22); and in the most comprehensive essay

[11]

"*Le ridicule*," René Rapin wrote, "*est ce qu'il y a de plus essencial à la Comedie*"; comedy, Joseph Addison plainly stated, "ridicules Persons by drawing them in their proper Characters"; since it is the business of comedy to copy the foolish and vicious originals of the age, John Dennis argued, "'tis the Business of the Copies to expose, and satyrize, and ridicule those foolish and vicious Originals"; "the general idea of Comedy," Hugh Blair wrote later in the century, "as a satyrical exhibition of the improprieties and follies of mankind, is an idea very moral and useful."[28] As these comments obstinately suggest, eighteenth-century writers and critics continued to link satire and comedy not out of confusion but because they continued to perceive satire and ridicule as basic ingredients of comedy. With a healthy dose of satire and ridicule, eighteenth-century comedy provides implicit judgments of unwelcome behavior; as Robert M. Torrance observes, however, the important point to remember is that "in a comedy of any distinction the character mocked for his insufficiencies, vices, and foibles is never delimited by them."[29]

---

on eighteenth-century comic terms, Corbyn Morris defined satire as "*a witty and severe Attack of mischievous Habits or Vices*" (*An Essay towards Fixing the True Standards of Wit, Humour, Raillery, Satire, and Ridicule* [London, 1744], 37).

28. *Oeuvres* (Paris, 1725), 2:196–97; *Spectator,* No. 249; *The Stage Defended* (1726), in *The Critical Works of John Dennis,* ed. Edward Niles Hooker (Baltimore, 1939–1943), 2:313; *Lectures on Rhetoric and Belles Lettres* (London, 1783), 2:528–29. Dennis had also written earlier that "Laughter [ridicule] is the Life, and the very Soul of Comedy. 'Tis its proper Business to expose Persons to our View, whose Views we may shun, and whose Follies we may despise; and by shewing us what is done upon the Comick Stage, to shew us what ought never to be done upon the Stage of the World" (*Defence of Sir Fopling Flutter* [1722], *Critical Works,* 2:245).

29. *The Comic Hero* (Cambridge, Mass., 1978), 5.

Introduction

The point that so many scholars of eighteenth-century satire have argued is an equally important one but, I think, wrongly stated. What changed during the eighteenth century was the perception of the comic, a change that affected satire *and* comedy. When critics talk about the shift toward comedy in the eighteenth century, they are actually talking about an important shift in notions of the comic that placed increasing prominence not upon "comedy" but upon that form of the comic identified in the eighteenth century as humor. It was a shift toward what Stuart M. Tave calls "the amiable humorist."[30]

The early eighteenth century was an unusually sociable age, and its emphasis on making man sociable to man brought with it a changing perception of the comic and the proper objects of laughter or ridicule.[31] Most early eighteenth-century writers believed that the moral function of comedy had been perverted during the Restoration, when virtue and infirmity had become objects of ridicule. Ridicule, Addison remarked, had been used "to laugh Men out of Virtue" and to mock our infirmities; "the Talent of turning Men into Ridicule and exposing to Laughter those one Converses with," he concluded, "is the Qualification of little ungenerous Tempers."[32] By mid century, however, laughter was perceived as natural rather than ungenerous and sociable

---

30. *The Amiable Humorist: A Study in the Comic Theory and Criticism of the Eighteenth and Early Nineteenth Centuries* (Chicago, 1960). Richard Keller Simon provides an excellent discussion of the comic at mid century in the first two chapters of *The Labyrinth of the Comic: Theory and Practice from Fielding to Freud* (Tallahassee, Fla., 1985).

31. As Tave demonstrates, "laughter" and "ridicule" were often used interchangeably during the eighteenth century (*The Amiable Humorist*, esp. pp. 28–39).

32. *Spectator*, No. 249.

rather than alienating. Laughter, more and more writers argued, gave a relish to social life, provided one chose the proper objects of laughter: folly rather than virtue, incongruity and affectation rather than inferiority or natural infirmity.

A particularly good example of the movement toward what Tave calls "the good-natured ideal" and the increasing emphasis on the positive social aspects of laughter by mid century is an essay on ridicule that appeared in the February 17, 1748, issue of the *Maryland Gazette*.[33] "Ridicule," the essay states,

> is an universal Ingredient in Conversation.... This seems to be the Salt and Seasoning of Life, giving to it a grateful Relish; hence we find it as natural for one Man to laugh at another, and to be mightily excited to Mirth, upon the Character and Behaviour of his Neighbour, as it is to breath the common Air....
>
> A Genius, or Turn for Ridicule, varies widely in different Men: Some dull Mortals there are, who may be said to have no perceptible Talent this Way, whose Life is one continued Series of lumpish Stupidity, or Moroseness. These Fellows are incapable of discerning the Ridiculous in any Thing; and tho' such Clod pates never join in the Laugh, yet by their stubborn Solemnity, or Blockishness, they afford a good Fund of Mirth for those around them. These are such inflexible Fellows as do not understand Railery.

The attitudes expressed in this essay, which would have been deplored earlier in the eighteenth century, had become commonplace by mid century. This changing perception of laughter was

---

33. See ch. 1 of *The Amiable Humorist*. Some of the phrases in this essay are reminiscent of passages from *The History of the Tuesday Club*, so it is tempting to identify Hamilton as the author of the piece. But his sentence structure is generally more loose than that in this essay; moreover, whenever he spoke of ridicule in the *History* he used it in a pejorative sense. This essay might well have been written, however, by another member of the Tuesday Club.

Introduction

accompanied by a changing perception of humor and by the emergence of humor as a distinct comic mode. Before the eighteenth century a "humorist"—a character whose behavior was controlled by his or her dominant humor—was a source of ridicule; early in the eighteenth century, however, a character's humor became a positive sign of his or her comic individuality. "*Humour* is from Nature," Congreve observed, and "shews us as we *are*."[34] Perhaps the best example of the changing attitude toward "humorists" in the early eighteenth century is Sir Roger de Coverley, "a great Humourist in all parts of his Life," Addison wrote, because his "Virtues, as well as Imperfections, are as it were tinged by a certain Extravagance, which makes them particularly his."[35] By mid century a "humorist" was increasingly perceived not simply as a character dominated by his or her humor but as the creator of humorous characters, a comic writer who, as Tave states, "relished varieties of character" and who chose the "liberal and expansive" comic mode of humor, which "emphasized variety and the individual rather than conformity and the class."[36] To this day, "humor seeks, not to expunge folly, but to condone and even to bless it, for humor views folly as endearing, humanizing, indispensable," and the humorist is a comic writer who recognizes the foolishness of others as well as himself or herself and offers "forgiving acceptance of foolishness in the whole human family of which we are all members."[37]

---

34. *Concerning Humour in Comedy* (1695), in *Theories of Comedy*, ed. Paul Lauter (New York, 1964), 209.
35. *Spectator*, Nos. 101, 106.
36. *The Amiable Humorist*, 97, 96.
37. Morton Gurewitch, *Comedy: The Irrational Vision* (Ithaca, N.Y., 1975), 9; George McFadden, *Discovering the Comic* (Princeton, 1982), 253. It is worth pointing out that these definitions of humor are much the same as Sutherland's definition of "comedy."

The Comic Genius of Dr. Alexander Hamilton

The movement toward humor in the eighteenth century affected comedy as well as satire, which is evident by the growing distinction early in the century between "true" and "false" satire. According to Addison and Steele, true satire was good-natured and generally placed; false satire was ill-natured and personal.[38] As Paulson argues, Addison and Steele's definition of true satire—essentially "another satiric weapon with which to discredit their opponents, the Tory satirists"—was "clubbable," not divisive.[39] The reaction against "false satire" was in part politically motivated but also in part "a rejection of the basic satirical assumptions of clear and fixed standards . . . against which the aberrations of man are measured with a just severity"[40] and a response to the growing sentiment that one's individual and natural aberrations should be regarded humorously, not maliciously. By mid century, Paulson asserts, "post-Addisonian writers . . . no longer accept[ed] the distinction between true and false satire: a satire *was* an ill-natured attack on a particular enemy of the satirist." Addison's notion of "true satire" had, in other words, been replaced by "comedy."[41]

Even if we more appropriately argue that humor, not "comedy," replaced satire by mid century (which is essentially Tave's argument), there is still something too neat about these distinctions, something that does not jibe with one's reading of Fielding's *Tom Jones* or Hamilton's *History of the Tuesday Club*. Is it really true that "comedy"—or humor, for that matter—*replaced*

---

38. See *Spectator*, Nos. 23, 35, 355, 451, and *Tatler*, No. 242.
39. *The Fictions of Satire*, 217, 219.
40. *The Amiable Humorist*, 24.
41. Paulson, *Satire and the Novel in Eighteenth-Century England*, 61; *The Fictions of Satire*, 218; see also Lockwood, "The Augustan Author-Audience Relationship," 651.

Introduction

satire by mid century? Is it true that by mid century writers typically regarded all satire as "an ill-natured attack on a particular enemy"? Is it true that "good-natured" and "satire" were incompatible, or have we perhaps misunderstood what writers such as Addison and Steele meant by good-natured? And is it true, as Tave and others have suggested, that satire's companion, wit, was *replaced* by its comic antithesis, incongruity, by mid century?[42]

Hamilton's comic works, written between 1746 and 1756, suggest instead that the many comic theories and comic forms prevalent during the first half of the eighteenth century were operating in full force, conjointly, by mid century. In the *Itinerarium* Hamilton ridicules the crude manners of colonial Americans and attacks various individuals such as Dr. William Douglass and the Reverend George Whitefield, yet the dominant comic mode in that work is humor. In his periodical pieces he broadly satirizes such things as curiosity and illiteracy but also sharply satirizes such figures as the Reverend Thomas Chase. And in *The History of the Tuesday Club* he defines "true satire" much as Addison did earlier in the eighteenth century: "The true Character and Spirit of Satyr," he says, "always ought to be generally placed, and rather seem to laugh in a pleasant manner, than grin with a Sneer"; if so, it "will never fail to please, with such as have any humor at all" (1:462). This passage demonstrates the continued appeal of Addison's definition of true satire at mid century as well as the changing perception of laughter and the growing relation between satire and humor, not "comedy." What is particularly striking about this passage, however, is that it comes from an au-

---

42. Tave in fact argues that the growing emphasis on humor and incongruity brought "the degradation of wit" by mid century (*The Amiable Humorist*, 43–87).

thor who also delighted in writing personal satiric attacks. That sort of satire exists side by side in the *History* with a broader and more genial satire. But even the more genial satire, good-natured as it is because it laughs at the universal passions and follies of all men and women rather than ridicules individuals, is not innocuous. Both types of satire thrive in *The History of the Tuesday Club* along with humor and a host of humorous characters who are embraced rather than satirized for their humors. And running throughout the entire narrative is an endless assortment of eighteenth-century wit, amicably coexisting with comic incongruity. Hamilton's *History* makes abundantly clear that wit was flourishing at mid century, as were both types of satire, and humor, and numerous other comic modes. What makes the comic works of Hamilton so sumptuous—or, one could argue, those of Fielding or Sterne—is not that one comic form had faded by mid century and had been replaced by another or that he chose one comic form over another, but that he lived at a time that witnessed an extraordinary convergence of comic forms and that brought an extraordinarily rich comic blend to his literature. Like his life and the age he lived in, Hamilton's comic world was inclusive, not restricted to one strain or another. The present study seeks to provide an itinerary to the expansive world of his life and literature.

CHAPTER ONE

A Life of Liberality

Alexander Hamilton had the good fortune to be born in Edinburgh on September 26, 1712, at the dawn of the period when Edinburgh would become one of the intellectual centers of Europe. He was born into the large family of Mary Robertson Hamilton and William Hamilton,[1] professor of divinity and prin-

---

1. The children of Mary Robertson Hamilton (c. 1675–Jan. 22, 1760) and William Hamilton (1669—m. Feb. 25, 1698—d. Nov. 12, 1732) were: Dr. John Hamilton (1698—m. Mary Scott, 1722—d. Mar. 28, 1768); Jean Hamilton (c. 1700—m. Hugh Cleghorn, July 6, 1718—d. *post* 1750); William Hamilton (c. 1701–*post* 1750); Ann Hamilton (1703—m. the Reverend John Horsely—d. 1735); Gavin Hamilton (1704—m. Helen Balfour, Mar. 24, 1732—d. Jan. 1, 1767); Margaret Hamilton (c. 1706—m. William Tod, May 16, 1731—d. 1743); the Reverend Robert Hamilton (May 19, 1707—m. Jean Hay, Mar. 31, 1745—d. Apr. 3, 1787); Janet Hamilton (c. 1710—m. the Reverend David Smith, Feb. 14, 1731—d. Jan. 7, 1773); Dr. Alexander Hamilton (Sept. 26, 1712–May 11, 1756); and the Reverend Gilbert Hamilton (May 16, 1715—m. Isabel Smith, Jan. 9, 1742, then Margaret Craidie, Mar. 4, 1754—d. May, 1772 (sources include George Hamilton, *A History of the House of Hamilton* [Edinburgh, 1933]; Hew Scott, *Fasti Ecclisiae Scoticanae* [Edinburgh, 1915–50]; Henry Paton, *The Register of Marriages for the Parish of Edinburgh, 1701–1750* [Edinburgh, 1908]; John Philip Wood, *Ancient and Modern State of the Parish of Cramond* [Edinburgh, 1794]; James MacVeigh, *The Scottish Nation* [Dumfries, Scotland, 1889]; Robert Chambers, *A Biographical Dictionary of*

cipal at the University of Edinburgh. William Hamilton was known for his "piety, learning, and moderation" during his tenure at the University of Edinburgh and during his five terms as leader of the General Assembly, "where his wisdom and moderation procured him the esteem of contending parties."[2] In public and in private life, "there was a sincerity, a kindness, and a vein of liberality in all he did and said."[3] Mary Hamilton's letters to her son display much the same sensibilities. Particularly at a time when moralists and pedagogues were encouraging greater communication between parents and children—and urging fathers especially to converse more frequently with their children and to supervise their upbringing[4]—there can be little doubt that both parents played active roles in helping to shape Hamilton's character. From them and from the experience of growing up in a large family he learned many things, but most of all an ethic of liberality that would serve him well as an adult.

Hamilton received a superb education at Edinburgh. After studying Latin at the High School of Edinburgh, he attended the University of Edinburgh and received his medical degree from

---

Eminent Scotsmen [Glasgow, 1835]; R. W. Innes Smith, *English-Speaking Students of Medicine at the University of Leyden* [London, 1932]; the Hamilton Letter Book; and Lemay, *Men of Letters in Colonial Maryland*, 213–56, which is also the best introduction to Hamilton's life and literature).

2. Wood, *Cramond*, 81; John Ramsay, *Scotland and Scotsmen in the Eighteenth Century* (Edinburgh, 1888), 1:227.

3. Ramsay, 1:228.

4. For a good discussion of the changing relationship between parents and children in eighteenth-century Scotland, see Craig Beveridge, "Childhood and Society in Eighteenth-Century Scotland," *New Perspectives on the Politics and Culture of Early Modern Scotland*, ed. John Dwyer, Roger A. Mason, and Alexander Murdoch (Edinburgh, 1980), 265–90.

that institution in 1737.⁵ In education as in other matters, eighteenth-century Scots shared "an almost religious attachment to their inherited ideal of a culture in which the general should take precedence over the particular and the whole over the parts."⁶ All students at the university enrolled in a broad curriculum, taking courses in Latin and Greek, philosophy, and the exact sciences. Courses in chemistry or mathematics drew heavily upon contemporary philosophy; indeed, "philosophy" itself meant not only courses in logic or metaphysics but also courses in natural philosophy and moral philosophy, the latter of which—the study of the ethical principles upon which conduct should be based— was of particular interest to eighteenth-century Scots.⁷

The dominant intellectual force at the University of Edinburgh from the day his father began teaching there to the day Hamilton received his medical degree was Sir Isaac Newton.⁸ To view Newton simply as the guru of empirical, inductive reasoning is to triv-

---

5. *List of the Graduates in Medicine in the University of Edinburgh from 1705 to 1866*, ed. S. Lewis (Edinburgh, 1867), 3. Like his older brother, Robert (appointed professor of divinity at Edinburgh in 1754 [see Scott, *Fasti Ecclisiae Scoticanae,* 1:46]), Hamilton probably entered the High School of Edinburgh at age nine (the usual age at that time) and spent the next four or five years there studying the Latin curriculum. (For further information on the high school curriculum at Edinburgh, see Alexander Law, *Education in Edinburgh in the Eighteenth Century* [London, 1965], 58–78.)

6. George Elder Davie, *The Democratic Intellect: Scotland and Her Universities in the Nineteenth Century* (Edinburgh, 1961), 4.

7. William R. Brock, *Scotus Americanus: A Survey of the Sources for Links between Scotland and America in the Eighteenth Century* (Edinburgh, 1982), 20.

8. A particularly good discussion of Newton's influence upon the undergraduate curriculum at Edinburgh is A. L. Donovan, *Philosophical Chemistry in the Scottish Enlightenment: The Doctrines and Discoveries of William Cullen and Joseph Black* (Edinburgh, 1975), 34–48.

ialize and even to misunderstand his influence upon students such as Hamilton. As I. Bernard Cohen argues, there has been "an excessive insistence on an out-and-out empirical foundation of seventeenth-century science."[9] Newton employed empirical observation not to establish but, in an almost biblical sense, to reveal universal truths. At the core of Newton's teaching lay his belief that "God created and directs nature through intelligent design"[10] and that the mathematical principles he revealed by experimentation served to reveal the divine order of things. Newtonianism was essentially conservative in nature, providing a "model and justification for social order, political harmony, and liberal, but orthodox, Christianity."[11] Empiricism for empiricism's sake, on the other hand, eventually led to the kind of radical materialist positions associated with the major *philosophes* in the second half of the eighteenth century.[12] That distinction was important to students such as Hamilton and the reason why he could later admire Newton and yet, without contradicting himself, denounce all rank "empyricks."[13]

---

9. *The Newtonian Revolution* (Cambridge, 1980), 8.

10. Richard H. Popkin, "Divine Causality: Newton, the Newtonians, and Hume," *Greene Centennial Studies: Essays Presented to Donald Greene in the Centennial Year of the University of Southern California*, ed. Paul J. Korshin and Robert R. Allen (Charlottesville, 1984), 45.

11. Margaret C. Jacob, "Newtonianism and the Origin of the Enlightenment," *Eighteenth-Century Studies*, 11 (1977), 1.

12. Jacob argues this point well in "Newtonianism and the Origin of the Enlightenment," 6–7.

13. Hamilton refers to "the illustrious Newton" in the *Itinerarium* (p. 86), and whimsically—but fondly—attributes "that great propensity in human nature, to unite and form into Clubs" to Newton's theory of attraction in *The History of the Tuesday Club* (1:25). His disdain for all "empyricks," or "physicall hereticks," runs throughout the *Itinerarium*, but see esp. pp. 65, 116–17.

A Life of Liberality

Newton's influence was especially felt by the medical faculty at the University of Edinburgh, all of whom had studied at Leyden under the man most responsible for applying Newton's principles to medicine, Hermann Boerhaave.[14] Established in 1726, the medical program at Edinburgh was patterned after the Leyden model, and by 1731, when Hamilton was enrolled in that program,[15] the University of Edinburgh could boast that it provided the most comprehensive medical education in all of Britain. Most students regularly attended lectures on anatomy and surgery, chemistry, botany, pharmacy, and the theory and practice of medicine.[16] Hamilton was most influenced by Alexander Monro, professor of anatomy, whose *Osteology* (1726), a study of the bones, provided the groundwork for Hamilton's thesis on bone disease, *De Morbis Ossium* (1737).[17] Having himself founded the Medical Society of Edinburgh in 1731, Monro encouraged Hamilton and five of his colleagues to organize a society for medical students. This society met informally for the first time in 1734 and helped to pave the

---

14. For Newton's influence upon Boerhaave, see G. A. Lindeboom, *Hermann Boerhaave: The Man and His Work* (London, 1968); the best discussion of Boerhaave's influence upon the medical faculty at Edinburgh is E. Ashworth Underwood, *Boerhaave's Men at Leyden and After* (Edinburgh, 1977), 88–125.

15. Monro's class lists indicate that Hamilton was enrolled in his anatomy class in 1731 (see Brock, *Scotus Americanus*, 178).

16. For further information on the sort of medical training Hamilton received at Edinburgh, see David Hamilton, *The Healers: A History of Medicine in Scotland* (Edinburgh, 1981), 109–24, and Donovan, *Philosophical Chemistry*, 34–48. In the *Itinerarium* Hamilton states that he "learnt pharmacy" in the shop of David Knox, an Edinburgh surgeon (p. 49), but he probably learned a good deal, too, from Andrew Plummer, professor of medicine and chemistry who essentially taught nothing but pharmaceutical chemistry (Donovan, 36–37), and from the *Edinburgh Pharmacopoeia* (3rd ed., 1737).

17. The complete title of Hamilton's thesis was *Specimen medicum inaugurale, de morbis ossium ipsam substantiam afficientibus, ex causis internis oriundis.*

way for the more formal organization, three years later, of what is now one of the most prestigious medical societies in Europe, the Royal Medical Society of Edinburgh.[18]

Hamilton also joined other societies of a more clubical nature during his years in Edinburgh. The eighteenth century, it has often been pointed out, was among other things the great age of clubbing. Most eighteenth-century British writers believed in "the innate sociability of man and the naturalness of society," and Scottish philosophers in particular increasingly stressed gregariousness as a social ideal during the eighteenth century.[19] In Scotland, where the Union of 1707 threatened to undermine the traditional fabric of Scottish culture, clubs served to maintain a sense of national identity and social cohesion and, at the same time, to promote an awareness of the social and intellectual changes taking place at home and throughout Europe. Scots therefore gravitated toward clubs during the 1720s and 1730s; in Edinburgh especially, a multitude of small clubs—usually no more than fifteen members each—began to proliferate while Hamilton was attending the university. These clubs generally represented a cross section of Edinburgh society: the list of members at any given club often included artisans and doctors, lawyers and ministers, Presbyterians and Episcopalians, even Whigs and Jacobites. Members typically met to discuss Scottish history as well as contemporary issues and developments—and, of course, to eat, drink, and simply enjoy each other's company. They had their fun, but the Edinburgh clubs took their clubbing seriously and established elaborate laws

---

18. Two useful studies of this society are James Gray, *History of the Royal Medical Society 1737–1937* (Edinburgh, 1952), and J. D. Holmes, "Early Years of the Medical Society of Edinburgh," *University of Edinburgh Journal*, 5 (1968), 333–40.

19. Gladys Bryson, *Man and Society: The Scottish Inquiry of the Eighteenth Century* (Princeton, 1945), 148, and 148–72.

to govern the conduct of their members. Social clubs were viewed not just as frivolous gatherings of select coteries but as models by which Scottish society as a whole could measure its character as well as its progress.[20]

Hamilton was likely a welcome visitor at several Edinburgh clubs, and he was a regular member of at least one—the Whin-Bush Club. Born in the shire of Clydsdale—a necessary prerequisite for admission—he became a standing member of the Whin-Bush Club in 1737. At his initiation the club's poet laureate, Allan Ramsay,[21] solemnly pronounced the following verses:

As this furz is ever green,
And this pipe streight white & clean,
May your virtue still remain,
Unchang'd, chast, pure, without a Stain,
Which, if it does, then you we dub,
A Standing member of this Club. (*HTC*, 1:59)

---

20. Davis D. McElroy surveys eighteenth-century Scottish clubs in three studies: "The Literary Clubs and Societies of Eighteenth-Century Scotland" (diss. Univ. of Edinburgh, 1952); *A Century of Scottish Clubs* (Edinburgh, 1969); and *Scotland's Age of Improvement: A Survey of Eighteenth-Century Literary Clubs and Societies* (Pullman, 1969). Less comprehensive than McElroy's studies but more sharply focused on the cultural significance of eighteenth-century Scottish clubs are portions of two excellent articles by Nicholas T. Phillipson: "Culture and Society in the 18th-Century Province: The Case of Edinburgh and the Scottish Enlightenment," *The University in Society: Europe, Scotland, and the United States from the 16th to the 20th Century*, ed. Lawrence Stone (Princeton, 1974), 2:407–48; and "The Scottish Enlightenment," *The Enlightenment in National Context*, ed. Roy Porter and Mikulas Teich (Cambridge, 1981), 125–47.

21. Best remembered for having influenced the revival of Scottish vernacular poetry in the eighteenth century, Ramsay delivered in club not just his own verses but many of the Scottish folk songs he collected in *The Tea-Table Miscellany* (1723–37) (Allan H. MacLaine, *Allan Ramsay* [Boston, 1985], 123). Hamilton and the Tuesday Club members later recited in club several of the songs included in Ramsay's collection.

"Tho these verses at first hearing, seemed to me alittle upon the hobbling order," Hamilton observed, "yet in my opinion they Contain an excellent Sentiment, and a most beautiful metaphor and Similie" (*HTC*, 1:59).

Hamilton describes the foundation of the Whin-Bush Club early in *The History of the Tuesday Club*, where he satirizes his country's preoccupation with Scottish history by tracing the Whin-Bush Club back to the halcyon days of the venerable Fethelmach, "famed for having Invented the high Relished Dish of Cock-a-leekie, and the Comfortable Soup called Dads and Blads" (1:43–44). Since Fethelmach's day, the club could boast of such distinguished personages as Daniel Hog, treasurer from 1569 to 1574, when he was "expelld the Club, for perpetual Sleeping and loud Snoring," and Laughlan McLean, master of ceremonies from 1534 to 1552, when he was "deposed for whoring" and succeeded by Jervais Fuckater, who was "killd by an Irishman for excessive farting and belching in Company" (1:65). According to Hamilton, "this venerable Club was under a total eclipse, during the Cromwellian usurpation, ... for Oliver Imagining that they were a Cabal a plotting against the common wealth, seized their Records, and dispers'd them, but, ... on the happy restoration of the Steuart family, ... those valuable records were again restored, to this venerable Club" (1:47).

Hamilton's account of the Whin-Bush Club's foundation is as whimsically distorted as most of the "historical" events in *The History of the Tuesday Club*. Yet the Whin-Bush Club did in fact exist by 1720, when Ramsay himself petitioned for membership in verse as follows:

> Native of Clydsdale's upper Ward
> Bred Fifteen Summers there,
> Tho, to my Loss I'm no a Laird

A Life of Liberality

> By Birth, my Title's fair
>   To bend wi' ye and spend wi' ye
>   An Evening, and gaffaw,
>   If Merit and Spirit
>   Be found without a Flaw.[22]

Like the Easy Club, which Ramsay had previously helped to form, the Whin-Bush Club met once a week to share a simple plate of bread and cheese, to discuss the latest events, and to indulge in a spirited guffaw or two. During the intense political divisiveness of the times, however, they wisely resolved not to talk politics,[23] an example that Hamilton and the other members of the Tuesday Club later had the good sense to follow on American shores.

Shortly after Ramsay dubbed him a standing member of the Whin-Bush Club, Hamilton put his affairs in order and, after a brief stay in London, headed for Maryland during the winter of 1738.[24] He left Scotland for practical reasons: his family was so large that his father, although modestly well off, could not afford

---

22. *The Works of Allan Ramsay*, ed. Burns Martin and John W. Oliver, Scottish Text Society (Edinburgh, 1945), 1:211. McElroy discusses Ramsay's admission into the Whin-Bush Club in *Scotland's Age of Improvement*, 14.
23. Phillipson, "Culture and Society in the 18th-Century Province," 434. For further details on how the members of the Whin-Bush Club generally passed an evening, see *HTC*, 1:51–67.
24. Letters from his sister Janet and his brother Gilbert ("an affable, easy, plain man" and minister of Cramond [Wood, *Cramond*, 82]) indicate that Hamilton stayed in London before leaving for Maryland (Janet [Hamilton] Smith to AH, Apr. 29, 1743; Gilbert Hamilton to AH, July 19, 1749). In a letter dated July 23, 1739, his mother informed him of a "terrible huriecane we had in this part of ye world, one ye 13 of Januarie," indicating that he probably left Britain before the end of 1738. After receiving his M.D. in 1737, Hamilton might well have spent some time in Holland studying under Boerhaave. His name does not appear, however, in Smith's *English-Speaking*

to provide for his fifth-born son; moreover, the country was so poor that his chances of establishing a profitable medical practice in Scotland were slim. Hamilton was part of a migration of Scottish physicians who came to America in the eighteenth century for "the simple [reason] . . . that Scotland was a poor country in which too many competed for too few resources."[25] Following the example of his oldest brother, John, who had established a successful practice in Maryland by 1738,[26] Hamilton chose the better prospects for professional advancement that America offered.

Hamilton arrived in Maryland at the beginning of what is now commonly referred to as the golden age of Chesapeake culture (1740 to 1770), but had anyone called it that in 1738 he probably would have taken his pulse and checked his temperature. Maryland culture had indeed developed in important ways by 1738. Most important, the undifferentiated society of seventeenth-century Maryland had changed by the 1720s to a society based on

---

Students of Medicine at the University of Leyden, and even though he defends Boerhaave's reputation more than once in the *Itinerarium* against disparaging physicians who claim to have studied under him, he makes no mention at those times of having studied under him himself.

25. Brock, *Scotus Americanus,* 18. Hamilton offers much the same explanation himself in the *History* (1:83–84). For a good overview of the Scottish influence upon American culture during Hamilton's time, see Andrew Hook, *Scotland and America: A Study of Cultural Relations, 1750–1835* (Glasgow, 1975), 1–16.

26. Dr. John Hamilton studied at Leyden and received his M.D. from the University of Edinburgh in 1719 (Smith, *English-Speaking Students of Medicine,* 107). Having settled in Calvert County, Maryland, by 1721 (Lemay, *Men of Letters,* 214), he was well established professionally and socially by the time his younger brother arrived. His obituary reads: "He has left, few, very few Equals, and none superior to him, in the Character of a skilful, and able Physician, and of an honest, humane, benevolent Man" (*Maryland Gazette,* Mar. 31, 1768). He appears in the *History* under the pseudonym of "Dr. Polyhistor" (see esp. 2:370).

A Life of Liberality

wealth, inheritance, and sharp class distinctions.[27] Under the influence of the Bordleys, Carrolls, and Dulanys, Annapolis in particular had gone through a period of rapid expansion shortly before Hamilton's arrival.[28] Yet Annapolis still offered newcomers only the scant cultural menu of horse racing, dancing at the local armory, or drinking and dining at one of its many taverns—no university, no circulating library, no theater, and no literary clubs or scientific societies. Hamilton was not impressed. He was used to Edinburgh, and by comparison the majority of the people and the living conditions in Maryland were, he felt, crude. When "three Pensylvanian dons" accosted him six years later at the beginning of his tour of the northern colonies and "enlarged upon the immorality, drunkenness, rudeness, and immoderate swearing so much practised in Maryland and added that no such vices were to be found in Pensylvania," he did not bother to refute them: "I heard this and contradicted it not," he observed in his travel diary (the *Itinerarium*), "because I knew that the first part of the proposition was pritty true" (pp. 14–15). While visiting New London he remarked that it was "just such another desolate ex[t]ensive town as Annapolis in Maryland, the houses being mostly wood" (p. 97).[29] And upon reapproaching Maryland toward the end of

---

27. Russell R. Menard argues this point well in "Population, Economy, and Society in Seventeenth-Century Maryland," *Maryland Historical Magazine,* 79 (1984), 71–92; see also Charles Albro Barker, *The Background of the Revolution in Maryland* (New Haven, 1940), 27–43, and David Curtis Skaggs, *Roots of Maryland Democracy* 1753–1776 (Westport, Conn., 1973), 30–56.

28. Nancy T. Baker discusses the developments that had taken place in Annapolis before Hamilton's arrival in "Annapolis, Maryland 1695–1730," *Maryland Historical Magazine,* 81 (1986), 191–209.

29. A good study of the housing and design of Annapolis by 1738 is John W. Reps, *Tidewater Towns: City Planning in Colonial Virginia and Maryland* (Williamsburg, 1972), 117–40. As Reps points out, the stately brick houses we associate with Annapolis did not arrive until the late 1740s and 1750s.

his tour, he joylessly but jokingly observed, "I now entered the confines of the three notched road by which I knew I was near Maryland. Immediately upon this something ominous happened, which was my man's tumbling down, flump, two or three times, horse and baggage and all, in the middle of a plain road. I likewise could not help thinking that my state of health was changed for the worse upon it" (p. 193).

Hamilton learned to cope with the crude living conditions in Maryland by laughing at them; more important, he helped to change those conditions so that by the time he died the idea of culture existing in Maryland was no longer a laughing matter. One thing he never learned to laugh at, however, and one thing he could not change was the Maryland climate. As he reported to his brother Gavin,[30]

> We have here in this Country very hot weather in the Summer time, of which you can have no Idea, I write to you now in my Shirt and drawers, with all the doors and windows open upon me to receive the breeze, and yet I sweat excessively, The Grass and herbage here would

---

30. A bookseller and printer in Edinburgh from 1733 to 1766, Gavin Hamilton challenged the copyright law of 1710 and won. His younger brother, Gilbert, wrote that "Gavin pushes a Brisk Trade—He had a plea to defend before the Court of Session against the Booksellers of London, who pursued him for reprinting English Books which they alledged were their property & having gained it he is pushing this new Scotts trade with vigour & success" (Gilbert Hamilton to AH, July 19, 1749). As a member of the Edinburgh Town Council (1732–46) he supervised public hangings, and as a staunch Whig he helped to suppress the Porteous riot of 1736. (For further information on Gavin Hamilton, see two studies by Warren McDougall: "Gavin Hamilton, John Balfour and Patrick Neill: A Study of Publishing in Edinburgh in the Eighteenth Century" [diss. Edinburgh Univ., 1974], and "Gavin Hamilton, Bookseller in Edinburgh," *British Journal of Eighteenth-Century Studies*, 1 [1978], 1–19.)

all dry to Snuff, were it not for the frequent heavy rains we have in the Summer time, which come up for the most part in the evening, with violent Thunder and Lightning, we are pestered here with vermin of various kinds, such as muscettoes, buggs & Ticks, which sticking in the Skin, pleague one Sufficiently and sometimes fester.

And the Maryland winters, he felt, were not much better:

Yet notwithstanding the Summer is so hot here, our winters are for the most part exceeding Cold, ... your breath will freeze upon the Sheets in a night, Cold Iron will take the Skin off if you handle it, ... It sometimes rains and freezes here at the same time, so that the trees in the woods are sometimes broke with the Iceicles upon them, Severall people here are what they call frost-bit, and Lose their limbs by gangrenes occasioned by the frost, ... and sometimes as one endeavours to warm himself, he shall be roased upon one Side and almost frozen on the other.

Aware that his brother might suspect him of stretching the truth, Hamilton concluded his letter by telling him to "ask any one that knows this Country and they will confirm what I have said, for I know some travellers are suspected of telling more than the truth" (AH to Gavin Hamilton, June 13, 1739).[31]

---

31. Hamilton's distraught weather report seems amusing today, but his account would indeed have been verified by many travelers who were equally distressed by the Maryland climate. Henry Callister, for instance, similarly complained (c. 1740) that Maryland was "full of Vermin of various sorts and sizes.... We are swarming with Bugs, Musketoes, worms of every sort both land & water, spiders, snakes, hornets, wasps, sea Nettles, Ticks, Gnats, Thunder & Lightening, excessive heat, excessive cold—irregularities in abundance, I mean according to our Notions of regularity" (Callister Papers, Maryland Diocesan Library; quoted and discussed in Lawrence C. Wroth, "A Maryland Merchant and his Friends in 1750," *Maryland Historical Magazine*, 6 [1911], 218–19).

The Comic Genius of Dr. Alexander Hamilton

Hamilton's work helped to take his mind off the weather. Good physicians were scarce throughout the colonies, and those with his training were much in demand.[32] In just a short time, he was evidently well received as a physician in Maryland: "We are all exceeding glead to here... of the good Caracter ye have got already," his mother wrote, "& yt ye are likely to get into business" (Mary Hamilton to AH, July 23, 1739). But the pay was poor and the hours were long. Like many colonial physicians, Hamilton worked double time as a physician and apothecary. During his first few years in Maryland, he made little money as a physician: "I find it a very hard matter to live well and grow Rich," he told a friend in Edinburgh, "and mind Chiefly my Gallipots and Vials, which are my bank Stock" (AH to John B——r, Nov. 6, 1743). His clientele rapidly grew, however, to include a wide range of Marylanders, including the wealthy planter Stephen Bordley and Governor Samuel Ogle.[33] Although he would never grow rich as a colonial physician, he was eventually able to live well off the proceeds of his practice.

Most of the time he was too busy to be homesick, but during his leisure hours Hamilton keenly missed the society of his friends

---

32. The deplorable state of the medical profession in colonial America has been well discussed by Richard Harrison Shryock, *Medicine and Society in America, 1660–1860* (New York, 1960), 1–18; Brooke Hindle, *Pursuit of Science in Revolutionary America, 1735–1789* (Chapel Hill, 1956), 36–58; and Whitfield J. Bell, "Medical Practice in Colonial America," *Bulletin of the History of Medicine*, 31 (1957), 442–53, and "A Portrait of the Colonial Physician," *Bulletin of the History of Medicine*, 44 (1970), 497–517. For further information on medicine in the colonial South, see Richard Beale Davis, *Intellectual Life in the Colonial South, 1585–1763* (Knoxville, 1978), 2:906–28.

33. For further details on Hamilton's medical practice, see Elaine G. Breslaw, "Dr. Alexander Hamilton and the Enlightenment in Maryland" (diss. Univ. of Maryland, 1973), 13–18.

A Life of Liberality

back home. Several months after his arrival he nostalgically invoked his brother Gavin to "be so good as Remember me to all the Members of the whin-bush Club, especially to the Right honourable, the Lord Provost,[34] and other magistrates and officers of that Ancient and honourable Society, Inform them that every friday, I fancy myself with them, drinking twopenny ale, and smoking tobacco, I Long to see those merry days again" (AH to Gavin Hamilton, June 13, 1739). "I find by your letters," his mother responded, "yt ye distance from your contry & frinds affects you much" (Mary Hamilton to AH, July 23, 1739). The letters from his family and the companionship of his brother John helped to alleviate his homesickness, but what Hamilton needed most was a good club.

In eighteenth-century America as well as in Britain, sociability was increasingly being viewed as the root of happiness.[35] And An-

---

34. George Drummond, six times Lord Provost of Edinburgh and arguably the most influential public figure in Edinburgh. That he and other magistrates were members of the Whin-Bush Club indicates that it was one of the leading social clubs of its day. One of Drummond's many accomplishments—and another direct link to Hamilton—was the role he played in establishing the medical school and the Royal Infirmary at Edinburgh (see Anand C. Chitnis, "Provost Drummond and the Origins of Edinburgh Medicine," *The Origins and Nature of the Scottish Enlightenment*, ed. R. H. Campbell and Andrew S. Skinner [Edinburgh, 1982], 86–97). Drummond wrote to Hamilton in Maryland asking him to solicit contributions for the infirmary; Hamilton had little success and sent his apologies to Drummond (AH to George Drummond, April 22, 1742).

35. A good discussion of this topic is David S. Shields, "Happiness in Society: The Development of an Eighteenth-Century American Poetic Ideal," *American Literature*, 55 (1983), 541–59. A thorough study of club life in colonial America remains to be written, but the following sources provide useful information on club life in colonial Maryland: Barker, *The Background of the Revolution in Maryland*, 52–61; Joseph Towne Wheeler, "Reading and Other Recreations of Marylanders, 1700–1776," *Maryland His-*

napolis, like Edinburgh, had become a center of club life. According to Hamilton, by 1720 there were "at least 40 clubs in that City" (*HTC*, 1:85). Unlike the Easy Club or the Whin-Bush Club, however, they "were all bouzing or toaping Clubs" (*HTC*, 1:85). These included "wine Clubs, punch Clubs, ... Syder Clubs, Rum Clubs, Bub Clubs, and Syllabub Clubs, The last of which were all female Clubs, tho' some Sorts of beaus and pritty fellows were admitted to them, who, in their mein and address approached nighly to the Feminine Gender" (*HTC*, 1:85). By 1728, Annapolis clubs had apparently found more to do than just drink: "I know not how it is in Virginia," one observer wrote, "but in Maryland I am told there are settled Clubs in every County, where they talk over Affairs."[36] In *The History of the Tuesday Club* Hamilton facetiously attributes this progress in the clubical state of affairs to the arrival of one man: that illustrious club hero George Neilson, an exiled Jacobite who, "having maturely considered, the wretched and Confused condition, that the Clubical constitutions were under in [Annapolis], ... set himself Strenuously about working a Reformation in these Clubs" (1:90). Until Neilson's arrival the Maryland "Royalist clubs" elected their kings simply according to who could drink the most. Seeking to reform their procedures, Neilson endured tremendous abuse by the members of these clubs: "They would call him a hundred abusive names in half an hour, such as lousy scabby scot, poor rascally pedlar, Itchified Son of a bitch, Scoundrel, knave, fool, ass, Goose, blockhead, ugly

---

torical Magazine, 38 (1943), 37–55, 167–80; Shunsuke Kamei, "Cultural Clubs in Colonial America, 1720–1750," *Studies in English Literature* (English Literary Society of Japan), English Number (1963), 37–70; and esp. Lemay, *Men of Letters*, and Davis, *Intellectual Life in the Colonial South*.

36. Henry Darmall, *A Just and Impartial Account of the Transactions of the Merchants in London* ... (Annapolis, 1728), 12.

"Mr Neilson's Anger Restrained by Philosophy."
Hamilton's Drawing in *The History of the Tuesday Club*.
(John Work Garrett Library, Milton S. Eisenhower Library,
The Johns Hopkins University)

beetle browd, squint eyed, Lenteren Jaw'd, Jacobitish, Skip kennel Scrub, nasty, blewbellied, blanket ars'd, hip-shotten, maggot eaten, round about, Snuff besmeard, flyblown Son of a whore" (1:98). One evening, unable to endure this abuse any longer, Neilson attacked his persecutors:

> Immediatly all was in an uproar, decanters, Glasses, and Tobacco pipes flew about like hail, his majesties guards at last seized upon Mr. Neilson, ... stuffed his mouth full of tallow and Candle wick, wrung his nose, broke his Sword, and tossed his whole box or mull of Snuff in his Eyes, and taking him by the legs and arms, carried him out of doors, and threw him headlong into a puddle, ... leaving him there, in a most miserable nasty pickle, his Scouts soon had Intelligence of it, and coming to his asistance, they beset, begirt and besieged the Club house; ... but being much annoyed with Stink-pots from the besieged, they were obliged to raise the Siege and march off. (1:98–99)

Following his ignominious ouster, Neilson and his supporters founded the Red-House Club in 1729, which expired with the death of its inimitable leader in 1736. But out of its scattered remains arose the Ugly Club, which Hamilton joined in 1739. Unlike the Ugly Club made famous by the *Spectator*, membership in the Annapolis Ugly Club was not determined by any physical deformity;

> it was Sufficient for [a member] Sincerely to profess and believe that he was not handsom, till he was declared to be a monstrous ugly fellow by the Ladies in public company.... A man was to show his Sincerity in this opinion of himself, by assuming a certain Slovenliness and peculiarity in his dress, by never throwing away his time at a looking Glass, and diligently evading all foppish and finical airs and affectation, ... but, if he ever observed any oddity of Gesture, affected by another man, such as a wink, a cast of the Eye, a sudden toss of the head, ... or wry twist of the mouth, ... these he was Strictly to Imitate, ... as being real deformities and deviations from nature in a much higher degree than bodily distortions and blemishes. (*HTC*, 1:117–18)

A Life of Liberality

From 1739 to 1744, this club met mainly "to argue and debate upon various Subjects, and to discuss points of a knotty and abstruse nature," but some of the members eventually became so contentious that "all Sort of Clubical cordiality and friendship, began to decrease, and at last was quite extinguished, so that the Members drop'd off one by one, and from a numerous Club, it dwindled to nothing, and at last expired" (*HTC*, 1:126–27).

Shortly before the Ugly Club disbanded, Hamilton also entered the contentious world of Maryland politics.[37] In 1743, "at the desire and Request of many of [his] fellow Citizens," he ran for the office of common councilman of Annapolis "in opposition to a certain creature of the Court" (AH to Gavin Hamilton, Oct. 20, 1743). Hamilton was not politically ambitious; he was, however, a gentleman, and in his day "the quality that most nearly epitomized what was needed to make a gentleman was 'liberality,'" including "a certain disposition... to undertake important responsibilities in the community at large."[38] Hamilton met his obligations as a gentleman, but Maryland elections were far from gentlemanly.[39] The election for common councilman in 1743 was fairly typical of other Maryland elections: "there arose such tumults at giving of the votes in the Mayors Court," he wrote

---

37. The struggles between the proprietary and anti-proprietary (Court and Country) parties in colonial Maryland have been enlarged upon in numerous works, but see esp. Ronald Hoffman, *A Spirit of Dissension: Economics, Politics, and the Revolution in Maryland* (Baltimore, 1973), 44–59; Skaggs, *Roots of Maryland Democracy*, 84–109; and Aubrey C. Land, *Colonial Maryland: A History* (Millwood, N.Y., 1981), 151–78.

38. Rhys Isaac, *The Transformation of Virginia, 1740–1790* (Chapel Hill, 1982), 131.

39. The turbulent nature of elections in colonial Maryland is well discussed in Robert J. Dinkin, "Elections in Proprietary Maryland," *Maryland Historical Magazine*, 73 (1978), 129–36.

Gavin, "that the majority of the Aldermen left the Bench in a passion.... In the afternoon the tumult was so high that the partizans went to Cudgelling and breaking of heads, ... and they have been afraid ever since to proceed upon the Election."⁴⁰ Eventually the election was decided in Hamilton's favor. At the time he questioned whether he would ever run for office again: "I doubt I shall stand again," he told Gavin, "for tho I be a Lover of Liberty, and abhor force or oppression of any kind, and especially when they are exercised by an Insolent Government party, yet I like better to be a peace maker, than an Instrument of disturbance in any Shape." Gentleman that he was, he kept his seat as common councilman for the rest of his life.⁴¹

But Hamilton's greatest concern in 1743 was not the health of the body politic; it was his own health. By the end of his first summer in Maryland he had told his mother that he was "very ill" (Mary Hamilton to AH, Apr. 1, 1740). Unaware that he was ill, his brother-in-law, the Reverend David Smith, had written to him, "Alas! how much scotch drollery is now transplanted into the American soil.... I suppose it will refine in proportion to its being cultivated under a more direct ray of Apollo" (David Smith to AH, Oct. 1, 1739). By the time he received Smith's letter nearly

---

40. This was hardly an isolated incident. A year later Hamilton wrote in his travel diary, "At Philadelphia I heard news of some conturbations and fermentations of partys att Annapolis concerning the election of certain parliament members for that wretched city and was sorry to find that these triffles still contributed so much to set them att variance, but I pray that the Lord may pity them and not leave them intirely to themselves and the devil" (p. 189).

41. The appointment as common councilman, Hamilton told his brother in the same letter, was "during life, or as long as one behaves well." Following Hamilton's death Charles Wallace was chosen common councilman of Annapolis "in the room of... the much regretted Dr. Alexander Hamilton, deceased" (*Maryland Gazette,* Feb. 10, 1757).

A Life of Liberality

four years later, Hamilton had developed increasingly severe symptoms of consumption. "As to the warmer Suns of America Increasing my Genius," he replied to Smith, "I Indeed cannot be Judge whether that has Improved or not, but this I am sure of, that these warmer Suns have much Impaired my health, for I have suffered much from the excessive heat of this Climate, being harassed every summer with a discharge of blood from my Lungs, and threatened very much with a Consumption, but I always recruit again in the winter, the cold with us then, being very Sharp, and the Sky clear" (AH to David Smith, [fall] 1743). By September 1743, Hamilton was in such a "Low State, with fevers and a bloody Spitting" (AH to Gavin Hamilton, Oct. 20, 1743), that he intended to return to Britain.[42] Over the next few weeks, however, he began to recuperate: "I am now Considerably better," he told Gavin, "but am followed up with an Incessant cough, which no medicine whatsoever can abate or deminish, this makes me apprehensive that the consequence will be a confirmed Consumption." Hamilton had good reason to feel apprehensive; he would die of consumption thirteen years later.

To improve his health, Hamilton spent the following summer away from the muggy Maryland climate touring the northern colonies. On May 30, 1744, he set out on horseback with his black slave Dromo on a four-month journey from Annapolis, Maryland, to York, Maine, and back, a trip totaling 1,624 miles. Along the way, he kept a diary of his observations as he visited Philadelphia, New York, Albany, New Haven, Providence, Boston, and many other cities and towns. By September 21 he was back in Maryland,

---

42. Hamilton announced his intention to leave in a broadside advertisement requesting "all Persons indebted to him to discharge their respective debts; and likewise such as have Demands upon him, to come and receive what is due" (Annapolis, Sept. 29, 1743).

noting in his diary "the washed countenances of the people standing att their doors and looking out att their windows, for they looked like so many staring ghosts. In short I was sensible I had got into Maryland, for every house was an infirmary, according to ancient custome" (p. 198). With his own health temporarily on the mend, however, Hamilton spent the next month revising his diary, and on October 29, 1744, he presented a fair copy of it to Onorio Razolini, a naturalized Italian citizen who was armourer and keeper of the stores of Maryland until he returned to Italy in 1748.[43] Hamilton's *Itinerarium* remained in Razolini's family until early in the twentieth century, when it was published for the first time.[44]

The Ugly Club had disbanded shortly before Hamilton began his tour, and following his return he helped to form the Tuesday Club, which met for the first time on May 14, 1745. For the next eleven years almost everyone of some importance in the northern

---

43. For further information on Razolini, see Donald Wallace, "Onorio Razolini, Pioneer Italian," *Sons of Italy Magazine*, 15, no. 10 (1942), 306; and 16, no. 2 (1943), 2–4; Giovanni E. Schiavo, *Four Centuries of Italian-American History* (New York, 1955), 110; and Donnell MacClure Owings, *His Lordship's Patronage: Offices of Profit in Colonial Maryland* (Baltimore, 1953), 49.

44. Albert Bushnell Hart suggested in the first edition of the *Itinerarium* that "It could hardly have been intended for publication at the time when written, for it is too free in comment on well known individuals" (*Hamilton's Itinerarium* [St. Louis, 1907], ix). He was probably right. But Hamilton's choice of Razolini, who apparently was not one of his closest friends, seems odd. The Tuesday Club existed for three years before Razolini returned to Italy, yet he never attended their meetings. Perhaps Razolini announced his intention of returning to Europe earlier than 1748, and perhaps Hamilton thought of having the *Itinerarium* published abroad, with Razolini acting as a liason. Be that as it may, the manuscript remained in Razolini's family until it was acquired by the London bookseller, Frank T. Sabin, early in the twentieth century (see Bridenbaugh, *Gentleman's Progress*, xxx-xxxi). The manuscript is now located at the Huntington Library.

A Life of Liberality

Chesapeake Bay area either joined or visited the Tuesday Club. In the beginning there were seven members besides Hamilton: John Bullen (d. 1764), captain of the Annapolis Independent Company, alderman, and commissioner of the Paper Currency Office; William Cumming (c. 1696–1752), a Scot who had been arrested during the Jacobite rebellion of 1715 and transported to Maryland (along with George Neilson), where he became a lawyer and a member of the Lower House; the Reverend John Gordon (1717–90), a Scot who became pastor of St. Anne's, Annapolis, and later of St. Michael's, Talbot County; Robert Gordon (1676–1753), a Scot who settled in Annapolis by 1719, where he was a merchant, judge of the Provincial Court, and commissioner of the Loan Office; John Lomas (d. 1757), an Annapolis merchant for many years before he moved to Glasgow in 1754; Witham Marshe (d. 1765), secretary to the Maryland Commissioners at the treaty of Lancaster in 1744 with the Six Indian Nations and later secretary for Indian affairs; and William Rogers (1699–1749), a native New Englander who moved to Annapolis by 1720 and served as chief clerk of the Prerogative Court.[45] A varied bunch, but many of them Scots and all of them public servants in one capacity or another.

As the Tuesday Club grew, its lists expanded to include many of colonial Maryland's most distinguished residents and visitors, such as the Reverend Thomas Bacon (c. 1700–68), rector of St. Peter's, Talbot County, musician, philanthropist, compiler of *Laws*

---

45. The source for much of the information on these members is Lemay, *Men of Letters*, 245–46, but see also Edward C. Papenfuse et al., *A Biographical Dictionary of the Maryland Legislature, 1635–1789*, 2 vols. (Baltimore, 1979, 1985), Nelson Waite Rightmyer, *Maryland's Established Church* (Baltimore, 1956), and Harry Wright Newman, *To Maryland from Overseas* (Annapolis, 1982). For John Gordon, see Mary M. Starin, "The Reverend Doctor John Gordon, 1717–1790," *Maryland Historical Magazine*, 75 (1980), 167–91.

of Maryland at Large, and one of colonial Maryland's most prolific authors; John Beale Bordley (1727–1804), judge, member of the Upper House, author, and member of the American Philosophical Society; the Reverend Thomas Cradock (1718–70), prominent Maryland clergyman and author; Jonas Green (1712–67), public printer of Maryland, poet, and publisher of the *Maryland Gazette;* the Reverend Alexander Malcolm (d. 1763), Maryland clergyman, author, and musician; the Reverend James Sterling (1701–63), Maryland clergyman, poet, and playwright; the sons of Daniel Dulany;[46] and numerous other members and visitors, not the least of whom was Benjamin Franklin.[47] All comers were welcome, and most men of any note who came to the Annapolis area visited the Tuesday Club.

The regular members—or the "longstanding members," as they liked to boast of themselves—were limited in number to fifteen. In *The History of the Tuesday Club* they appear under pseudonyms typifying their characters and roles in the club: John Beale Bordley

---

46. Each of these men has been the topic of one or more good studies: Bacon (Lemay, *Men of Letters,* 313–42; William E. Deibert, "Thomas Bacon, Maryland Clergyman," *Maryland Historical Magazine,* 73 [1978], 79–86); Bordley (Olive Moore Gambrill, "John Beale Bordley and the Early Years of the Philadelphia Agricultural Society," *Pennsylvania Magazine of History and Biography,* 66 [1942], 410–39; David Hackett Fischer, "John Beale Bordley, Daniel Boorstin, and the American Enlightenment," *Journal of Southern History,* 28 [1962], 327–42); Cradock (David Curtis Skaggs, "Thomas Cradock and the Chesapeake Golden Age," *William and Mary Quarterly,* 3rd Ser., 30 [1973], 93–116); Green (Lawrence C. Wroth, *A History of Printing in Colonial Maryland, 1686–1776* [Baltimore, 1922], 75–95; Lemay, *Men of Letters,* 193–212); Malcolm (James R. Heintze, "Alexander Malcolm: Musician, Clergyman, and Schoolmaster," *Maryland Historical Magazine,* 73 [1978], 226–35); Sterling (Lemay, *Men of Letters,* 257–312); and the Dulanys (Land, *The Dulanys of Maryland*).

47. An interesting article on Franklin's association with the Tuesday Club is Robert R. Hare, "Electro Vitrifrico in Annapolis: Mr. Franklin Visits the Tuesday Club," *Maryland Historical Magazine,* 58 (1963), 62–66.

(Quirpum Comic, Master of Ceremonies); Stephen Bordley (Huffman Snap); John Bullen (Bully Blunt, also Sir John Oldcastle, Club Champion); Charles Cole (Nasifer Jole, President); William Cumming, Sr. (Jealous Spyplot, Sr., Attorney General); William Cumming, Jr. (Jealous Spyplot, Jr.); Edward Dorsey (Drawlum Quaint, Speaker); Richard Dorsey (Tunbelly Bowzer); Walter Dulany (Slyboots Pleasant); Jonas Green (Jonathan Grog, P.P.P.P.P.—Purveyor, Punster, Punchmaker General, Printer, and Poet—and later P.L.M.C.—Poet Laureate and Master of Ceremonies); Thomas Jennings (Prim Timorous, Sergeant at Arms); John Lomas (Laconic Comas, Orator); Alexander Malcolm (Philo Dogmaticus, Chancellor); William Thornton (Solo Neverout, also Protomusicus, Chief Musician and Attorney General); and, of course, Hamilton himself (Loquacious Scribble, Secretary and Orator).[48] Other longstanding members came and went, but these were the mainstays.

As the club's secretary, Hamilton spent an enormous amount of time over the next eleven years recording and fictionalizing the proceedings of this comical cast of characters. First, he recorded the club's minutes at or shortly after each meeting. He then compiled the "Record of the Tuesday Club," a careful revision of the minutes. In the fall of 1752 he "began to Collect and Compile [a draft of] the History of the Club" (*HTC*, 3:118), which he continued working on until early 1754. From late 1754 until his death

---

48. Stephen Bordley (c. 1710–64), lawyer, attorney general, commissary general, member of Lower House; Charles Cole (d. 1757), an Annapolis merchant; William Cumming, Jr. (1724–93), planter and attorney; Richard Dorsey (1714–60), magistrate and clerk of the Paper Currency Office; Walter Dulany (d. 1773), merchant, naval officer, and landowner; Thomas Jennings (d. 1759), chief clerk of the Land Office; William Thornton (d. 1769), sheriff of Anne Arundel county (Papenfuse, *Biographical Dictionary;* obituaries in the *Maryland Gazette,* July 7, 1757, Aug. 30, 1759, Sept. 11, 1760, Feb. 9, 1769).

"Loquacious Scribble Esqr, Secretary and Orator
of the Ancient and Honorable Tuesday Club."
Hamilton's Drawing in *The History of the Tuesday Club*.
(John Work Garrett Library, Milton S. Eisenhower Library,
The Johns Hopkins University)

A Life of Liberality

two years later he revised and rewrote the entire manuscript. This final, fictionalized account of the club's proceedings, *The History of the Tuesday Club,* is three volumes and nearly 1,900 manuscript pages. From fact to fiction, Hamilton must have written nearly 5,000 pages concerning the club's history.[49]

And his comical club companions gave him much to write about. Every other Tuesday for eleven years, longstanding members, honorary members (those who could attend whenever in Annapolis without having to entertain the club), and visitors met, normally at the home of the "high steward" for the night, to share a side of bacon, some bread and cheese, a bowl of punch, but mostly each other's company and conversation. Hamilton establishes the formula for a boon club companion early in *The History of the Tuesday Club,* maintaining that "none but your merry, droll, facetious, Jocose, good humored, risible companions, punsters, comical Story tellers, and *Conundrumifiers,* ought to be members of those nocturnal assemblies, called Clubs, for the

---

49. Volume 1 of the Tuesday Club minutes (from May 14, 1745, to Feb. 25, 1755) is located in the John Work Garrett Collections, Milton S. Eisenhower Library, Johns Hopkins University; volume 2 of the minutes (from May 27, 1755, to Feb. 11, 1756) is at the Library of Congress, Peter Force Collection, Series 8D, Item 170. Hamilton's revision of the minutes (from May 14, 1745, to Apr. 22, 1755), the "Record of the Tuesday Club," is at the Maryland Historical Society, MS 854. The "Record" and the second volume of minutes are included in Elaine G. Breslaw's edition of the *Records of the Tuesday Club of Annapolis, 1745–56* (Urbana and Chicago, 1988). Only portions of the draft of the *History* have been located: the table of contents, dedication, and first two pages of the preface have been mistakenly included in the first two gatherings of the "Record"; the remaining portion of the preface is also at the Maryland Historical Society, Dulany Papers, MS 1265; and the only extant portion of the drafted text is included at the end of volume 3 of the *History* (Garrett Collections). For further details on Hamilton's composition of the Tuesday Club manuscripts, see my edition of *The History of the Tuesday Club.*

Quintessence, marrow and main fulcrum of Clubs consists in gayiety, Jollity, pleasantry and Jocosity" (1:72). On the other hand, he concludes that

> Those Solitary, moaping, morose, humdrum fellows, who evade, shun, run and fly, from all company, hate the Sight of men, as if they were Tygers, bears, Serpents, hobgoblins, Rhinoceroses and Panthers... are mortal and Irreconcileable enimies to all Clubs, Jovial meetings, and humerous Conversations.
>
> When I see a fellow of this Stamp, with his Clouded brows, and Lowring countenance, *monstrum deforme Ingens,* I Imagine I behold a black cloud, rising from the dirty blustering South east, saturated with hollow murmuring Smouldering blasts, sending before it grumbling, tumbling, Jumbling thunder, and Infectious puffs of pestilential Steams, darkening the face of the fair day with polluted murky and Stiffling vapors, exhalations and damps, saturated, loaded, Impregnated and overcharged, with morbific Sulphureous atoms, bursting from the mouth of Tartarus it self. (1:69–70)

The Tuesday Club was no place for such humdrum fellows. As Hamilton's fellow clubbist, the Reverend Thomas Cradock, asked in one of his sermons,

> Were we not form'd for Society?... And can that Society be carried on without a chearful and benevolent Disposition? How can a Man be desirous to promote the Happiness and Benefit of his Neighbour, when he has not a Soul susceptible of generous Sentiments... and looks with an evil Eye on every Thing hearty and sociable? Can that Soul promote Harmony that hath no Harmony in itself?... No; the morose, surly, uncheartul Man can never answer the End of his Creation;... He may say what he will; but if he wants a merry Heart, he wants a very great Characteristic of a human Mind.[50]

---

50. "Innocent Mirth Not Inconsistent with Religion," in *Two Sermons, with a Preface Shewing the Author's Reasons for Publishing Them* (Annapolis, 1747), 2–3.

A Life of Liberality

Like the Edinburgh clubs, the Tuesday Club framed an elaborate set of laws—fifty-two in all—to govern the conduct of their members. Most of these laws were violated at one time or another, but the "gelastic law" (from the Greek "to laugh") was always upheld. This law stated "That if any Subject... be discussed, that levels at party matters, or the administration of the Government of this Province, or be disagreeable to the Club, no answer shall be given thereto, but after such discourse is ended, the Society shall laugh at the member offending, in order to divert the discourse" (*HTC,* 1:151). In passing this law, Hamilton wrote, the club had shown "deep Judgement and Sagacity," since "men are much sooner laughed out of their follies and faults, than cured of them by grave admonition and advice" (*HTC,* 1:151). This law was intended mainly to prevent the divisiveness of Maryland politics from dividing the club, but the Tuesday Club put it into effect whenever any member waxed too serious about any topic, political or otherwise. One such occasion was during the mock trial of the club's chief musician, William Thornton, who had failed to serve the club on his appointed day. A portion of that trial follows:

> President: Pray Sir, answer me plainly, wherefore did not you serve the Club, upon that day, on which you was appointed to serve as high Steward?
> Protomusicus: Why really Sir, if I must declare to your honor the plain truth, It was matter of Conscience, mere matter of Conscience, that day on which I was appointed to serve this here Club, being a fast day ordained by the Church....
> President: But good Sir, allow me to Inform you that your time for serving this Club, was not in the day but the evening of the day.
> Protomusicus: Honorable Sir, the Evening and the morning make the day with me (here Mr Neverout Quoted Scripture)
> President: But Sir, how a matter of Conscience, what do you mean by a matter of conscience?

Protomusicus: Sir I hope I am not here before a Court of Inquisition.
Chancellor: Yea Sir; but you are before a court of Inquiry.
Huffman Snap: It is my humble opinion Sir, that this here Club has nothing to do with conscience.
Chancellor: Right, conscience is only my province as Conscience keeper.
Jonathan Grog: If this here Club has nothing to do with Conscience, it must of Consequence be an unconscientious Club.
Omn: Ha, Ha, Ha, He, Hi.
Mr. Attorney Spyplot: Mr President Sir, I think the Gentleman's excuse is a very reasonable one, for which, Sir, my reasons——(here he was Interrupted)
Huffman Snap: I have observed Sir, that this is the first time that this gentleman has set up for conscience.
Mr Attorney Spyplot: Sir,—I Intended to urge a few reasons which——
Tunbelly Bowzer: The Gelastic Law, the Gelastic Law; ha, ha.
Omn: Haw, Haw, Haw, Haw, Haw, hoh, hoh, hoi. (2:90–91)

This debate continued awhile longer, but Jealous Spyplot, who had been effectively silenced for taking himself too seriously, dared not open his mouth again. The gelastic law worked on him and more than once on Loquacious Scribble and the other club members, and perhaps more than any other law it embodied the spirit of cordiality that for many years sustained the Tuesday Club.

The combined talents of the members of the Tuesday Club provided an almost limitless fund of entertainment. Those members familiar with law—and some not so familiar—entertained the club by conducting numerous mock trials; those with a flair for speechmaking—and some flaired better than others—entertained the club with their rhetorical effusions; and those gifted with musical talents—and some not so gifted—entertained the club by reciting popular songs and by performing their own compositions in club to the accompaniment of several of the club's members. (Hamilton regularly played violoncello.) Thomas Bacon, Alexander Malcolm, and Hamilton were the chief composers, in that order of musical ability. Their baroque anniversary odes for 1750, 1751, and 1753 "show that a high level of musical sophistication existed in the American colonies well before the formal establishment of a concert tradition."[51] Hamilton's anniversary ode for 1750 demonstrates, if not the exceptional harmonic organization of Bacon's 1751 ode, "interesting, often expressive, and well formed" melodies, although "corrections to his manuscript show that someone [probably Bacon] attempted to make musical sense out of some of the stranger passages."[52] Hardly one of the musical geniuses of his time, Hamilton was nonetheless a competent musician who contributed his share to the club's musical entertainment.

But the greatest source of entertainment in the Tuesday Club was the wit of its two principal comedians, Hamilton and Jonas Green—Loquacious Scribble and Jonathan Grog. As club orator, Hamilton took every occasion to impress the club with his erudition by haranguing them with numerous bombastic speeches, especially at each of the club's anniversaries, when he annually delivered a learned and lengthy speech commemorating the grandeur of the occasion. At those times his rhetorical talents were

---

51. John Barry Talley, *Secular Music in Colonial Annapolis: The Tuesday Club, 1745–56* (Urbana and Chicago, 1988), 121. Talley provides modernized transcriptions of all the songs and odes recited in the Tuesday Club and valuable comments on each. The original scores appear in my edition of the *History*.
52. Talley, 114, 116.

The Comic Genius of Dr. Alexander Hamilton

"Jonathan Grog Esqr, Poet Laureat and
Master of Ceremonies of the Tuesday Club."
Hamilton's Drawing in *The History of the Tuesday Club*.
(John Work Garrett Library, Milton S. Eisenhower Library,
The Johns Hopkins University)

A Life of Liberality

complemented by the literary talents of Jonas Green, whom Hamilton fondly portrays as follows in *The History of the Tuesday Club:*

> This Gentleman is of a middle Stature, Inclinable to fat, round faced, small lively eyes, from which, as from two oriental portals, Incessantly dart the dawning rays of wit and humor, with a considerable mixture of the amorous leer, in his countenance he wears a constant Smile, having never been once seen to frown; his body is thick and well set, and for one of his make and Stature he has a good Sizeable belly, ... and his darling liquor of late is Grog, he professing himself to be of the modern Sect of the Grogorians, and as some think the patron and founder of that Sect in Annapolis, ... he is a very great admirer, Improver and encourager of wit, humor and drollery, and is fond of that Sort of poetry which is called Doggrell, in which he is himself a very great proficient, and Confines his genius Chiefly to it, tho sometimes he cannot help emitting some flashes of the true Sublime, in his Club Compositions; ... in fine, to sum up all he is really a good humored, smooth tempered, merry, Jocose, and Innofensive companion, a man of the most happy Clubical Genius that ever was known, and a Great promoter Improver and encourager of Clubific felicity, for were there 50 Clubs in the place, he'd be a member of every one of them. (1:345–46)

As the club's poet laureate, Jonathan Grog traditionally delivered his anniversary ode following Loquacious Scribble's anniversary speech. He further entertained the club on many other nights with his witty verses and his numerous practical jokes, puns, and conundrums. Hamilton and Green, the two club "Conundrumificators," regularly amused the club with these "wit stretchers," but Green was the indisputable master, and the more bawdy of the two: "Why is the king's prick," he asked the club, "in marking down a Sheriff like an Elephant?"—to which Jealous Spyplot, Sr., rightly answered, "Because it always *Stands*" (2:116). "I shall beg leave to observe," Hamilton notes, "lest it should escape the observation of the Reader, that there seems to be an uncommon delicacy and Elegance in most of the Conundrums, composed by Jonathan Grog Esqr, as may be seen in the one Just now mentioned, Concerning *The king's prick,* which is not only a perfect Conundrum, but Contains also a delicate pun, as the word *Prick* may be Interpreted various ways" (2:117).

Although it might be hard to tell from a brief sampling of their elegant wit, Hamilton and Green are the best comic team in colonial literature, and the Tuesday Club was perhaps "the most brilliant imitation of the European gentleman's club in America."[53] As Anna Wells Rutledge has stated, it is doubtful that "any of the numerous clubs in contemporary America had as sprightly and talented a membership as the Tuesday Club of Annapolis. Surely none has left such records for posterity. We can only be grateful that [they] had so talented a secretary who not only recorded their literary effusions, but also acted as a 'candid cameraman' of his day and caught them at their fun."[54]

The team of Hamilton and Green brought their brand of wit not only to the Tuesday Club but also to the *Maryland Gazette,* which Green began publishing in 1745. Green evidently considered it his function primarily to print the news at home and abroad, and to use his paper as a forum to discuss issues that concerned Marylanders. Yet he also welcomed literary contributions and managed to inject a spicy touch of satire into the pages of the *Gazette* by enlisting the services of his friends, particularly Hamilton. From 1746 to 1750 Hamilton contributed several pieces to the

---

53. Elaine G. Breslaw, "Merrymaking in Old Annapolis: The Tuesday Club," *Baltimore Sun Magazine,* Mar. 24, 1974, 22.

54. "A Humorous Artist in Colonial Maryland," *American Collector,* 16 (1947), 15.

A Life of Liberality

Gazette, including an essay on the impertinent question, "What News?" (Jan. 7, 1746); a cure for distempered authors and a mock advertisement to catch a runaway wit (Feb. 4, Mar. 18, 1746); an essay on curiosity (Jan. 27, 1747); a dream vision on the fate of the contributors to the *Gazette* (June 29, 1748); a tale for melancholic scribblers (Aug. 31, 1748); a piece on odd orthography (Apr. 12, 1749); and a parody of Masonic ceremonies (Jan. 24, 1750). These pieces, mostly satiric, helped to make the *Maryland Gazette* one of colonial America's most entertaining newspapers.

While writing for the *Maryland Gazette,* serving the Tuesday Club, and administering to his patients, Hamilton also found time, on Friday, May 29, 1747, to marry Margaret Dulany, daughter of Daniel Dulany the Elder. His marriage to the "vivacious" Miss Dulany was "the social event of the season"[55] but much lamented by Stephen Bordley, who had been hopeful that Hamilton would remain, like himself, one of the Tueday Club's few surviving bachelors:

> Yet in vain was that hope, [he wrote to Witham Marshe,] since I am now obliged to hold out alone against that numerous and powerful host we... formerly provoked by our united hostilities,—for poor Hamilton is gone!—not dead, but married, he was the day before yesterday obliged to surrender discretion to throw himself up to the money of Peggy Dulany, and is already become what you would from

---

55. Land, *The Dulanys of Maryland,* 191. The *Maryland Gazette* for June 2, 1747 reported, "Friday last Dr. Alexander Hamilton, of this City, was married to Miss Margaret Dulany, (Daughter to the Hon. Daniel Dulany, Esq;) a well accomplish'd and agreeable young Lady, with a handsome Fortune." As was customary among upper class families, they probably had a private wedding at the Dulany home, with Hamilton's friend, the Reverend John Gordon, presiding (Breslaw, "Dr. Alexander Hamilton and the Enlightenment in Maryland," 47).

your knowledge of the lady now suppose him to be, a very grave sober fellow.[56]

As Bordley well knew, Hamilton's marriage to Margaret Dulany, a person whose "infectious gaiety... charmed men and women of all ages,"[57] could only enhance his fortune and lift his spirits. Except for Bordley and the club's president, Charles Cole,[58] all the other regular members of the Tuesday Club eventually married as well, and, as Aubrey C. Land clubically observes, "somehow each survived the ordeal and the Tuesday Club flourished in spite of the changed status of individual members."[59]

As much as Bordley and some of his club companions liked to joke about the glories of bachelorhood, in Hamilton's day it was no joking matter that any man of sound mind and sound body, aged thirty-five, would choose to live in Maryland for nine years unmarried. Throughout the colonies "unmarried persons were regarded as pitiable encumbrances," and in Maryland "the tax imposed upon bachelors... indicates the widespread feeling that the man without a family was evading a civic duty, and numerous expressions of commiseration reveal the prevailing notion that the husbandless woman had no purpose in life."[60] On April 26, 1749, the *Maryland Gazette* reprinted a petition of the Petticoat Club

---

56. Bordley Letter Book, 1740–1747, Maryland Historical Society, May 30, 1747.
57. Land, *The Dulanys of Maryland*, 115.
58. Cole's obituary, however, stated that "This Gentleman was a Batchelor, who, it is said, Repented of nothing in his latter Years, so much as that he had not Married while he was Young" (*Maryland Gazette*, July 7, 1757).
59. *The Dulanys of Maryland*, 189.
60. Julia Cherry Spruill, *Women's Life and Work in the Southern Colonies* (1938; rpt. New York, 1969), 137. Spruill's book is the only study thus far that attempts to present a comprehensive view of women in the colonial

A Life of Liberality

(from the *New York Gazette),* claiming that, despite their best efforts to marry, many women were "frustrated of this our laudable design, by the unsufferable stupidity and obstinacy of a set of men called *Old Batchelors,* who know and ought to do better, and who, in contempt of the laws both of God and Nature, and to the inexpressible damage of this province, do oblige us, contrary to our desires and inclinations, to remain useless, and ever burthensome members thereof." Following the lead of the Petticoat Club, on September 26, 1749, "the Single Ladies of Annapolis" informed the president of the Tuesday Club

> That whereas it has been observed by sundry persons as well as your petitioners, that a Singular and Surprizing Success, has all along attended such happy females, as your honor has been pleased to pitch upon, as the toasts of the honorable Chair, every one of whom in a short time, after having been thus adopted by your honor, has Successfully and happily been provided, with a much more Eligible State, than that of a Single Life,
>
> Your petitioners therefore, earnestly pray, that your honor, instead of conferring your favors in so partial a manner, would, in Commiseration of our desperate Situation, Include us all in the circle of your favor, that the benign Influence of your honor's maritiferous notice, may henceforth equally shine upon us all, which benevolent Condescention of your honor, will have a tendency to multiply the Inhabit-

---

South. The following works, however, provide useful information on the lives of women in the Chesapeake society of Hamilton's day: Kathryn Allamong Jacob, "The Women of Baltimore Town: A Social History, 1729–1797" (M.A. thesis, Georgetown Univ., 1975), and "The Woman's Lot in Baltimore Town: 1729–1797," *Maryland Historical Magazine,* 71 (1976), 283–95; and Daniel Blake Smith, *Inside the Great House: Planter Family Life in Eighteenth-Century Chesapeake Society* (Ithaca, 1980). A good review of the scholarship—or the lack of it—in this area is Anne Firor Scott, *Making the Invisible Woman Visible* (Urbana, 1984), 243–58.

ants of this City, as well as to better our present forlorn Situation. (*HTC*, 1:523)

The Petticoat Club was downright angry, the Single Ladies of Annapolis only mildly sarcastic, but both petitions convey a real anxiety about the purpose of unmarried people in colonial America.

Being of sound mind, Hamilton shared that anxiety, but being of unsound body, he felt he could not in good conscience marry before 1747. When Gavin informed him that one young lady from Edinburgh had promised to wait six years for him, Hamilton was flattered by the offer but afraid that he might not even be alive in six years:

> but Granting I was to last 6 years, [he told Gavin,] and Miss P——e was to have me, I am afraid she would soon repent of her bargain, finding that Instead of the office of a wife, she must exercise that of a nurse, to a peevish Valetudinarian, so, not without Lamenting the Impossibility of my ever enjoying any such good fortune, as that of being link'd in the bands of matrimony to so fair and so virtuous a Lady, I wish her a much happier fate in a husband, and desire she would not throw away the Inestimable time of her youth, in waiting upon such an Insipid fellow, as I, but catching time by the forelock, take the first advantagious offer that comes in her way, where youth, Good health, Sense, and some of our earthly mammon, (of which possessions I cannot pretend to,) may conspire to render her life happy and unmolested. (AH to Gavin Hamilton, Oct. 20, 1743)

Clearly, Hamilton was not one of those obstinate bachelors the Petticoat Club complained about. He enjoyed the company of the ladies, but, he told a friend in Edinburgh, "I am not well in health, and for that reason Chiefly continue still a Batchellor" (AH to John B——r, Nov. 6, 1743). Fortunately, by 1747 he was in good enough health to marry one of colonial Maryland's comeliest and wealthiest young women.

A Life of Liberality

Had he waited another nine years, he could not have chosen a better wife. Hamilton's friend, Charles Carroll, described in a letter to his son the qualities that most gentlemen looked for in a wife:

> Without yr wife be virtuous, sensible, good natured, complaisant, Complying & of a Chearfull Disposition, you will not find a Marryed State a Happy one. Next to these Family & Fortune Come under Consideration.... Beauty is not to be under valued, But it is too transient & Lyable to too many Accidents to be a substantial motive to Mariage, & yet it Affects our Propensity to Lust so strongly, that it makes most Matches, & most of those Matches miserable unless when Beauty is gone, Virtue, good sense, good nature, Complaissance & Chearfullness Compensate the loss. An Agreeable genteel & neat woman with these qualities is therefore to be sought by a man of Sense.[61]

Margaret Dulany was all of these. As numerous passages from the *Itinerarium* suggest, Hamilton particularly admired a woman with sense and spunk.[62] Although his wife could not match his education—only the Dulany males attended universities; the girls attended finishing schools—she evidently could match his spirit. Hamilton, moreover, became wealthy only by association with his wife. Theirs was likely a more equal marriage than was typical at the time, and although they had no children—at least none that survived birth—they apparently enjoyed their life together.[63]

---

61. Letter dated Sept. 1, 1762, "Extracts from the Carroll Papers," *Maryland Historical Magazine*, 11 (1916), 272.
62. Hamilton repeatedly expresses his admiration for "sprightly, sensible" women in the *Itinerarium* (see pp. 138, 146, 171, 194).
63. For a good discussion of marital life in colonial Chesapeake society, see Blake, *Inside the Great House*, 126–74. Hamilton's mother wrote more than once that she had received letters from him and his wife attesting to

His marriage into the Dulany family produced several changes in Hamilton's life, the first of which was his adoption of the Anglican faith. Early eighteenth-century Scottish culture was "a thoroughly Calvinist culture,"[64] and Hamilton, like most Scots, was raised a Presbyterian. By 1747, however, he had long since stopped believing in the depravity of man and other Calvinist doctrines and was well on his way toward becoming a Presbyterian only in name.[65] In 1744 he recorded in his travel diary a conversation he had concerning his religion with a devout Presbyterian woman during his stay in Philadelphia:

> "You, sir," said she, "was educated a Presbyterian, and I hope you are not like most of your country men of that perswasion who, when they come abroad in the world, shamefully leave the meeting and go to church." I told her that I had dealt impartially betwixt both since I

---

their happiness together (see Mary Hamilton to AH, July 15, 1748, Feb. 15, 1749, and Oct. 25, 1749). Hamilton's will, dated October 18, 1747, leaves all of his property to his wife, unless there should be a posthumous child, who was to receive two-thirds of his estate (Maryland Hall of Records, lib. 30, fol. 106). This suggests that his wife could have been pregnant when Hamilton made out his will; if so, neither that child nor any other children that might have been born to them survived birth. Margaret Dulany (d. 1791) remarried in 1757 following Hamilton's death. She and her second husband, William Murdock, had two children, Rebecca and Margaret.

64. Charles Camic, *Experience and Enlightenment: Socialization for Cultural Change in Eighteenth-Century Scotland* (Chicago, 1983), 26. A good study of the influence of Presbyterianism on eighteenth-century Scottish culture is J. H. S. Burleigh, *A Church History of Scotland* (London, 1960), 261–85.

65. Hamilton called the doctrines of "justification, sanctification, adoption, regeneration, repentence, free grace, reprobation, [and] original sin" "chimerical knick knacks," "the monstruous and deformed offspring of scholastick, theologicall heads," worth contemplating "at no other times but when [he] took a cathartick or emetick in order to promote the operation if it proved too sluggish" (*Itin.*, 163, 121).

A Life of Liberality

came to the place, for I had gone to neither. "That is still worse," said she. (p. 27)

Like his Latitudinarian friend, the Reverend Thomas Bacon, Hamilton had come to believe in a rationally ordered universe, one in which the "revealed Law of God" was consistent with the "Law of Nature."[66] For Hamilton, as for Bacon, God was a benevolent deity who had made all people "dependent one upon the other, and by a mutual Exchange of Service and Assistance, to contribute to the Comfort and Support of each in Particular, as well as the general Benefit of the Whole."[67] These were good clubical sentiments. The Anglican church, which stressed a similar brand of "rational piety,"[68] came close enough to Hamilton's own beliefs that, even though he considered some of the church's sacraments foolish, he was able to join in faith.[69]

It simply made good sense, moreover, to practice the Anglican faith in a predominantly Anglican colony, and Hamilton was an eminently sensible man. When his brother-in-law, the Reverend

---

66. Thomas Bacon, *Four Sermons, Upon the Great and Indispensable Duty of All Christian Masters and Mistresses to Bring Up Their Negro Slaves in the Knowledge and Fear of God* (London, 1750), 1st sermon, 35.
67. Bacon, *Four Sermons*, 2nd sermon, 56.
68. Henry F. May, *The Enlightenment in America*, (New York, 1976), 67.
69. Hamilton disapproved of certain "High Church maxims" and considered "the promoters and favourers of these doctrines to be every whit as absurd and silly as the doctrines themselves" (*Itin.*, 109). In the *History* he parodies the thirty-nine articles of the Anglican Church, listing the Tuesday Club's forty-two mock maxims and pointing out that "These Clubical maxims, or rather articles, ... are as Consistent and harmonious among themselves, as the 39 Articles of the Church of England ... and as nicely Calculated for ... laying a firm foundation for eternal wrangles and disputes, In fine, they equal them in every respect, and excell them in one material point, vizt: in number, there being three more of them, and the number three is granted by many Subtile doctors to be a mystical and mysterious number" (3:149).

David Smith, wrote asking him to help a friend find a position in Maryland, Hamilton replied, "If [he] Intends to exercise the office of a Presbyterian preacher here, I wish him good fortune, but a good Income he never can have in that Capacity, where the Established Church is that of England," and he suggested that "If he could conscientiously take orders from a Bishop, ... he might probably Jump in to a living, of 40, or 50 hogsheads of Tobacco a year, which is worth near 200 pound Sterling Sallary, and which many less deserving men than he, here Enjoy" (AH to David Smith, [fall 1743]). When he married Margaret Dulany, Hamilton essentially took his own advice and joined the Anglican church, which was more accepted socially and more consistent with his own Latitudinarian tastes.[70] Two years later he was elected vestryman of St. Anne's Parish, a position he held until March 30, 1752.[71]

Hamilton's marriage to Margaret Dulany also produced significant changes in his financial and political status. By now he was making a good living as a physician-apothecary; his marriage into the Dulany family, however, made him financially secure. One of

---

70. It has been suggested more than once that Hamilton was a deist, but that seems unlikely. To be a deist in colonial Maryland was no more socially prudent than to be a Presbyterian (see Herbert M. Morais, *Deism in Eighteenth-Century America* [1934; rpt. New York, 1960], 13–28). And in the *History* Hamilton ridicules deists by hoping that the conclusion of William Warburton's *The Divine Legation of Moses* will "come out some time or other, to the Confusion of all Deists and freethinkers" (1:24).

71. St. Anne's Parish Vestry minutes, Maryland Hall of Records. Gerald E. Hartdagen discusses the significance of this office in "The Vestry as a Unit of Local Government in Colonial Maryland," *Maryland Historical Magazine*, 67 (1972), 363–88, and "The Anglican Vestry in Colonial Maryland: A Study in Corporate Responsibility," *Historical Magazine of the Protestant Episcopal Church*, 40 (1971), 315–35, 461–79.

colonial Maryland's principal landowners, Daniel Dulany helped his daughter and new son-in-law purchase nearly a thousand acres of land in the Annapolis area, four smaller tracts north of the Severn River, and a house lot in Annapolis.[72] Politically, too, Hamilton was strongly influenced by Dulany, the most respected figure in the proprietary camp.[73] Like Dulany, Hamilton was a Whig, but a moderate one.[74] One would suspect that, as a Whig who supported government by Parliament rather than the sort of feudalism practiced by Lord Baltimore, Hamilton would side with the Country rather than the Court party. Indeed, the letter concerning his election as common councilman in 1743 (quoted above) suggests that he did lean in that direction. But despite his Whiggish sentiments, Hamilton's experience as an observer and as a participant in the tumultuous world of Maryland politics had led him to lean increasingly toward moderation and stability, and consequently toward the proprietary camp. With the aid of the Dulanys (Daniel Dulany died shortly before the election, but Hamilton had the continued support of Dulany's sons), in 1753 Hamilton represented the Court party in the election for the

---

72. Maryland Hall of Records, Deeds, 1747, R.B. no. 2, 424–25, 428–29, 436–39, 441–44.

73. Dulany had at one time opposed proprietary interests in Maryland, but by 1747 he was a staunch supporter of Lord Baltimore's government (see Land, *The Dulanys of Maryland*, 62–85).

74. The Whiggish ideals espoused in the colonial South by men like Dulany are well discussed in H. Trevor Colbourn, *The Lamp of Experience: Whig History and the Intellectual Origins of the American Revolution* (Chapel Hill, 1965), 134–57. In the *History* Hamilton remarks that the members of the Whin-Bush Club (including himself) were all "Sober discrete moderate whigs" (1:53; cf. 1:173). Yet he also pokes fun at the kind of political grumblings that threaten to arise in the Tuesday Club from members who are "too strait laced in their whiggish principles" (1:361; cf. 1:250, 488).

Lower House seat of his recently deceased friend, Robert Gordon. Once again, the election was contested, but Hamilton was officially sworn in on October 19, 1753.[75] He served as a member of the Lower House until the Assembly adjourned on July 25, 1754, when he resigned, probably because of poor health.

Hamilton much preferred the convivial world of clubbing, and in 1749 he and several Tuesday Club members founded a Freemasons' lodge in Annapolis.[76] So much has been written about the anxieties that Freemasonry caused the church or the state and about all the nefarious rituals that Freemasons reputedly conducted behind closed doors[77] that the least sensational but perhaps most essential fact about Freemasonry has often been overlooked: in an age when clubbing was the thing to do, being a Freemason was as much a part of the normal social fabric of eighteenth-century life as being a member of any other club. "Though I am no free mason myself," Hamilton had written in the *Itinerarium* before his induction, "I believe the free masons to be an innocent and harmless society that have in their constitution nothing mysterious or beyond the verge of common human understanding, and their secret, which has made such a noise, I

---

75. *Archives of Maryland,* 50:xii, 168, 172, 175, 179, 180, 217. An excellent study of the struggle for power in the Lower Houses of Assembly in the southern colonies is Jack P. Greene, *The Quest for Power: The Lower Houses of Assembly in the Southern Royal Colonies, 1689–1776* (Chapel Hill, 1963).

76. Other Tuesday Club Freemasons included Jonas Green, John Lomas, Alexander Malcolm, John Gordon, Thomas Bacon, and Edward Dorsey. For further information on the foundation of the Annapolis lodge, see Lemay, *Men of Letters,* 239–40.

77. The popular literature of Freemasonry dicusses these issues at length, but the best scholarly analysis of the various controversies that Freemasonry provoked during the eighteenth century is Margaret C. Jacob, *The Radical Enlightenment: Pantheists, Freemasons and Republicans* (London, 1981).

A Life of Liberality

imagine is just no secret att all" (p. 19). To be sure, Freemasons encouraged and no doubt were amused by the misconceptions that the uninitiated entertained about their being a clandestine organization. That, after all, was part of the fun of belonging to that particular club, and Freemasons such as Hamilton did their best to exploit those misconceptions if only to better relish the joke. In *The History of the Tuesday Club* he more than once feigns ignorance about the "mysteries" of Freemasonry, observing, for instance, that clubs composed of Freemasons could not "by many connoiseurs... in a strict sense [be] reckoned Clubs," since they deal "in mysteries, which they keep Intirely to themselves" (1:86).[78] As Grand Master of the Annapolis lodge, Hamilton very well knew that he was not part of a mysterious, subversive organization but of a right honorable club.

The Annapolis lodge published three Masonic sermons, including the Reverend John Gordon's *Brotherly Love Explained and Enforc'd* (Annapolis, 1750), which developed the popular argument that man was a sociable being naturally inclined to acts of benevolence.[79] Gordon dedicated his sermon to the "Right Worshipful Alexander Hamilton M.D., Master," who appended to the sermon his own "Discourse Delivered from the Chair, in the Lodge-Room at *Annapolis*, by the Right Worshipful the Master,

---

78. The relationship between Freemasonry and the *History* is more thoroughly discussed in Robert Micklus, "The Secret Fall of Freemasonry in Dr. Alexander Hamilton's *The History of the Tuesday Club*," *Deism, Masonry, and the Enlightenment: Essays Honoring Alfred Owen Aldridge*, ed. J. A. Leo Lemay (Newark, D., 1987), 127–36.

79. The other two sermons, also dedicated to Hamilton, are William Brogden, *Freedom and Love. A Sermon ... in the Parish Church of St. Anne ...* (Annapolis, 1750), and Thomas Bacon, *A Sermon, Preached at Annapolis ... before a Society of Free and Accepted Masons ...* (Annapolis, 1753).

to the Brethren of the Ancient and Honourable Society of *Free and Accepted* Masons." The purpose of his discourse, Hamilton says, is to provide

> Instructions, concerning the Nature and Design of our *Ancient Craft;* which, whatever superstitious Notions the Vulgar may entertain of it; whatever Sarcasms or Sneers it may meet with, from those who are abundantly wise in their own Conceit; however it may be misapprehended, even by unskilful or indolent *Masons,* or misrepresented by malicious, profligate, or unworthy *Brethren;* may justly be defined, *A Plan or Scheme, originally intended to promote and establish LIBERTY, in the largest and most extensive Sense of the Word:* Hence conducive to the Advancement of the Practice of *Morality* and *Virtue,* to the cherishing and fomenting of *Brotherly Love, Charity,* and a general and diffusive *Love to Mankind;* to the Improvement of *Rational Religion,* or a due Reverence to the *Omnipotent Architect* and *Author of Nature;* in fine, to the Expulsion of *Barbarism* of every Kind, by hewing off our rough Corners, polishing and humanizing *Man,* and working strenuously to promote, improve, and encourage all *Liberal Arts* and useful Learning.

Hamilton then elaborates upon the three types of liberty—"Civil, Religious, and Moral"—that all virtuous Masons should practice, keeping in mind that all three should be subjected to the "Touchstone of *Reason."* He further adds that it is "one great Part of the Work of a *true Mason"* to encourage freedom of expression in the arts, since

> Men are naturally inquisitive, curious, and fond of new Discoveries; and therefore in a free State, where Wit and Invention are left at large, and there is full *Liberty* of speaking and writing, they will vigorously set about the Discovery of what may be curious, instructive, and profitable; and here a Fountain will be opened of useful Learning and Knowledge.

A Life of Liberality

But in the arts as in all phases of our lives, "true *Liberty* does not consist in an unlimited *Freedom of the Will*"; a man is not free, Hamilton argues, "unless his Conduct and Actions are conformable to the Dictates of a well-informed Conscience, and the *Lights of Reason*." It is evident, then,

> that before we can, with any Propriety, be denominated *free*, we must be the *Subjects of a free State*, reason *freely* without Heat or Rancour, on Points of *Religion*; and above all, be free from the miserable Thraldom of *vicious Passions*, and *weak unmanly Affections:* This last is indeed the chief Part of a *Mason's Work*, because he must necessarily advert to this, before he can acquire the Character of a *just* and *upright Man*, before he can *love the Public*, pursue *universal Good*, and promote the *general Interest*.

In Hamilton's day the precepts outlined in his discourse provided the framework by which not just all Freemasons but all enlightened men sought to structure their lives. The "upright man," in control of his passions and guided by the "Lights of Reason" in his pursuit of liberty, was obliged, as Hamilton concludes his discourse by saying, to perform works of "*Charity, Benevolence,* and *Brotherly Love*." Hamilton did his best to follow this ethic of liberality, and so did his fellow Masons and Tuesday Club members.

One of Hamilton's more charitable acts of brotherly love was his defense of his old medical school classmate, Dr. Adam Thomson, in 1751.[80] On November 21, 1750, Thomson had lectured on smallpox inoculation at the Philadelphia Academy's Public Hall and had then published his *Discourse on the Preparation of the Body*

---

80. Hamilton's health was so poor in 1743 that Thomson had thought of moving to Annapolis to replace his former classmate, "who they did not expect would live" (*Itin.*, 31).

[65]

for the Small-Pox: and the Manner of Receiving the Infection (Philadelphia, 1750). In his discourse Thomson made no effort to conceal his contempt for what he considered empirical quacks who performed inoculations without any knowledge of medical theory. Inoculation, he complained,

> seems to be considered by many as a mere chirurgical Operation, accordingly we see almost everyone who knows how to handle a Lancet intrusted with the whole Management of it; ... what ought to be done on this Occasion for the Safety and Security of the Patient, a judicious and skilful Physician only can judge, ... and yet of all Professions in America the true Qualifications of a Physician are the least examined into, ... [which] may, perhaps be occasioned in some Measure, by a Notion ... that Physic is not a *real Science,* founded on just and rational Principles, but a Sort of *Knack* to be got entirely by Practice, which an ignorant, illiterate Person, may as readily attain, as one of Learning and Knowledge, who has taken due Pains to study it.

Unsure, perhaps, of whom he was calling ignorant, several local physicians responded to Thomson's discourse.[81] But the most severe response was Dr. John Kearsley's *A Letter to a Friend: Containing Remarks on a Discourse Proposing a Preparation of the Body for the Small-Pox* (Philadelphia, 1751), in which Kearsley attacked Thomson's writing style, his method of inoculation, and his lack of learning and originality.

In support of Thomson, Hamilton published *A Defence of Dr. Thomson's Discourse on the Preparation of the Body for the Small Pox, and the Manner of Receiving the Infection* (Philadelphia, 1751). In this twenty-seven page pamphlet (addressed as a letter to an un-

---

81. See *Pennsylvania Journal,* Dec. 13, 20, and 25, 1750; Jan. 1, 8, and Apr. 18, 1751.

A Life of Liberality

named Philadelphia colleague),[82] Hamilton dismisses most of the newspaper articles as "not at all to the Purpose" but simply the "ill natured Sneers and rude Reflections" of a pack of "Physical Dunces." One of these dunces, he facetiously claims, has recently reported to him a

> newly discovered Method of curing dangerous Dysenteries, by Means of a certain pneumatic Operation. He informed me of "a Patient, dangerously ill with a *Bloody Flux,* at the Point of Death, who, finding some Difficulty in Respiration, desired his Servant... to apply his Mouth to his, and blow with all his Force into his Lungs, which the good natured Fellow did several Times; and, to the great Surprize of every Body, the seemingly forlorn Patient recovered." Whether such a Whimsical Cure as this be natural, I leave you to judge: For I shall make no Remark upon it; only, I think, the Gentleman might easily make an Improvement on this Discovery by applying his Mouth to a certain Part, through which he might convey his Air or *Flatus* more immediately into the Place, where that Distemper has it's Seat.

According to Hamilton, these "forward Prigs, who every where *set up for* Physicians, and trifle with Men's Constitutions, without the least Grain of ... Learning and Common Sense," are despicable "Quacks, Imposters, and Empirics," although some might claim that they are "a *right* worthy and venerable Society, who have been often useful in their Calling by multiplying the Fees of Grave-Diggers, Sextons [and] Undertakers." Rather than simply call Thomson names, Hamilton suggests that they try his methods, stating that "things of this Nature ought to be proved, or disproved, by Experience." Hamilton grants that medical theory

---

82. Lemay reasonably conjectures that Hamilton addressed his letter to Dr. Phineas Bond, who had studied under Kearsley and whom Hamilton admired (*Men of Letters,* 241).

must be proven by practical experience. But "bare Experience, without a rational Theory, is what all Empiricism is founded upon," and those who assert "*that a just Skill in* Physic *is to be acquired only by bare Experience and repeated Practice*" do not know the difference, he says, "betwixt the Terms *Quack* and *Physician.*" Physicians, whether university trained or independently trained, have done their reading; all others, Hamilton concludes, are mere "*Guess-Doctor*[s], or Empiric[s]."

As for Kearsley's complaint about Thomson's lack of originality, Hamilton states that this

> is a very merry Objection: For, granting it to be true, may not an Author write well, and yet say nothing new? Must a Performance... be rejected and condemned, because *really* there is *nothing* new propos'd?—If this Rule was to hold, I doubt we should lose many good and valuable Pieces, and retain many trifling Performances, which are altogether Novel, on Account of the strange unprecedented Nonsense they are stuffed with.

Although hardly original, Thomson's findings were based not upon haphazard experimentation but upon his careful study of Boerhaave—"the greatest Physician," Hamilton claims, "since the Days of *Hippocrates*"—and tested by experience. Hamilton felt that Kearsley owed his friend an apology, and eventually Kearsley did apologize for attacking Thomson.[83]

In the spring and summer of 1755 Hamilton became involved in another dispute, one that lay more outside his field of expertise. A letter from his brother John indicates that Hamilton provided medical assistance in the spring of 1755 to Sir Peter Halket, a family friend and one of Gen. Edward Braddock's officers, at Brad-

---

83. For further details on this dispute, see Lemay, *Men of Letters*, 240–44, and Douglas Gordon Carroll, Jr., *Medicine in Maryland, 1634–1900* (Baltimore, 1984), 16–18.

dock's camp in Alexandria, Maryland.[84] A few weeks later, on July 9, 1755, Braddock's army was decimated by the French at the Monongahela River near Fort Dusquesne. In only three hours Halket and nearly four hundred men were killed, over five hundred others wounded. To help defend his friend's reputation—Halket was rapidly becoming the scapegoat of the disaster in British papers—Hamilton interviewed several of the surviving officers of Braddock's army following their retreat into Maryland and in the summer of 1755 sent a seventeen-page account of the battle to his brother Gavin so that he could inform Halket's family of what actually transpired "at that bloody & Tragical Action."

Hamilton's letter places the blame squarely on Braddock's shoulders, stating that Braddock was "haughty and Imperious," "puff'd up with pride and intoxicated with power." Rather than bargain with the Indians, "he threatened... to put them all to the Sword, if they did not immediately join him, and absolutely for-[bade] them to Scalp the prisoners or Slain." The Indians simply "laugh'd at his threats" and refused to support him. According to Hamilton, Braddock treated the majority of his officers with similar contempt:

> with Sir Peter Halket, a Gentleman remarkable for his Civility and good nature, he was Scarce [on] Speaking terms, . . . he show'd no more respect to [Sir John St. Clair, the Quarter Master General] than

---

84. John Hamilton to Gavin Hamilton, May 7, 1755. Another letter from John to Gavin, dated October 6, 1755, suggests that Alexander had written to Gavin about the battle. These two letters and Hamilton's letter, undated and awkwardly transcribed in another hand, are at the National Library of Scotland ("Copie Letters to Baillie Hamilton Concerning the Battle in America," MS 6506; microfilm copy at the Maryland Historical Society). Breslaw provides transcriptions of these letters and discusses the events relating to them in "A Dismal Tragedy: Drs. Alexander and John Hamilton Comment on Braddock's Defeat," *Maryland Historical Magazine*, 75 (1980), 118–44.

if he had been his Lacquai, and he was only barely civil from the teeth outwards to Major George Washington, ... a Youth of an undaunted and brave Spirit, whose deserts are beyond my expression, and to whose care alone it was owing that this General was carried alive out of the Field of Battle.

When Halket tried to reason with him, Braddock "ordered him to go to his Station and give his advice when it was asked"; Halket replied "That he valued not his own life, ... but he was grieved, much grieved, to have ... [to witness] the certain destruction of so many brave men, who deserved a better fate." Moments later, Halket was shot to death and Braddock's army was in complete disarray. "By the whole conduct of this affair," Hamilton states, "it would appear, that the bad Success was chiefly owing to the rash and headstrong Conduct of the General." At the conclusion of his letter Hamilton notes that, like the Indians, "our Backwoods-men here and Huntsmen and many of our American Militia understand [how to] maintain a kind of Running Fight, Skulking behind Trees and Bushes." That, he points out, is the only way to fight successfully on American terrain, and "his Majesty's Regular Troops" had better start paying attention.

The summer of 1755 was a difficult one not only for Braddock's army but for Hamilton as well. During the previous winter his health had taken a turn for the worse: "I was then sent for by his wife," John told Gavin, "without his knowledge. He was Sick, but not so apprehensive of danger as his wife & her Brothers were, [which] made them send Express for me" (John Hamilton to Gavin Hamilton, May 7, 1755). By the time he wrote to Gavin in the spring, John felt confident that their younger brother had "perfectly recovered." But by the following fall he informed Gavin, "Our Brother Alexr. is still in a drooping condition, tho' better than he has been during the heat of the Summer. His ailment is such as he may suffer under yet, long before it gets the better of him, but cant well be cured as it is of the Tabid [consumptive] kind viz. an Ulcer in his Kidney" (John Hamilton to Gavin Hamilton, Oct. 6, 1755). As his brother probably knew, Hamilton would not last much longer.

Hamilton's condition increasingly prevented him from joining his club companions, and perhaps out of respect for his absence, the Tuesday Club did not even meet in June 1755. He returned on August 26, 1755, when he served as high steward and reintroduced one of the club's original members, Witham Marshe, and continued to attend irregularly during the next few months. But by February 11, 1756, he turned the record book over to his friend, William Lux,[85] with a letter asking him to

> take 'special Care [of the Records], let them be well kept, and produced at next Sederunt.... For the loss of these Archives, (in my Opinion) would be greater to Posterity than the Loss of the whole Transactions of Alexander the Great; for I think Charles Cole the great to be a greater Man than the former, in so far as he has done less Harm to Mankind; the Office of the first being that of a Cutthroat, and the Occupation of the other the keeping of a Store in a reputable and Merchantlike Manner, in North East Street in Annapolis, and (the most glorious of all his Occupations) the Ruling of the ancient and honorable Tuesday Club these ten years past, with Justice Equity and Moderation.

Even though he was forced to abdicate his position as record keeper, Hamilton continued to work on *The History of the Tuesday*

---

85. William Lux of Annapolis, an Annapolis merchant who left his entire estate to his "dearest friend and relation," William Lux of Baltimore (Maryland Hall of Records, Wills, 1772, vol. 38, p. 824). Hamilton's letter is the last entry in the second volume of minutes.

Club right up until his death. Dr. Upton Scott,[86] a club member who administered to Hamilton along with his brother John, wrote that Hamilton suffered from "excruciating pains" during his final months:

> His Brother directed the Treatment, & visited him occasionally, whilst it was my melancholy duty to daily watch the progress of his disease, & by my friendly attention render him all the aid & consolation which the Nature of his complaint would admit of. A liberal Use of Opiates was requisite to make life bearable, & when relieved from pain he amused himself by writing this History, indeed the love of whimsicall drollery was so predominant in his constitution, that, a few days before his death, when I called upon him, I found him just finishing a Story that he had been employed in writing, which he read to me with as much Glee & delight as he was wont to do at the Club, laughing at the same time most heartily.

As Scott states in his letter, Hamilton was the "Life & Soul" of the Tuesday Club. Things were not the same without Loquacious Scribble. The club met for the last time on February 10, 1756, even though Hamilton did not die until Tuesday, May 11, 1756, which would have been the club's eleventh anniversary. In the *Maryland Gazette* for May 13, 1756, Hamilton's good friend, Jonas Green, lamented the passing of the man they had all come to love:

> On Tuesday last in the Morning, Died... Alexander Hamilton, M.D. aged 44 Years. The Death of this valuable and worthy Gentle-

---

86. Scott (1724–1814) was a prominent Maryland physician and the first president of the Medical and Chirurgical Faculty of Maryland. His glowing obituary appeared in the *Maryland Gazette,* Mar. 3, 1814. Scott's letter, which calls Hamilton "the most eminent Physician in Annapolis" and attests to his "strict honour & integrity," is at the Maryland Historical Society, Howard Family Papers, MS 469. An abridged version of it appears at the front of the "Record," Maryland Historical Society, MS 854.

A Life of Liberality

man is universally and justly lamented: His medical Abilities, various Knowledge, strictness of Integrity, simplicity of Manners, and extensive Benevolence, having deservedly gained him the Respect and Esteem of all Ranks of Men.—No man, in his Sphere, has left fewer Enemies, or more Friends.[87]

---

87. Another obituary for Hamilton, written by his brother-in-law Walter Dulany, states: "In his Conversation he was instructive, full of Vivacity, & most peculiarly engaging. He had exquisite Parts & was very assiduous in his Studies, by which means he became accomplish'd in all the Refinemts. of Polite Literature.... His talents were happily adapted to every Branch of Science & his active Soul cou'd never be satisfy'd with Superficial Enquiries or rest 'til he had a Compitent knowledge of his Subject" (Maryland Historical Society, Dulany Papers, MS 1265).

CHAPTER TWO

Delightful Instruction
The *Itinerarium*

Hamilton's *Itinerarium*, a travel diary of his journey from Annapolis, Maryland, to York, Maine, and back during the summer of 1744, has been called "the best single portrait of men and manners, of rural and urban life, of the wide range of society and scenery in colonial America."[1] Yet it is only passingly mentioned—and often not mentioned at all—in most studies of colonial literature and culture.[2] That is hardly surprising, since travel literature as a whole has received little serious attention from lit-

---

1. Lemay, *Men of Letters in Colonial Maryland,* 229. The circumstances concerning Hamilton's trip, the composition of the *Itinerarium,* and its publication are discussed in ch. 1.
2. The best critical discussion of the *Itinerarium* is Lemay, *Men of Letters,* 218–29, but see also Elaine G. Breslaw, "Dr. Alexander Hamilton and the Enlightenment in Maryland," 30–46; Steven E. Kagle, *American Diary Literature, 1620–1799* (Boston, 1979), 63–67; and the introductions to the two editions of the *Itinerarium:* Albert Bushnell Hart, *Hamilton's Itinerarium* (St. Louis, 1907), ix–xxiv; and Bridenbaugh, *Gentleman's Progress: The Itinerarium of Dr. Alexander Hamilton, 1744,* xi–xxx.

erary scholars.[3] How can travel literature be considered serious literature at all, the argument runs, when so much of it consists of closet performances intended only for private audiences, when it provides merely a factual account of real events rather than the creative fruits of an author's imagination, and when it is often composed at such scattered intervals that it cannot possibly possess the unity and coherence we expect from serious literature.[4] Our reluctance to discuss travel literature as serious literature was not shared, however, by authors and reviewers in the eighteenth century, when the travel narrative was a respected and enormously popular literary genre.[5] "There would not, perhaps, be a more pleasant, or profitable study, among those which have their prin-

---

3. Two excellent studies, however, are available: Charles L. Batten, Jr.'s brief but well researched *Pleasurable Instruction: Form and Convention in Eighteenth-Century Travel Literature* (Berkeley, 1978); and Barbara Maria Stafford's massive *Voyage into Substance: Art, Science, Nature, and the Illustrated Travel Account, 1760–1840* (Cambridge, Mass., 1984). Also informative are R. W. Frantz, *The English Traveller and the Movement of Ideas, 1660–1732* (1934; rpt. Lincoln, 1967); Percy G. Adams, *Travelers and Travel Liars, 1660–1800* (Berkeley, 1962), *Travel Literature and the Evolution of the Novel* (Lexington, Ky., 1983), and "Perception and the Eighteenth-Century Traveler," *The Eighteenth Century: Theory and Interpretation*, 26 (1985), 139–57; Kagle, *American Diary Literature*; John Butt, *The Mid-Eighteenth Century* (Oxford, 1979), 244–65; Wayne Franklin, *Discoverers, Explorers, Settlers: The Diligent Writers of Early America* (Chicago, 1979); and Michael McKeon, *The Origins of the English Novel, 1600–1740* (Baltimore, 1987), 100–105.

4. Kagle discusses these and other reasons why travel literature has been undervalued by literary critics in *American Diary Literature*, 20–24, and "The Diary as Art: A New Assessment," *Genre*, 6 (1973), 416–27.

5. As McKeon points out, late in the seventeenth century the Royal Society issued specific instructions concerning the composition of only one prose form—the travel narrative—which established it as one of the most respected literary genres and "the richest example of the interplay of critical theory and practice" during the early eighteenth century (*The Origins of the English Novel*, 101–102, 118).

ciple end in amusement," Fielding wrote, "than that of travels or voyages, if they be writ, as they might be, and ought to be, with a joint view to the entertainment and information of mankind."[6] "A book of travels, in which materials are in general important, and well managed," one reviewer concurred,

> is one of the most entertaining and instructive of literary productions. There is a happy mixture in it of the *utile* and the *dulce;* it amuses and captivates our fancy, without the fiction of romance; it gives us a large proportion of moral and political information, without the tediousness and perplexity of system. It promotes and facilitates the intercourse of countries remote from each other; it dispels from our minds unreasonable and gloomy antipathies against those manners, customs, forms of government, and religion, to which we have not been bred: it makes man mild, and sociable to man; it makes us consider ourselves and all mankind as brethren, the workmanship of one Supreme benign Creator.[7]

Addison voiced the sentiments of many early eighteenth-century readers when he said, "There are no books which I more delight in than in travels."[8] Later in the century, from 1773 to 1784, the two most frequently borrowed books from the Bristol Library were Patrick Brydone's *Tour through Sicily and Malta* (1773) and John Hawkesworth's *Account of the Voyages... in the Southern Hemisphere* (1773).[9] Little wonder, then, that while Fielding was paid a respectable one thousand pounds for *Tom Jones*, Hawkesworth received an exorbitant six thousand pounds for his

---

6. *The Journal of a Voyage to Lisbon*, ed. Harold E. Pagliaro (New York, 1963), 23.
7. *Critical Review*, 30 (1770), 195–96.
8. *Tatler*, no. 254
9. Paul Kaufman, *Borrowings from the Bristol Library, 1773–1784* (Charlottesville, Va., 1960), 122.

Voyages.[10] From the beginning of the century until the end, the books most in demand and those that reaped the greatest profits were travel narratives.

The reasons for the "unparalleled popularity"[11] of nonfiction travel literature during the eighteenth century are numerous. As the passages quoted above suggest, the travel narrative particularly appealed to an age that held as virtually sacrosanct Horace's literary dictum that all good literature should delight and instruct. A well-written travel account did both: it instructed without resorting to the formality of political treatises or philosophical essays, and it entertained without resorting to the frivolous fictions of popular romances. Traveling and travel reading, moreover, naturally appealed to an age that stressed sociability as a key—if not *the* key—to happiness.[12] Melancholic or physically ill people were encouraged to travel not simply to find a rest cure in a more congenial climate but because travel forced them to get up and socialize, to broaden the scope of their associates, and at the same time to broaden their knowledge of social and intellectual developments in other parts of the world. Also, by merging artful narrative with scientific data, the travel narrative thrived during an age that firmly believed in the interdisciplinary nature of the arts and sciences and in the ideal of the "universal man" who could master many subjects. And it thrived for a more simple reason, too: it catered to an obvious craving among eighteenth-

---

10. Adams, *Travelers and Travel Liars*, 224.
11. Batten, *Pleasurable Instruction*, 1; Adams, too, observes that "in the history of ideas no other period seems to have felt so much the influence of these unofficial reporters" (*Travelers and Travel Liars*, 6).
12. Two good discussions of the eighteenth-century emphasis on sociability are Bryson, *Man and Society: The Scottish Inquiry of the Eighteenth Century,* 148–72, and Shields, "Happiness in Society: The Development of an Eighteenth-Century American Poetic Ideal."

century readers to discover the unusual. With harmonious phrases such as "whatever is, is right" constantly ringing in our ears, we tend to minimize the paradoxical position that oddity held in the literature of an age that prized symmetry. For travel writers, as for natural philosophers, "anomalies were the object of experience,"[13] and although travel literature could hardly be called a subversive genre, it did appeal to the natural curiosity of many eighteenth-century readers who wished to be informed of the anomalous, and not simply the harmonious, aspects of human existence.

But what appealed most to eighteenth-century readers—and what modern readers, I think, have the most difficulty coming to terms with in approaching travel literature as serious literature—was the sheer factuality of travel accounts. The travel narrative was ideally suited to an age that valued empirical observation as the means to understanding truth. As Paul Fussell, Jr., suggests, "There is something about both the actual experience of travel and the literary experience of the travel report . . . that comes very near the heart of the dominant eighteenth-century idea of knowledge as a sequential accumulation of particulars collected from a multifarious but verifiable objective reality."[14] In the eighteenth century the ability to communicate objective data artfully became the *summum bonum* of serious literature, and it was largely because of the travel writer's

---

13. Simon Schaffer, "Natural Philosophy," *The Ferment of Knowledge: Studies in the Historiography of Eighteenth-Century Science*, ed. G. S. Rousseau and Roy Porter (Cambridge, 1980), 80.

14. "Patrick Brydone: The Eighteenth-Century Traveler as Representative Man," *Literature as a Mode of Travel: Five Essays and a Postscript*, intro. Warner G. Rice (New York, 1963), 54–55. J. Paul Hunter similarly argues that the "characteristic mode of the [eighteenth] century" was the "acquisitive mode," which was particularly manifested in travel literature (*Occasional Form, Henry Fielding and the Chains of Circumstance* [Baltimore, 1975], 219).

nonmetamorphic scrutiny of the particulars of this world that truth telling was elevated to aesthetic status. Resisting allegorical or any other nonoptical transformational modes, the traveler in search of fact relied on an exploratory method consonant with that of empirical science.... The [traveler's] enterprise, like the scientist's, was predicated on the belief that he could discover a tangible (not an illusory) world exuberant with details and alive with individualities that would withstand customary patterning, generalization, or schematization.[15]

Barbara Maria Stafford calls this type of perception the "scientific gaze," which she distinguishes from Michel Foucault's "clinical gaze." Her point, however, is much the same as Foucault's: that during the eighteenth century there arose an "objectively based correlation [between] the visible and expressible," and that "an absolutely new use of scientific discourse was then defined: a use involving fidelity and unconditional subservience to the coloured content of experience—to say what one sees."[16] This "scientific gaze" informs most eighteenth-century literature in ways that we have only begun to appreciate, but especially the travel diary, which emphasized the correlation between objective viewing and objective expression more than any other literary genre.

If, then, Hamilton's *Itinerarium* is indeed the "best travel book" in colonial America,[17] it is important to examine the reasons why. J. A. Leo Lemay and Carl Bridenbaugh have discussed several of the ways in which the *Itinerarium* portrays people and manners in colonial America.[18] That, to be sure, is what makes it

---

15. Stafford, *Voyage into Substance*, 1–2.
16. *The Birth of the Clinic: An Archaeology of Medical Perception* (New York, 1973), 196.
17. Geoffrey D. Needler, "Linguistic Evidence from [Dr.] Alexander Hamilton's 'Itinerarium,'" *American Speech*, 42 (1967), 211.
18. *Men of Letters*, 218–29; *Gentleman's Progress*, xi-xxx.

Delightful Instruction

particularly valuable to students of American culture. But if it is more than just an excellent colonial American travel diary—if it is a first-rate eighteenth-century travel diary, period—we need to address some larger questions as well. Most important, to what extent does it reflect the method of perception typical of the age in which Hamilton lived? And to what extent does it employ the conventions and meet the critical standards imposed upon travel literature during the eighteenth century? In the following pages I hope to answer those questions and to examine further Hamilton's portrayal of colonial life in the *Itinerarium*.

Foucault defines two types of perception in the eighteenth century: the "horizontal gaze" of the natural historian, which he says dominated most of the century; and the "vertical" or "clinical gaze" of the physician, which he says emerged toward the end of the century.[19] Stafford has convincingly shown that Foucault's "clinical gaze"—the ability to plunge vertically, to perceive and interpret internal rather than merely external phenomena—existed much earlier in the eighteenth century than he suggests; she therefore uses the broader term, "scientific gaze," to describe a method of perception that is both horizontal and vertical, a method of perception, she demonstrates, that permeated several disciplines in the eighteenth century including travel writing.[20] Hamilton is a good example of a mid-century travel writer who employs both types of perception. At the University of Edinburgh, an eighteenth-century haven of natural philosophy, he was trained to focus upon external phenomena with the "horizontal gaze" of a natural historian and then, as a medical student who

---

19. Foucault elaborates upon these terms in *The Birth of the Clinic*.
20. Stafford develops the distinctions between her thesis and Foucault's throughout *Voyage into Substance*, but see esp. p. 320.

[81]

dissected human and other animal bodies, to focus upon internal phenomena with the "vertical gaze" of a physician. In the *Itinerarium,* his first major literary effort after receiving his medical degree, Hamilton fuses both types of perception.

Like most eighteenth-century natural historians, Hamilton seeks primarily to describe, not to classify external phenomena in the *Itinerarium.* "It would be an error," Jacques Roger points out, "to forget, as Foucault seems to do, that for many important naturalists of the age the most necessary task was not to classify, but to describe living [things]."[21] The same can be said of most eighteenth-century travel writers and travel diaries, except they were also concerned with describing non-living things. Hamilton's *Itinerarium,* for one, is loaded with precise descriptions of the various city designs, churches, fortifications, houses, landscapes, and natural objects he sees during his tour. He writes, for example, that

> the city of Albany lyes on the west side of Hudson's River upon a rising hill about 30 or 40 miles below where the river comes out of the lake and 160 miles above New York. The hill whereon it stands faces the south east. The city consists of three pritty compact streets, two of which run paralell to the river and are pritty broad, and the third cuts the other two att right angles, running up towards the fort, which is a square stone building about 200 foot square with a bastion att each corner, each bastion mounting eight or ten great guns, most of them 32 pounders.... There are three market houses in this city and three publick edifices, upon two of which are cupolos or spires, vizt., upon the Town House and the Dutch church. The English church is a great, heavy stone building without any steeple, standing just below the fort.... This city is inclosed by a rampart or wall of wooden palisadoes about 10 foot high and a foot thick, being the

---

21. "The Living World," *The Ferment of Knowledge,* 265.

trunks of pine trees rammed into the ground, pinned close together, and ending each in a point att top.... At each 200 foot distance round this wall is a block house, and from the north gate of the city runs a thick stone wall down into the river, 200 foot long, at each end of which is a block house. (pp. 71–72)

In Salem, Massachusetts, he similarly describes one of the houses he visits, Browne Hall, and its surrounding landscape:

[This] house stands upon the top of a high hill and is not yet quite finished. It is built in the form of an H with a middle body and two wings. The porch is supported by pillars of the Ionick order about 15 foot high, and betwixt the windows of the front are pilasters of the same. The great hall or parlour is about 40 foot long and 25 wide, with a gallery over the first row of windows, and there is two large rooms upon a floor in each of the wings, about 25 foot square. From this hill you have a most extensive view. To the southwest you see the Blue Hills about 36 miles' distance, to the east the sea and severall islands, . . . and all around you a fine landskip covered with woods, a mixture of hills and valleys, land and water, upon which variety the eye dwells with pleasure. (pp. 120–21)

Occasionally, too, Hamilton describes natural objects—particularly stone formations—simply for their intrinsic interest as natural objects. At Staten Island, for instance, he remarks, "I took notice of one intire stone there about 10 foot high, 12 foot long, and 6 or 7 foot thick. At one end of it grew an oak tree, the trunk of which seemed to adhere or grow to the stone" (p. 39). Hamilton's interest in natural objects *as objects* anticipates a growing interest in these phenomena during the Enlightenment, when "individual components of matter [were seen as] eloquent of their own history."[22] But whether it be natural or man-made objects,

---

22. Stafford, *Voyage into Substance*, 284.

cities or scenery, Hamilton describes all of the external phenomena he perceives in great detail. This was typical of the "horizontal gaze" of the natural historian, and in an age that stressed empirical observation, it was exactly the sort of thing most readers of travel narratives expected and relished.

Hamilton also exhibits the "vertical gaze" of the physician in the *Itinerarium* by penetrating beneath the exteriors of many of the objects he perceives. Indeed, one could argue that traveling and travel writing are by definition constant acts of penetration, constant probings into various phenomena. The traveler penetrates the landscape and moves not simply over but *through* space. His or her language reflects that movement, as when Hamilton reports that he rode "thro very barren waste land" and "thro a plain of 6 or eight miles long where was nothing but oak brush or bushes two foot high, very thick" (p. 93). Like other travelers, Hamilton also moves through many of the objects he initially perceives externally. When he attends the Reverend William Hooper's church at Boston, he describes first its exterior, then steps inside and carefully describes the pulpit all the way down to the pulpit cushion (p. 109). During his visit to Albany, he begins by describing the city and the cleanliness of the houses. But rather than stop there, his gaze moves inward, examining the floors, "laid with rough plank which, in time, by constant rubbing and scrubbing becomes as smooth as if it had been plained"; the bedrooms, curiously placed in "alcoves so that you may go thro all the rooms of a great house and see never a bed"; the china in the cabinets; and the kitchens, whose walls are adorned with dishes "in the manner of pictures, having a hole drilled thro the edge of the plate or dish and a loop of ribbon put into it to hang it by" (p. 72). In effect, Hamilton's gaze moves not only into the houses but into the alcoves, into the cabinets, even into the holes on the plates. Although these passages fall short of the kind of extensive probing into substrata typical of clinical dissections or eighteenth-century mineralogical treatises, they do demonstrate the physician's—and, as Stafford repeatedly stresses, the travel writer's—habitual penetration into the interiors of the phenomena he or she perceives.

Hamilton's method of perception is typical of the "scientific gaze" of eighteenth-century travelers. His perception of natural scenery, however, is less typical of a traveler writing in 1744. Eighteenth-century travel writers were expected to provide observations on nature, but few travel narratives written before mid century display any interest in uncultivated scenery.[23] The *Itinerarium,* however, is an exception to the rule. As Lemay observes, no colonial writer before Hamilton "was so interested in the wilderness as wilderness, so fascinated by scenery for its picturesqueness, or so absorbed by the variegated face of the American landscape."[24] Hamilton describes in detail the waterfalls north of Albany, the sea beating against the Connecticut coast, fields of wheat and barley in New Jersey, even a barren stretch of land in Long Island. But what attracts his eye most is the awesome scenery along the Hudson Valley. He describes Buttermilk Island as "a very wild, romantick place surrounded with huge rocks, dreadfull precipices, and scraggy broken trees" (p. 77), and Cook's Island as "a small rock about 10 paces long and 5 broad upon which is buried a certain cook of a man of war. . . . His sepulchre is sur-

---

23. George B. Parks develops this point in "The Turn to the Romantic in the Travel Literature of the Eighteenth Century," *Modern Language Quarterly,* 25 (1964), 22–33. Batten similarly states that it was not until the 1770s that "travelers for the first time turned extensively . . . to descriptions of the beauties of nature" (*Pleasurable Instruction,* 97).

24. *Men of Letters,* 224.

rounded with 10 or 12 small pine trees about 20 foot high which make a grove over him. This wild and solitary place," Hamilton says, with its

> huge precipices and inaccessible steeps..., infused in my mind a kind of melancholly and filled my imagination with odd thoughts which, att the same time, had something pleasant in them. It was pritty to see the springs of water run down the rocks, and what entertained me not a little was to observe some pritty large oaks growing there, and their roots to appearance fixed in nothing but the sollid stone where you see not the least grain of mould or earth. (pp. 55–56)

In this passage Hamilton broadly associates melancholy, solitude, and sublimity with nature in a way that would become increasingly familiar at the turn of the nineteenth century.[25] Yet the measurements he provides at the beginning of the passage and the sharply focused observation of the roots in solid stone at the end serve to frame even his Romantic reveries in the "scientific gaze" of the eighteenth century.

These descriptions of Romantic landscapes would have helped to satisfy the eighteenth-century craving for the unusual in travel narratives. Hamilton further satisfies that craving when he turns from describing various phenomena to describing people. People bring out the comic side of his descriptive powers, and he effectively burlesques the travel genre's preoccupation with the unusual by playing the wide-eyed traveler who carefully describes the many extraordinary characters he meets during his fantastic

---

25. Hamilton also wrote a poem celebrating solitude, antiquity, and the wildness of nature, which he included in a letter to his brother-in-law, the Reverend David Smith (AH to David Smith, [fall] 1743.) "If these verses are bad," he told Smith, "dont tell any body they are mine." They are not particularly bad, so I have not violated his trust in exposing them.

voyage. Most of these characters are genuinely odd in some way, not just character types. Some merely possess strange mannerisms or odd physical characteristics, such as the Reverend John Milne, who, "att every the least triffling expression and common sentence in discourse,... would shrug up his shoulders and stare one in the face as if [he] had uttered some very wonderful thing" (p. 66); Dr. James McGraw, an Irishman who said surprisingly little, but when he did he "leaned over the table and streeched out his neck and face, goose-like, as if he had been going to whisper in your ear," and who, "when he drank to any in the company,... would not speak but kept bowing and bowing... till the person complimented either observed him of his own accord or was hunched into attention by his next neighbour" (p. 83); or a young woman who "seemed very handsom in every respect and, indeed, needed neither stays nor hoop to set out her shapes,... [but] had a vile cross in her eyes which spoilt... the beauty and symmetry of her features" (p. 134). Several are vintage eighteenth-century grotesques, such as the hectoring Scotsman who, "having a homely carbuncle kind of a countenance with a hideous knob of a nose,... screwd it into a hundred different forms while he spoke and gave such a strong emphasis to his words that he merely spit in one's face att three or four foot's distance.... The company seemed to admire him much," Hamilton says, "but he set me a staring" (p. 42). And many are true originals. Hamilton reports that one evening in New York he heard a young man sing in the most unfathomable key ever heard. "I sat for some time," he incredulously observes,

> imoveable with surprize. The like I never heard, and the thing seemed to me next a miracle.... The whole company were amazed that any person but a woman or eunuch could have such a pipe and began to question his virility; but he swore that if the company pleased he

would show a couple of as good witnesses as any man might wear. He then imitated severall beasts, ... and all to such perfection that nothing but nature could match it. When the landlord (a clumsy, tallow faced fellow in a white jacket) came to receive his reckoning, our mimick's art struck and surprized him in such a manner that it fixed him quite, like one that had seen the Gorgon's head, and he might have passed for a statue done in white marble. (pp. 84–85)

Two days later, he reports having dinner with a doctor who had agreed to dine with him and his friend Stephen Bayard only if they would assure him that no peas would be served. They did, but just as they began eating, the peas were nevertheless served, "att which the doctor began to stare and change colour in such a manner," Hamilton says, "that I thought he would have been convulsed, but he started up and ran out of doors so fast that we could never throw salt on his tail again.... This was the oddest antipathy ever I was witness to" (p. 87). And just a few days later he comes across a seventy-five-year-old man who entertains him by "jumping half a foot high upon his bum without touching the floor with any other part of his body. Then he turned and did the same upon his belly" (p. 92). But perhaps the oddest character of all is the one Hamilton encounters at the end of his marvelous journey. Shortly before reentering Maryland, he recalls,

> I met a monstrous appearance, by much the greatest wonder and prodigy I had seen in my travells, and every whit as strange a sight by land as a mermaid is att sea. It was a carter driving his cart along the road who seemed to be half man, half woman. All above from the crown of his head to the girdle seemed quite masculine, the creature having a great, hideous, unshorn black beard and strong course features, a slouch hat, cloth jacket, and great brawny fists, but below the girdle there was nothing to be seen but petticoats, a white apron, and the exact shape of a woman with relation to broad, round buttocks. I would have given something to have seen this creature turned topsy

turvy, to have known whether or not it was an hermaphrodite, having often heard of such animals but never having seen any to my knowledge; but I thought it most prudent to pass by peaceably, asking no questions lest it should prove the devil in disguise. (p. 194)

Strange and wondrous indeed, yet real and precisely described: the very stuff of eighteenth-century travel narratives—burlesqued.

Whether serious or facetious, Hamilton generally manages to focus the reader's attention upon what he sees, not upon himself or his interpretation of what he sees. As Stafford argues, during the eighteenth century "an admirable campaign was waged to get at the truth of the phenomenal world without imprisoning it in self-revelatory idiosyncrasy."[26] Readers of travel narratives were primarily interested in exploring the phenomenal world, and travel writers who spent too much time talking about such things as what they wore or what they said, or too much time interpreting phenomena or revealing their feelings about what they saw, were viewed as self-indulgent egotists. But for their narratives to appear credible, travel writers were forced to tell them in the first person: "'I said, and I did, and I went'—how shall I get rid of it?" one travel writer wondered, "for the soul of me I can't tell!—it hurts myself—how then must it affect my readers?"[27] Thus, an eighteenth-century travel writer had to walk a fine line:

> he had to include a sufficiently detailed record of his experiences to prove that he actually visited the [places] he described, but he could not tell too much about himself and his adventures. If his narrative

---

26. *Voyage into Substance*, 1. The Royal Society helped to initiate this campaign late in the seventeeth century, when it instructed authors of travel narratives only to shape and sort out details, not to moralize upon their observations (see McKeon, *The Origins of the English Novel*, 103).

27. Samuel Paterson, *Another Traveller!* (1767–1769), 1:35–36.

appeared too circumstantial, he would usually be attacked as an egotist; if it seemed too contrived, he would frequently be criticized as a writer of fiction... interested in entertaining readers at the expense of their instruction.[28]

A travel narrative that was too self-revealing or too contrived was panned by eighteenth-century reviewers because it failed to provide useful instruction and because, by diverting the reader's attention from the phenomenal world to the subjective world of the writer, it failed as an instrument of perception.

Hamilton manages to avoid these charges by objectively reporting the phenomena he sees and by seldom allowing himself to become the center of attention in the *Itinerarium*. When he does, it is usually to emphasize his own incongruous appearance, not to aggrandize himself. The travel writer, Hawkesworth wrote, should "never be the object of admiration, and seldom of esteem."[29] Decked out in his green velvet coat and laced hat, and sporting his pistols and sword, Hamilton is more an object of wonder and puzzlement than of admiration and esteem as he tours the northern colonies. When he arrives at Trenton, he is "treated... with a dish of staring and gaping from the shop doors and windows" (p. 31). Near Greenwich Village the "wild and rustick" country children "stared like sheep" upon him, "being amazed at [his] laced hat and sword" (pp. 54–55). And near Providence he reports that the people "were as simple and awkward as sheep, and so wild that they would not appear in open view but kept peeping att [him] from behind doors, chests, and benches" (p. 150). Rather than simply stare and gape at him, one

---

28. Batten, *Pleasurable Instruction*, 63.
29. *Adventurer*, 4.

Delightful Instruction

more cultivated Boston woman approaches Hamilton's friend Samuel Hughes to ask a few questions about him:

> "Lord!" said she, "what strange mortall is that?" " 'Tis the flower of the Maryland beaux," said Hughes. "Good God!" said the belle, "does that figure come from Maryland?" "Madam," said Hughes, "he is a Maryland physitian." "O Jesus! A physitian! Deuce take such odd looking physicians." (p. 139)

"When he told me of this conference," Hamilton writes, "I desired Hughes

> to give my humble service to the lady and tell her that it gave me vast pleasure to think that any thing particular about my person could so attract her resplendent eyes as to make her take notice of me in such a singular manner, and that I intended to wait upon her that she might entertain her opticks with my oddity, and I mine with her unparallelled charms. (p. 139)

To the average person on the streets, Hamilton's appearance is just as odd as many of the odd characters he describes. It is all a matter of perspective. Indeed, a large part of what makes passages like these so humorous is that Hamilton inverts the typical perspective of travel writers: here the observer becomes the observed, and all get to play the optical game of eighteenth-century travelers—the observance of oddity.

Hamilton frequently emphasizes not only the oddity of his appearance but also the awkwardness of his behavior. In Boston, for instance, an attractive young lady entertains him one evening by displaying her assorted talents, musical and otherwise. "I told her that she playd the best spinett that I had heard since I came to America," Hamilton says. Her father asks him if that is the best he can do for a compliment, which, he says, "dashed me a little,"

> but I soon replied that the young lady was every way so deserving and accomplished that nothing that was spoke in her commendation could in a strick sense be called a compliment. I breathed a little after this speech, there being something romantick in it and, considering human nature in the propper light, could not be true. The young lady blushed; the old man was pleased and picked his teeth, and I was conscious that I had talked nonsense. (p. 138)

While dining with his landlady and her daughters at Narrows Ferry, New York, he behaves less romantically but even more awkwardly:

> As I sat down to dinner I observed a manner of saying grace quite new to me. My landlady and her two daughters put on solemn, devout faces, hanging down their heads and holding up their hands for half a minute. I, who had gracelessly fallen too without remembering that duty according to a wicked custom I had contracted, sat staring att them with my mouth choak full.... [During dinner] the landlady called for the bedpan. I could not guess what she intended to do with it unless it was to warm her bed to go to sleep after dinner, but I found that it was used by way of a chaffing dish to warm our dish of clams. I stared att the novelty for some time, and reaching over for a mug of beer... my bag sleeve catched hold of the handle of the bed pan and unfortunately overset the clams, at which the landlady... muttered a scrape of Dutch of which I understood not a word except mynheer, but I suppose she swore, for she uttered her speech with an emphasis. (p. 40)

In these and similar situations, Hamilton, in his typical pose as the wide-eyed traveler, sits staring at these unusual customs, when actually the only person behaving oddly here is himself.

When Hamilton does occupy center stage, then, it is generally to invert the optical lens of the traveler and to poke fun at the oddity of his own appearance and behavior. More often, though,

Delightful Instruction

he prefers to divert the reader's attention from himself altogether. During his stay at Philadelphia, for instance, he reports,

> I dined att a taveren with a very mixed company of different nations and religions. There were Scots, English, Dutch, Germans, and Irish; there were Roman Catholicks, Church men, Presbyterians, Quakers, Newlightmen, Methodists, Seventh day men, Moravians, Anabaptists, and one Jew. The whole company consisted of 25 planted round an oblong table in a great hall well stoked with flys. The company divided into committees in conversation; the prevailing topick was politicks and conjectures of a French war. A knott of Quakers there talked only about selling of flower and the low price it bore. The[y] touched a little upon religion, and high words arose among some of the sectaries. . . . A gentleman that sat next me proposed a number of questions concerning Maryland. . . . In my replys I was reserved, pretending to know little of the matter as being a person whose business did not lye in the way of history and politicks. (p. 20)

Against this motley, noisy background, Hamilton says virtually nothing. While dining in the home of a Boston family who embrace Whitefield's doctrines, he similarly relates what others had to say, but he "thought fit only to be a hearer" (p. 112). Toward the end of his tour, he again observes, "I dined att Cockburn's [in Philadelphia] where was a sett of very comical phizzes and a very vulgar unfurbished conversation which I did not join in but eat my dinner and was a hearer" (p. 191). In these and other scenes, Hamilton's restraint obviously serves to emphasize his gentlemanly superiority to the noise and clamor around him.[30] But it

---

30. As Lawrence C. Wroth has stated, throughout the *Itinerarium* Hamilton "shows himself to be aware of his superiority in position, experience, and education to most of the people he casually encounters," but as he rode along "his gentry was less in his mind than his curiosity and his hu-

also establishes him as an objective observer, and it constantly deflects the reader's attention from the narrator to the world around him. It functions, in other words, as more than just a character trait; it helps to keep the reader's eye on the phenomenal world outside the narrator in a way that eighteenth-century readers and reviewers of travel narratives would have applauded.

Hamilton's unobtrusiveness as a narrator and his precise descriptions of usual and unusual people or things were two qualities that eighteenth-century reviewers expected from travel narratives. They are two qualities, moreover, that establish him as a reliable observer of colonial life, along with another quality that reviewers expected: a middle prose style that was neither too specialized nor too common for the average reader. As part of an overall effort to "instruct without pedantry and entertain without familiarity," eighteenth-century travel writers aimed at "a kind of middle rank between the solidity of studied discourse and the freedom of colloquial conversation."[31] The *Itinerarium* generally hits that mark. Even when Hamilton's gaze is most scientific his language is never overspecialized; and he seldom slips into low or vulgar language himself. He does, however, display a greater interest in colloquial expressions and common language than would have suited most eighteenth-century reviewers, who would have wondered why he would bother to note that his black servant, Dromo, "desired the skipper [of a Rhode Island ferry] to 'trow away his stones, de horse be better ballast" (p. 101); or that he "was saluted with How' s't ni tap" (p. 34) by an Indian as he

manity, ... [and] when he was supercilious it was without the smug superiority of the intellectual" (review of Bridenbaugh's edition, *William and Mary Quarterly*, 3rd Ser., 6 [1949], 125–26).
31. Batten, *Pleasurable Instruction*, 46; [Andrew Swinton or William Thomson], *Travels into Norway, Denmark and Russia* (London, 1792), vii.

Delightful Instruction

passed through Princeton; or even that "the common stile of salutation upon the road [near Brandywine, Pennsylvania] was How d'ye? and How is't?" (p. 16).[32] They also would have questioned why he would bother to record the low conversations of the many Dutch, Irish, and Scottish colonials he met along his way, including that of a certain innkeeper at New York named Todd. "As to cuikry," Todd informs his company one evening,

> I defaa ony French cuik to ding me, bot a haggis is a dish I wadna tak the trouble to mak. Look ye, gentlemen, there was anes a Frenchman axed his frind to denner. His frind axed him "What ha' ye gotten till eat?" "Four an' twenty legs of mutton," quo' he, "a' sae differently cuiked that ye winna ken whilk is whilk." Sae whan he gaed there, what deel was it, think ye, but four and twenty sheep's trotters, be God. (pp. 42–43)

Todd was just about to continue "this tale of a tub," Hamilton says, when he was called into another room, where his company heard him roaring, "dam ye bitch, wharefor winna ye bring a canle?" (p. 43). Eighteenth-century reviewers probably would have questioned Hamilton's judgment in recording conversations as vulgar as this one. As Wayne Franklin observes, however, for colonial travelers "language seemed capable of domesticating the strangeness of America,"[33] and, one might add, of domesticating the crudeness. Throughout the *Itinerarium* Hamilton's own urbane middle style frames, domesticates, and at the same time accentuates the strangeness of colonial speech much like the framework device later employed by tall tale writers.

---

32. For further discussion of the language in the *Itinerarium* and a useful list of the Americanisms it contains, see Needler, "Linguistic Evidence from [Dr.] Alexander Hamilton's 'Itinerarium,'" 211–18.

33. *Discoverers, Explorers, Settlers: The Diligent Writers of Early America*, 5.

As the examples quoted thus far demonstrate, Hamilton generally acts as a detached observer of colonial life, whether as a viewer or a listener. But despite his objectivity and gentlemanly restraint, Hamilton's attitudes are unmistakable. He is a comic variation of what Charles L. Batten, Jr., calls the "splenetic traveler," a figure that would become increasingly familiar in the second half of the eighteenth century. Batten identifies the splenetic traveler according to the older sense of the word: as a melancholic, misanthropic observer who is "impervious to the seductive allure of outward appearances," and therefore one "whose observations and reflections must be trusted."[34] Hamilton, however, is another type of splenetic traveler, more in the modern sense of the word and, I think, more trustworthy: neither melancholic nor misanthropic, but rather a comic observer of people and manners that irritate him. To a large extent, the *Itinerarium* is a running comic commentary on the major and minor irritants to a colonial gentleman. Hamilton, after all, was a gentleman living in an age when "differences in rank were taken for granted . . . to a degree which contemporary Americans find hard to imagine," and "without realizing it [he] was witnessing in the American colonies the beginnings of one of the greatest revolutions of modern times— the breakdown of the medieval class structure and the liberation of the common man."[35] The many breaches in privilege and decorum produced by this social revolution irritated him to no end, but he felt secure enough in his position as a gentleman that he

---

34. *Pleasurable Instruction*, 74.
35. May, *The Enlightenment in America*, 27; Bridenbaugh, *Gentleman's Progress*, xxv. Kagle's discussion of the *Itinerarium* further develops Bridenbaugh's argument (*American Diary Literature*, 63–67).

Delightful Instruction

chose mainly to display them with unruffled amusement in the *Itinerarium*—except when they struck too close to home.

Ironically, one of the minor irritants in the *Itinerarium*—minor because he takes it less seriously than others—is the breakdown of class distinctions Hamilton witnesses during his tour. Early in his diary he reports having observed a comical "boxing match" between a master and his servant in the streets of Philadelphia:

> The master was an unweildy, pott-gutted fellow, the servant muscular, rawbon'd, and tall; therefor tho he was his servant in station of life, yet he would have been his master in single combat had not the bystanders asisted the master.... The servant, by his dialect, was a Scotsman; the names he gave his master were no better than little bastard, and shitten elf, terms ill apply'd to such a pursy load of flesh. (p. 24)

Later in the *Itinerarium* Hamilton receives a lesson in semantics from a lowly innkeeper at Providence: "I found this fellow at the door," he says,

> and asked him if the house was not kept by one Angel. He answered in a surly manner, "no." "Pardon me," says I, "they recommended me to such a house." So as I turned away, being loath to lose his customer, he called me back. "Hark ye, friend," says he in the same blunt manner, "Angell don't keep the house, but the house keeps Angell." I hesitated for some time if I should give this surly chap my custome but resolved att last to reap some entertainment from the oddity of the fellow. (p. 149)

For Hamilton, a gentleman secure in his position, situations such as these, although mildly annoying, were finally neither threatening nor foreboding but simply amusing.

Hamilton is similarly amused in the *Itinerarium* by what he considered the pretentious behavior of black servants.[36] At Newtown, Maryland, he observes that one black woman, a "female baboon," "had more attendants and hangers on att her levee than the best person (of quality as I may say) in town. She was very fond of the compliments and company of the men and boys but expressed... an utter aversion att women and girls, especially negroes of that sex" (p. 11). At Long Island he overhears his black servant Dromo "discoursing" with a black girl:

> "Dis de way to York?" says Dromo. "Yaw, dat is Yarikee," said the wench, pointing to the steeples. "What devil you say?" replys Dromo. "Yaw, mynheer," said the wench. "Damme you, what you say?" said Dromo again. "Yaw, yaw," said the girl. "You a damn black bitch," said Dromo and so rid on. (pp. 40–41)

This passage further demonstrates Hamilton's keen interest in various colloquialisms and dialects. But it also demonstrates his amusement at the very thought that these two lower class black servants could "discourse" intelligently about anything. And he considers Dromo's living quarters at Marblehead equally entertaining: "a most spacious [room], furnished alamode de cabaret with tables, chairs, a fine feather bed with quilted counterpine, white callicoe canopy or tester, and curtains, every way adapted for a gentleman of his degree and complexion" (p. 119).

Hamilton did not intend these remarks as racial slurs. For him, race was not the issue here. The idea of any members of the lower

---

36. Like many enlightened gentlemen, as a matter of principle Hamilton disapproved of all forms of slavery, yet his attitudes toward blacks are ambivalent at best. For a good discussion of that ambivalence during the Enlightenment, see David Brion Davis, *The Problem of Slavery in Western Culture* (Ithaca, N.Y., 1966), 391–421.

Delightful Instruction

classes, black or white, male or female, overstepping their bounds offended his sense of social, not racial, propriety. Throughout the *Itinerarium* he deals with this as a gentleman would, humorously exposing and delighting in the pretentious behavior of the lower classes regardless of race.[37] His tone becomes more caustic, however, when he discusses the pretentions of those who threaten to intrude upon his social sphere, such as the numerous "fops" at New York who "held their heads higher than the rest of mankind and imagined few or none were their equals." This sort of behavior, he observes, inevitably proceeds from an

> ignorance of the world, and low extraction, which indeed is the case with most of our aggrandized upstarts in these countrys of America who never had an opportunity to see, or if they had, the capacity to observe the different ranks of men in polite nations or to know what it is that really constitutes that difference of degrees. (p. 186)

Hamilton considered the pretentious behavior of the lower classes humorous indeed, since they posed no immediate threat to his way of life, but these sorts of "aggrandized upstarts" were already knocking at his door and he was not eager to greet them smiling.

Hamilton was similarly disturbed by the many breaches in decorum he observed in the colonies. He considered some of the customs that had been introduced in the colonies offensive yet amusing, such as "the farce of kissing most of the women [at Al-

---

37. Hamilton's attitude toward cultivated Indians, however, is a notable exception. He considers the majority of Indians "a lazy, indolent generation [that] would rather starve than work att any time" (p. 172), but he speaks approvingly of an Indian chief he meets in Rhode Island who "lives after the English mode" (p. 98) and of "a parade of Indian chiefs" in Boston wearing "laced hats, and some of them laced matchcoats and ruffled shirts" (p. 112). For Hamilton, the only noble savage was a cultivated one.

bany, their] manner of salutation.... This might almost pass for a pennance," he says, "for the generality of the women here, both old and young, are remarkably ugly" (p. 63); or the custom of shaking the hand of a new acquaintance, which he also considered indecorously forward. But he was not at all amused by some of the crude behavior he observed in all walks of colonial life. In the eighteenth century, Richard L. Bushman writes, "the ideal of cultivation... became inextricably associated with human progress itself. The degree to which a person, a people, or a place had achieved gentility and urbanity was a measure of progress from barbarism to civilization."[38] Hamilton felt that many of the people and places he visited were eons away from any semblance of cultivation. Early in the *Itinerarium* he reports having been invited to dinner by a kind but crude elderly couple:

> They desired me to eat, but I told them I had no stomach. They had no cloth upon the table, and their mess was in a dirty, deep, wooden dish which they evacuated with their hands, cramming down skins, scales, and all. They used neither knife, fork, spoon, plate, or napkin because, I suppose, they had none to use. I looked upon this as a picture of that primitive simplicity practiced by our forefathers long before the mechanic arts had supplyed them with instruments for the luxury and elegance of life. (p. 8)

Although less primitive, an even more offensive form of crudeness existed in Hamilton's own social sphere. One evening in New York, during a conversation concerning "hystericks and vapours in women," a certain Mr. Hog, in front of his wife and children, remarked "that a good mowing was a cure for such complaints." Hamilton enjoyed "polite smutt" (p. 177) as much as the next gen-

---

38. "American High-Style and Vernacular Cultures," 358.

tleman, but not in the company of ladies: "this kind of talk," he concludes, was apparently "what [Hog's] wife had been used to, but it is an inexcusable piece of rudeness and rusticity in the company of women to speak in this manner" (p. 177). Earlier in New York, Hamilton's goose-necked companion, Dr. James McGraw, complained that "he was troubled with the open piles and with that, from his breeches, pulled out a linnen handkercheff all stained with blood and showed it to the company just after [they] had eat dinner." McGraw's crude behavior, Hamilton says, "exceeded every thing I had seen for nastiness, impudence, and rusticity" (p. 86). In conversation as in dining, Hamilton preferred the refinements of civilization to this sort of "elegant company" (p. 7).

One type of impudent behavior particularly irritated Hamilton: the inquisitiveness of many colonials he met. "Although this characteristic marks the increasing democratization of manners in America," Lemay writes, "it was an affront to an aristocratic gentleman," and Hamilton was "duly affronted."[39] He was polite enough not to pry into other people's business "lest [they] should think [him] impertinent" (p. 4), and he expected the same from those he met. But wherever he went he was pestered by inquisitive colonials who wanted to know his name, where he came from, what his business was, and where he was going. "I did not know that I had any relations in [New London]," he remarks, until "a parcell of children ... saluted me with 'How d'ye, unkle?'" (p. 160). When an equally curious and naive New Englander asks him if there are not "a great many dangerous wild beasts in [the Maryland] woods," Hamilton informs him that "the most dangerous wild beasts in these woods were shaped ex-

---

39. *Men of Letters*, 221.

actly like men, and they went by the name of buckskins, or bucks, tho they were not bucks neither but something... betwixt a man and a beast" (p. 123). And when an old gentleman asks him where he is from and where he is going, Hamilton says, "I answered him I came from Calliphurnia and was going to Lanthern Land. He swore damn his old shoes... if he had not been a sailor all his life long and yet never had heard of such places" (p. 92). But the most persistent busybody he meets is the one who accosts him on his way to Portsmouth and bombards him with one question after another "in the rustick civil stile":

> "Pray sir, if I may be so bold, where are you going?" "Prithee, friend," says I, "where are you going?" "Why, I go along the road here a little way." "So do I, friend," replied I. "But may I presume, sir, whence do you come?" "And from whence do you come, friend?" says I. "Pardon me, from John Singleton's farm," replied he, "with a bag of oats." "And I come from Maryland," said I, "with a portmanteau and baggage." "Maryland!" said my companion, "where the devil is that there place? I have never heard of it. But pray, sir, may I be so free as to ask your name?" "And may I be so bold as to ask yours, friend?" said I. "Mine is Jerry Jacobs, att your service," replied he. I told him that mine was Bombast Huynhym van Helmont, att his service. "A strange name indeed; belike your a Dutchman, sir,—a captain of a ship, belike." "No, friend," says I, "I am a High German alchymist." "Bless us! You don't say so; that's a trade I never heard of; what may you deal in sir?" "I sell air," said I. "Air," said he, "damn it, a strange commodity. I'd thank you for some wholesom air to cure my fevers which have held me these two months." (p. 124)

In these instances, Hamilton adroitly resorts to the put on to put off his inquisitors. But he is less amused when he overhears other people talking about him. At a tavern in New York he overhears a fellow whom he presumes is one of Governor Clinton's spies asking questions about him and disrupts the conversation:

Delightful Instruction

> Todd [the tavernkeeper] informed him who I was upon his asking the question. "You mean the pock-fretten man," said he, "with the dark colourd silk coat. He is a countryman of mine, by God, one Hamilton from Maryland. They say he is a doctor and is travelling for his health." Hearing this, "this is afternoon's news," thinks I, "for the G[overno]r," and just as the inquisitor was desiring Todd to speak lower, he was not deaf, I bolted out upon them and put an end to the enquiry, and the inquisitor went about his business. (p. 80)

Young or old, bumpkins or spies, far too many colonials, Hamilton felt, simply did not know how to mind their own business.

Yet these sorts of brash inquisitors were relatively harmless, and in most instances Hamilton manages to amuse himself by answering their questions whimsically rather than caustically. He found it more difficult, however, to deal whimsically with another type of brash American—the big mouth. Too many colonials, he thought, had too much of nothing to say. One such character is Marcus Van Bummill, a drunken, blustering fool who accompanies Hamilton part of the way up the Hudson River and stupidly lectures him on one subject after another. "Understanding that I was a valitudinarian," Hamilton writes,

> he began to advise me how to manage my constitution. "You drink and whore too much," said he, "and that makes you thin and sickly. Could you abstain as I have done and drink nothing but water for 6 weeks, your belly and cheeks would be like mine, look ye, plump and smooth and round." With that he clapt his hands upon his belly and blowd up his cheeks like a trumpeter. (p. 51)

Rather than inform Van Bummill about the true nature of his illness, Hamilton quietly discredits him by noting in passing that he "brought on board with him a runlett of rum," not water, and that he went after the first thing in skirts, a "remarkably ugly

[Dutch woman], upon whom [he] cast a loving eye and wanted much to be att close conference with" (pp. 51, 52). Before he and Van Bummill part company, his puffed-up companion also treats him to a "learned discourse" on the medical profession:

> "You are a doctor," says he to me; "what signifys your knowledge? You pretend to know inward distempers and to cure them, but to no purpose; your art is vain. Find me out a doctor among the best of you that can mend a man's body half so well as a joiner can help a crazy table or stool.... Experience has taught me to shun [doctors] as one would impostors and cheats, and now no doctor for me but the great Doctor above." (p. 54)

Van Bummill is an ignorant clod, and rather than waste his time disputing him, Hamilton practices his usual restraint and lets Van Bummill talk himself into oblivion. During his stay at Boston, Hamilton encounters another know-nothing, a Mr. Clackenbridge, who argued "against all the company, but like a confused logician, he could not hold an argument long but wandered from one topic to another, leading us all into confusion and loud talking.... My head being quite turned... with this confused dispute," Hamilton says,

> I got into a strange fit of absence, for having occasion to go out of the company two or three times..., I heedlessly every time went into a room where there was a strange company... and twice sat down in the midst of them, nor did I discover I was in the wrong box till I found them all staring att me. For the first slip I was obliged to form the best apology I could, but att the second hitt I was so confused and saw them so inclinable to laugh that I run out at the door precipitatly without saying any thing and betook me to the right company. (p. 144)

At Newport, Rhode Island, however, after listening to a whole club of Van Bummills and Clackenbridges dispute about "declarations, recantations, letters, advices, remonstrances, and other such damnd stuff of so little consequence to the benifit of mankind," Hamilton manages to find the right door and irritably leaves the club, "disgusted with such a stupid subject of discourse" (p. 152).

Even more irritating than the big-mouths who knew nothing were the many "superficiall philosophers" (p. 197) in the colonies who knew very little yet had the audacity to foist what little they did know upon others. At the Elk River in Maryland, the ferryman, who doubles during his off hours as a pimp, tries to impress Hamilton by quoting "a few hexameter lines out of Lilly's Grammar" (p. 9). In New York he meets a certain Major Spratt, a drunken, carbuncular, phthisical-looking poet who considers himself the finest rhymer in the Western Hemisphere. Having recently composed some ingenious lines on his dead neighbor, Spratt recites them for Hamilton and his friends:

> "Gentlemen," said he, "pray take notise now, give good attention. [This] is perhaps the concisest, wittiest, prittiest epigram or epitaph, call it what you will, that you ever heard. Shall I get you pen and ink to write it down? Perhaps you mayn't remember it else. It is highly worth your noting. Pray observe how it runs,—
> Here lyes John Purcell;
> And whether he be in heaven or in hell,
> Never a one of us all can tell." (p. 81)

Trailing these lines of glory, Hamilton journeys to Boston, where one evening he endures the half-baked ramblings of an Irish minister, who

> seemed to be one of those conceited priggs who are fond of spreading out to its full extent all that superficial physicall knowledge which they have acquired more by hearsay than by application or study.... We had a load of impertinence from him about the specific gravity of

air and water, the exhalation of vapours, the expansion and condensation of clouds, the operation of distillation, and the chemistry of nature. In fine it was but a very puerile physicall lecture and no sermon att all. (p. 110)

Hamilton notes that even a scholar at Ipswitch, who had professedly read everything, merely "affected being a schollar... and used a great many hard words in discourse, which he generally missapplied" (p. 122). From pimps to poets, preachers to scholars, this sort of "pseudosophia" (p. 83), Hamilton felt, was threatening to bury the American colonies in a load of superficial nonsense.

Hamilton was particularly vexed by the extent to which this superficial learning had permeated the medical profession in colonial America. As I demonstrated earlier in this chapter, his manner of perceiving and describing the phenomenal world in the *Itinerarium* is typical of the empirical age in which he lived. But he would have gagged had anyone called him an "empyrick," a class of physicians he considered little better than butchers. Like most eighteenth-century physicians, Hamilton valued empirical observation as a means of complementing medical theory, but he was appalled by the number of "empyricks" in America who had little or no understanding of the latter.[40] In Albany, he complains, the doctors are "all empyricks, having no knowledge or learning

---

40. The disdain Hamilton expresses toward "empyricks" in the *Itinerarium* was voiced by physicians on both sides of the Atlantic and, in fact, was the central medical controversy in the eighteenth century. For a good discussion of this controversy, see Shryock, *Medicine and Society in America, 1660–1860*, 48–54. In 1751 Hamilton further attacked these "Physical Dunces" in his *Defense of Dr. Thomson's Discourse on the Preparation of the Body for the Small pox* (Philadelphia, 1751). Hamilton's defense of Thomson is discussed in ch. 1.

Delightful Instruction

but what they have acquired by bare experience" (p. 65). The most formidable "empyrick" he encounters during his tour is the Boston physician, Dr. William Douglass, an unusually learned "empyrick" but, Hamilton says,

> the most complete snarler ever I knew.... He is of the clinical class of physicians and laughs att all theory and practise founded upon it, looking upon empyricism or bare experience as the only firm basis upon which practise ought to be founded.... This man I esteem a notorious physicall heretick, capable to corrupt and vitiate the practise of the place by spreading his erroneous doctrines among his shallow bretheren. (pp. 116–17)

When Douglass attacks Boerhaave in Hamilton's presence, calling him "a mere *helluo librorum,* an indefatigable compiler that dealt more in books than in observation," Hamilton becomes so annoyed with him and his "awkward imitators" that he temporarily abandons his habitual reserve and becomes openly hostile, defending Boerhaave as "by far the greatest genius that ever appeared ... since the days of Hippocrates" (pp. 131, 132).[41] "I must say," he explains,

> it raised my spleen to hear the character of such a man as Boerhaave picked att by a parcell of pigmies, mere homuncios in physick, who shine no where but in the dark corner allotted them like a lamp in a monk's cell, obscure and unknown to all the world excepting only their silly hearers and imitators, while the splendour of the great character which they pretend to canvass eclipses all their smaller lights like the sun, enlightens all equally, ... and is known by every one who has any regard for learning or truth. (p. 132)

---

41. Boerhaave's influence upon Hamilton's medical training is discussed in ch. 1.

Hamilton's contempt for these "half learned physicall priggs" (p. 138) is matched only by his contempt for "hair brained [religious] fanaticks" and the "spirit of enthusiasm" (p. 10). As Gary B. Nash argues, the Great Awakening was not simply a religious movement; it was a "reckless social thrust" toward social leveling by revivalists such as Whitefield.[42] Not surprisingly, when Whitefield visited Maryland, a predominantly Anglican, proprietary colony that had developed a strong sense of privilege, he came away disappointed and empty handed.[43] In a letter to George Drummond, Lord Provost of Edinburgh, Hamilton apologized for having been unable to raise contributions for the infirmary at Edinburgh but added that a "common orator" such as himself could hardly be expected to persuade Marylanders to contribute when "our famous Enthusiast, and erratic preacher, Whitefield, could not work upon them, so as to open their purses" (April 22, 1742). Their stinginess was a sign that Marylanders such as Hamilton found Whitefield's brand of religious enthusiasm repugnant to their sense of religious and social propriety. "He is a mortal," Hamilton wrote to his brother-in-law after

---

42. *The Urban Crucible: Social Change, Political Consciousness, and the Origins of the American Revolution* (Cambridge, 1979), 204, 211. David S. Lovejoy also examines the Great Awakening as a serious threat to the social stability of colonial America (*Religious Enthusiasm in the New World: Heresy to Revolution* [Cambridge, Mass., 1985], 178–94). Jon Butler has challenged this notion in "Enthusiasm Described and Decried: The Great Awakening as Interpretative Fiction," *Journal of American History,* 69 (1982), 305–25; the reaction against Whitefield by Maryland society, however, supports Nash's and Lovejoy's claims.

43. A good study of a typical upper-class Marylander's (and a good friend of Hamilton's) rejection of Whitefield is Richard J. Cox, "Stephen Bordley, George Whitefield, and the Great Awakening in Maryland," *Historical Magazine of the Protestant Episcopal Church,* 46 (1977), 297–307.

hearing Whitefield preach, "who not only has a sufficient Stock of Enthusiasm, (I wont say pious effrontery or Impudence, far Less will I tax the man with hypocrisy) but has along with it the action and Carriage of an orator to perfection, and what Influence that has upon weak minds, you know as well as I" (AH to the Reverend David Smith, [fall] 1743). Rather than liberate others, according to Hamilton men like Whitefield work at "Enslaving mankind, and reducing those that before were a free and generous people to worse than Common pack horses" (*HTC*, 2:299). This kind of enslavement, Hamilton felt, had spread throughout the colonies and was most recently manifested by

> the strange madness that had possessed some people att Ipswitch occasioned by one [Richard] Woodberry, a mad enthusiast, who, pretending to inspiration, uttered severall blasphemous and absurd speeches, asserting that he was the same to day, yesterday, and for ever, saying he had it in his power to save or damn whom he pleased, falling down upon the ground, licking the dust, and condemning all to hell who would not do the like. (pp. 119–20)

To Hamilton's dismay, many of his listeners were taken in by Woodberry's rantings. "This is a remarkable instance," Hamilton concludes, "to what lengths of madness enthusiasm will carry men once they give it a loose [rein]" (p. 120).[44]

Thus, the portrait that our splenetic traveler draws of colonial life in the *Itinerarium* is not a particularly flattering one. To be sure, Hamilton meets several people along the way whom he admires and trusts and visits numerous clubs that provide the benefits of civilization, but on the whole the *Itinerarium* portrays

---

44. For further examples of Hamilton's disapproval of Whitefield and the "New-light-men," see esp. pp. 8–9, 117, and 161; see also *The History of the Tuesday Club*, 1:44, 127, and 166.

colonial life as crude and unmannerly. Hamilton concludes the *Itinerarium* by saying that "as to politeness and humanity" life throughout the colonies was "much alike"—meaning crude—"except in the great towns where the inhabitants are more civilized, especially att Boston" (p. 199). The average colonial in the *Itinerarium* is impertinent, uncouth, and easily duped by men such as Whitefield who possess a modicum of learning. Most colonials, moreover, are easily prone to lie, and although naive in other areas, they are conniving sharpers in money matters. "A Pensylvanian," Hamilton observes, "will tell a lye with a sanctified, solemn face; a Marylander, perhaps will convey his fib in a volley of oaths; but the effect ... is the same tho' the manner of operating will be different" (pp. 28–29). The people of Rhode Island, "in their dealings one with another, and even with strangers, in matters of truck or bargain have as bad a character for chicane and disingenuity as any of our American colonys" (p. 157); and the people of Philadelphia also possess "that accomplishment peculiar to all our American colonys, viz., subtilty and craft in their dealings" (p. 193). Like other eighteenth-century gentlemen, Hamilton "thought of men in their economic capacities as essentially selfish beings" and considered the rising market economy at Philadelphia and other cities a threat to social order.[45] "I still retain a little of my native honesty," he wrote to an old friend at Edinburgh, "not haveing quite lost myself in the American Subtilty and selfishness" (AH to John B———r, Nov. 6, 1743). Hamilton was an Old World gentleman living in a crude and pushy New World, and he did not like the directions in which he was being pushed.

---

45. J. E. Crowley, *This Sheba, Self: The Conceptualization of Economic Life in Eighteenth-Century America* (Baltimore, 1974), 101. Crowley provides an excellent discussion of the growing concern about economic self-interest in colonial America (see pp. 96–124; he mentions Hamilton on p. 99).

Delightful Instruction

For the most part, though, Hamilton tempers his spleen with an urbane sense of humor that makes the *Itinerarium* a delight to read. He sometimes openly attacks the Douglasses or Whitefields who are more his equals socially, but usually he expresses a gentlemanly restraint and amusement at the numerous irritants that pester him. When three know-nothing, arrogant "Pensylvanian dons" try their best to irritate him by comparing Maryland with Pennsylvania—all, of course, to Maryland's disadvantage—Hamilton remains humorously unruffled:

> They inlarged upon the immorality, drunkeness, rudeness and immoderate swearing so much practised in Maryland and added that no such vices were to be found in Pensylvania. I heard this and contradicted it not, because I knew that the first part of the proposition was pritty true. They next fall upon the goodness of the soil as far more productive of pasturage and grain. I was silent here likewise, because the first proposition was true, but as to the other relating to grain, I doubted the truth of it. But what appeared most comical in their criticisms was their making a merit of the stonnyness of the roads. "One may ride," [one said,] "50 miles in Maryland and not see as many stones upon the roads as in 50 paces of road in Pensylvania." This I knew to be false, but as I thought there was no advantage in stonny roads, I even let them take the honour of it to themselves and did not contradict them. (p. 15)

As this decorously understated three-part joke indicates, Hamilton regarded others—and himself—as constant sources of entertainment.[46] And eighteenth-century readers and reviewers

---

46. Hamilton's ability to turn the joke inward upon himself marks an important shift in the objects of laughter in colonial humor (see Robert Micklus, "Colonial Humor: Beginning with the Butt," *Critical Essays on American Humor*, ed. William Bedford Clark and W. Craig Turner [Boston, 1984], 139–54).

would have been equally entertained by his depiction of colonial life in the *Itinerarium*. They probably would have objected to the commonness of some of the language and scenes he records, and they might have suggested that he make more of an effort at times to keep his opinions to himself[47]—critics, of course, are never completely satisfied with anything—but they would have commended the precision and abundance of his descriptions, his usual unobtrusiveness, and the middle style of his own prose, and on both sides of the Atlantic the *Itinerarium* would have been received as, if not the best travel diary in the colonies, then certainly the most delightfully instructive one.

---

47. As Batten observes, the final test of any good travel narrative during the eighteenth century was the accuracy of an author's observations, not his reflections; but travel writers were not discouraged from offering reflections, provided there was not a disproportionate number of them (*Pleasurable Instruction*, 84). Hamilton offers a few more reflections than eighteenth-century readers might have preferred, but there is clearly a preponderance of observations to reflections in the *Itinerarium*.

CHAPTER THREE

"*A Few Crude Thoughts*"
Periodical Pieces

Mr. Green,

    As you publish a *News paper* weekly, for our Entertainment, without which, perhaps, this dull Place would be still duller; and as at some times you seem to be at a Loss for better and more pertinent Subjects, than *Letters from the King to the Queen, From the Dauphin to his dear Mamma,* ... and tiresome Scrolls of *Blank Verses,* to fill up *Blanks* in your *Gazette;* I, for this Reason, and out of Pity to your *Alphabetic Engine,* which some time ago groaned in dire Labour, and brought forth *monstrous Births* of *Poetry,* have shuffled together a few crude Thoughts in *Prose,* which, if you please, you may dignify with a Place in your Paper, when you can find nothing better to insert.[1]

---

1. Quoted from Hamilton's essay "What News?" (*Maryland Gazette,* January 7, 1746). My reasons for attributing this and the other pieces discussed in this chapter to Hamilton are simple: the similarities in content, tone, and style between these pieces and his other writings, particularly *The History of the Tuesday Club,* as well as similarities between the pieces themselves. Hamilton's generally loose sentence structure, like Addison's, rests heavily upon parallel structures: most of his sentences begin with the main clause, then move along sequentially, clause added onto clause, relying upon hypotaxis, duplicate predicates, and various pairings of phrases, nouns, adjectives, and other parts of speech. As critics have often pointed out, the stylistic ideal being aimed at by Addison and his imitators was not one of economy

The Comic Genius of Dr. Alexander Hamilton

Out of commiseration for Jonas Green and the readers of the *Maryland Gazette,* Hamilton on several occasions "shuffled together a few crude Thoughts" to fill in the blanks of Green's paper. Unlike the *Itinerarium,* his satiric pieces were designed to provide a minimum amount of instruction and a maximum amount of entertainment to a culture sorely in need of diversion. More than any other contributor to the *Gazette* during the early years of Green's editorship, Hamilton helped to keep the drowsy god at bay and to make the *Gazette* one of the liveliest papers in colonial America.

While other Marylanders were contributing competent but tiresome Addisonian essays on topics such as history, taste, and flattery to the *Maryland Gazette,* Hamilton chose to liven things up a bit during the winter of 1745–46 by helping to stage a literary battle in the *Gazette* between the "Baltimore Bards" and the members of the Tuesday Club. "Much about this time," he writes in *The History of the Tuesday Club,* "appeared an epidemical distemper in the Club" that produced violent "fits of Rhiming" (1:175). Even Solo Neverout (William Thornton),

> who had never before shown the least genius or turn to Rhiming, . . . was so Infected as to break all at once into blank verse, and with great

---

but one of rhythmical copiousness. But Hamilton exaggerated the devices typical of Addisonian prose to such an extent that his style is finally his own. His sprawlingly loose yet carefully balanced sentences are like no other writer in the *Maryland Gazette.* Lemay (*Men of Letters in Colonial Maryland,* 229–39) has previously identified Hamilton as the author of five of the selections discussed in this chapter (the essay "What News?" by "KLMN PQRST," the nostrum by "Theophilus Polypharmacus," the advertisement by "Jehoiakim Jerkum," the dream vision by "Quevedo," and the piece on orthography by "Philotypographus"). The other selections discussed in this chapter are new attributions.

violence and vociferation, exclaimed to the Surprize of all present,
> With dowble Lustre, Beckie's beauties shine.

And when he was desired to proceed farther, and make a Couplet of it, he bawld out in a furious manner,
> Rise Jupiter, and snuff the moon! (1:175)

This "poetical Contagion," Hamilton says, began in Baltimore with Bard Mevius (the Reverend Thomas Cradock), who, listening one day to the Reverend George Whitefield, "was diverted in his attention to the Sweet words of that Inspired Saint, by some Ladies, who sat in a pew Just before him, with the whiteness and beautiful Length of whose Necks... he was so miraculously Charmed, that, Intirely forgetting where he was, he fell directly to Composing [the following] verses" (1:176):

> Plac'd as I was, such charms within my view,
> Say, Whitefield, what could all thy Rhet'ric do?
> In vain the nonsense trickl'd from thy tongue,
> In vain with canting harmony you sung;
> Their blooming beauties more perswasive prov'd,
> My heart with greater energy they mov'd,
> Their Swan-like necks my ravish'd eyes did bliss,
> Courted the touch, and tempted me to kiss. (1:185)

Mevius's epigram naturally inspired Hamilton and his club companions to exercise "the acuteness of wit and Genius pritty Smartly upon this unfortunate Bard" (1:177). Hamilton attached to the poem a set of facetious queries and an equally splendid piece of doggerel "hammered out" by the "conjoint muses" of the club, then returned the poem to Cradock along with a letter bawdily chastizing him for "seeing the most powerful Charms of the Ladies behind" (1:186–88). Cradock's champion, Bard Bavius (the Reverend Thomas Chase), a "Gygantic auxiliary Bard," wittily responded, "The lovely Sex, my friend, are charms all o'er, / And strike behind as powerful as before.... / Then friend be wise, your ill plac'd Jeers give oer, / Who sees no Charms behind, sees none before" (1:178, 189). Cradock and Chase then wrote a "Sublime panegyric," "The Baltimore Belles" (1:179), which prompted one of the Tuesday Club's members, a Dr. Philalethes,[2] to publish in the December 17, 1745, issue of the *Maryland Gazette* "*An infallible Receipt to cure the afflicting and epidemical Distempers of* Love, *and the* Poetical Itch." "Take half a Grain of . . . common Discretion," Philalethes suggests,

> two Grains of moderate vulgar Sense and Solidity, . . . half a Dram of . . . solid Thought and Reflection, three Drams of common Modesty, . . . and a Pound of honest Industry and Diligence; beat all stoutly in a Mortar well propp'd with a good Understanding, and when all is reduced to a Powder, give it frequently only to the Quantity of half a Dram for a Dose; taking care all the while it operates, to stop well all the Crevices and Cracks of the Patient's intellectual Chamber, or *Cranium*, . . . lest the poisonous Blast and Air of Ignorance, Self-Conceit, and Idleness, should get Access, and frustrate the Operation of the Medicine.

"According to the humor of great Physicians, who commonly prefer their own Nostrums, to those of all the faculty besides" (1:181), Hamilton published his own remedy in the February 4, 1746, issue of the *Maryland Gazette*. As Dr. Theophilus Polypharmacus, he reports having visited Bard Bavius in his bedchamber, where he found him still suffering from a "*Furor Poeticus*" and

---

2. Probably Hamilton's brother John, the only other doctor who was at this time a member of the Tuesday Club. Hamilton's publishing his own remedy a few weeks later was thus a curious combination of satirical, professional, and fraternal one-upsmanship.

"A Few Crude Thoughts"

"The Phrensy of a Baltimore Bard."
Hamilton's Drawing in *The History of the Tuesday Club*.
(John Work Garrett Library, Milton S. Eisenhower Library,
The Johns Hopkins University)

"*Febris Amatoria.*" The distracted poet, he says, bawled out several passages from "The Baltimore Belles," beginning with "*A well-turn'd Praise requir'd the nicest Skill, / And he who writes ill-natur'd must write ill,*" upon which he "blooded him, blister'd his Head, and administred a few Doses of my worthy Friend's Medicine." But Philalethes' remedy proves to no avail, and Bavius babbles out, "M——a *sings, now bid the* Muses *hear, / Or call* Apollo *from the* Chrystal Sphere." "I immediately apprehended a *Calenture,*" Polypharmacus says, "when he talked of *Chrystal Spheres,* and therefore ordered frequent and copious Injections of Warm Glysters." The evacuations that result cause poor Bavius to sink from the mock sublime to the bathetic. At last Polypharmacus discovers an effectual remedy:

> Take four Lines out of any of *Pope's poetical Works,* six Lines of *Milton's Paradise Lost,* eight Lines of *Garth's Dispensary,* guarded with four Lines of *Butler's Hudibras;* let the Doctor or Apothecary read these very loud to the Patient, every Time he bursts forth into his Exclamations, in the hearing of some discreet Persons, *Judges of Poetry,* 'til the *Contrast* produces a Laugh in the Company. When the Patient's raving Nonsense, and the true Sublime of these *great Wits,* have been sufficiently prepared, and their Parts broke and blended together, by the Gelastic Conquassation of the Air, put them into a large bellied long-necked Matrass, and there will arise a most furious Fermentation, from the *Antipathy* and heterogene Nature of the Ingredients; when this ceases, it will produce a *Neutrum quid,* or a Substance neither saturated with the *Salt of good Sense,* nor flattened with the *Phlegm of Nonsense.*

Hamilton's nostrum apparently exhausted Chase's fund of gentlemanly raillery. He responded with a "dirty Epistle to the City of Annapolis," an "extraneously extravagant" "prophylactic dissertation" instructing Jonas Green to put these ignorant critics into

"A Few Crude Thoughts"

his "press or typographical machine" while "an operator with a Spatula was to extract excrementitious matter from their fundament" (1:189, 182–83). That was a mistake. The March 18, 1746, issue of the *Maryland Gazette* printed a mock advertisement for a runaway wit, written mainly by Hamilton and signed "Jehoiakim Jerkum":[3]

> Ran away from the Subscriber, and left nothing behind him but his Senses, a *dapper-witted, finical Fopling,* known by the Name of *Bard,* alias *Bavius,* he wore, when he went away, *a string of Bells,* which make a hideous jingling, and discordant noise, his Speech is frothy and incoherent, inclining more to *Rhime* than *Reason,* ... [and] he deals much in insignificant Rhimes, being far gone in the *poetical Itch....* His Performances are little understood by any body, least of all by himself, not upon Account of sublimity of Stile, and fine Sentiments, but rather a dark indefinite Expression, and a motly Rabble of confus'd Ideas, and unnatural Comparisons and Allusions; He may, therefore, probably have sundry things about him, such as *Bundles of Papers,* scribbled over with *poetical Trumpery,* and Conceits of his own Composition, so monsterously form'd and void of Sense, as to be utterly unintelligible.... I cannot give any Account of his *Parentage* and *Country,* and despair of ever being able to succeed in such an Attempt, considering what some intelligent Persons have lately advanced, that he never had any *Ancestors,* because he is universally acknowledged to be an *Original....* His Discourse is entirely *excrementitious,* and he throws out his *Sarcasms,* as a *Scavenger* would do *Tubs of Sir-Reverence,* for his whole Talk and especially his Compositions turn upon *B—sh—tt—ng* and being *B—sh—t, treading*

---

3. In *The History of the Tuesday Club* Hamilton states that Jehoiakim Jerkum "is thought to have been personated, by one or more of the Longstanding members, of the ancient and honorable Tuesday Club, taking upon them the Character of a Master advertising his run away Servant" (1:183). The "one" was clearly Hamilton himself, although he perhaps had some help with the finishing touches.

upon a T—d, pulling it out of his own Bosom and dropping it into a Lady's, eating and chewing it as one would do a Sugar Plumb. He is a nasty Fellow, for the *Sphincter Ani,* or *Bum Muscle,* in him being preternaturally relaxed, he is very apt to bewray himself in Company, and being somewhat foolish, is insensible of his Misbehaviour, and lays all the blame upon others. He seldom is heard to praise any Person but himself, his whole Drift is Defamation and Censure, and that frequently convey'd under the sham Name of *Panegyrick,* to which he is a mighty Pretender.

Hamilton punningly concludes that "any Person who goes upon the *chace* after him, such Person or Persons apprehending him, because it is a difficult matter so to do, shall have, as a *Reward,* all the Profits arising from his *Poems,* made over to him and his, or them and their Heirs, for One hundred Years to come." It perhaps goes without saying that, as a result of this advertisement, "the Baltimorian muses gave up the Ghost" (1:189).

This exchange between the Baltimore Bards and the Annapolis Wits demonstrates not only how adeptly Hamilton could flay a fool but also how easily gentlemanly "repartee and railery" (1:177) could turn into blistering ridicule and satire in his day if one rallied the wrong person. As Stuart M. Tave asserts, raillery was "the aristocratic social mode of intelligence" during the eighteenth century.[4] Cradock enjoyed raillery; indeed, he probably wrote the initial epigram and passed it about not only to display his wit but to provoke a bout of raillery during a dull spell. This was all part of the "innocent mirth" he extolled as a clergyman,

---

4. *The Amiable Humorist,* 16. In the " 'true Art of Raillery,' " Tave writes, a gentleman showed that he was "in good humor with the person he rallie[d]"; his raillery was "without edge" and "gently undisruptive of self-esteem" (p. 17; *Spectator,* No. 422). The distinction between "raillery" and "railing" is well discussed in Elkin, *The Augustan Defence of Satire,* 17.

and part of what eventually made him a welcome member of the Tuesday Club.[5] Chase, however, who developed quite a reputation for himself as a "pugnacious parson,"[6] was apparently much offended by Hamilton's nostrum, which was designed to expose both Chase's pretentiousness and that of the "great wits" who criticized his performances. Rather than swallow the good doctor's medicine, he responded with an abusive letter on the members of the Tuesday Club, who then responded with an even more offensive advertisement. Although the dispute began with good-natured raillery, it ended with a severe satiric attack upon a man who was too thin-skinned to withstand raillery like a gentleman.

A decade later, when Hamilton wrote about the dispute in *The History of the Tuesday Club*, he resumed a more broadly satiric strain:

> So the Baltimore Bards & the Critics of the Tuesday Club strenuously contended who should outrhime, and who should outcriticise each other, and some who thought them wiser than themselves admired much their wit, while others who had no opinion of their wisdom laughed at their folly and assurance, and condemned them much, as Idle and mischievous, in trowbling people that thought no harm with such poetical Jargon, which set many tongues a wagging in a Scan-

---

5. Cradock was admitted an honorary member of the Tuesday Club in 1753 and dubbed "Mevius Pumpkin" for his past performances and his round, jocular face. For a good discussion of Cradock's more substantive contributions to the intellectual temper of his times, see Skaggs, "Thomas Cradock and the Chesapeake Golden Age," 93–116. Cradock's sermon on "innocent mirth" is quoted in ch. 1.

6. One of Chase's most intense legal disputes concerned James Richard, the messenger who delivered the Tuesday Club's witticisms to the Baltimore Bards. This and other of Chase's entanglements are discussed in Rosamond Randall Beirne, "The Reverend Thomas Chase: Pugnacious Parson," *Maryland Historical Magazine*, 59 (1964), 1–14.

dalous manner, ... not to mention the Idle habit some contracted by it, in squandering their time in Composing of Silly rhimes, vainly Imagining that they had a poetical turn, tho they found themselves at last miserably mistaken, and were obliged to bear the Laugh of the public with patience, seeing they had drawn it upon themselves, by their own folly and vanity. (1:177–78)

Although he had sharply ridiculed Chase at the time of the dispute, when he recounted the incident years later Hamilton realized that everyone involved had become caught up in an equally ridiculous display of folly and vanity.

Shortly after silencing the Baltimore Bards, Hamilton again turned to writing about what he considered the greatest enemy of sociability—ungoverned curiosity.[7] Addison and Steele had both sanctioned curiosity as a gentlemanly attribute: Steele announced that Mr. Spectator's "prevailing Passion" was curiosity, and Addison approvingly added that "Curiosity is one of the strongest and most lasting Appetites implanted in us."[8] Hamilton would have agreed, but he also considered no appetite more repugnant than ungoverned curiosity. In his essay on curiosity, published January 27, 1747, in the *Maryland Gazette* and mockingly signed "O. O.," he depicts curiosity as a Chimera-Hydra of "strange Shape and Proportion," constantly sprouting heads and resembling "more the random Draught of a distracted Fancy, than any Thing natural." This monster "has many Tongues and many Ears," he says, "but no Eyes, for she gives and takes every Thing upon bare *Hearsay,* and knows nothing of *ocular Evidence.*" She artfully manages to infiltrate all levels of society and to mimic all levels of

---

7. Hamilton's disdain for inquisitive colonists is discussed at length in ch. 2.
8. *Spectator,* Nos. 156, 237.

language to perfection, but she employs her powers of mimickry corruptly: "she speaks soft and fair before Faces, but behind Backs throws out loud Peals of poisonous Defamation to every common Ear"; among polite company, "she will faintly extoll some of their Vertues, but be sure to mix with her Encomiums a competent Number of *Ifs, Onlies,* and *Were it nots,* by which means she makes the whole a couched *Lampoon*"; among lawyers "she prompts Vollies of Quibbles, idle Clamour, Detraction, and personal Scurrilities"; in politics her noxious influence appears in the words of "pretended *Patriots*" who "have babeled lustily for the Good of their Country, which they never consulted in any Thing but noisy Clamour and vain Speeches"; and even "among the Vulgar and low Set of People" she can "assume a very dirty obscene Dialect; in such places as *Billingsgate,* her Phrases and Tropes of Eloquence are broad and coarse: *Son of a B*——, ... *stinking Trull, d——n'd Whore's bird,* are there her favourite Epithets." As these passages indicate, Hamilton repeatedly attacked curiosity not only because he considered it indecorous and generally repugnant to good company but because, perhaps more than any other form of socially disruptive behavior, it corrupted the very function of language as a means of rational discourse.

Unlike Steele, therefore, who viewed the inquisitive person as a sort of harmless pest, subject to railery for a lack of judgment and an inability to discriminate between useful and useless information,[9] Hamilton considered the curious person an obnoxious toad who destroyed intelligent conversation. In his essay on the impertinent question "What News?" published January 7, 1746, in the *Maryland Gazette* and uninformatively signed KLMN PQRST, he conveys his irritation toward those who propose this

---

9. *Spectator,* No. 228.

question in company "because they can think of nothing better to say." Hamilton considers "the *impertinent Coxcomb* generally the most incorrigible *Ignoramus* in the Company," not only because of his impertinence but because of the effects of his impertinence. When this question is "proposed to a silly Fellow, gifted with the Talent of Loquacity," his listeners "are presently surfeited with an idle Discourse, which consists of nothing but Fiddle-faddle, or a tedious Story, without Connection or Symmetry of Parts, which answers no Purpose, either to instruct or entertain; and while the Fool is laughed at for his Simplicity, his Vanity suggests to him, that the Company are pleased with his fine Humour, and his own stunning *Horse-Laugh* drowns all the rest." Others respond to this question by providing a litany of news, which Hamilton considers "a most nauseous Piece of Impertinence" and the product of "*Barren Wits* and *Common-place Talkers*" who are "incapable of thinking to the Purpose, or furnishing a Stock from their own sterile Fancies fit for Conversation." Often, too, there is "a Set of busy Enquirers, who spontaneously make use of little sly Arts and Fetches, to discover one another's Thoughts of this or that Person"; such "groveling Mortals" store these juicy bits of gossip until the next tattler comes along, and upon his asking "What News?" the rumors and slander fly about. "This is a Character so base and infamous," Hamilton concludes, "that we cannot but detest it."

In the June 29, 1748, issue of the *Maryland Gazette*, Hamilton published "the colony's best belletristic essay,"[10] a dream vision concerning the contributors to the *Gazette* and signed "Don Fran-

---

10. Lemay, *Men of Letters*, 233. Lemay provides an excellent discussion of this essay in *Men of Letters* (233–38) and the complete text of Hamilton's dream vision in "Hamilton's Literary History of the *Maryland Gazette*."

cisco de Quevedo Villegas." Hamilton signaled the satiric intent of his piece by identifying himself with the author of the sharply satiric and enormously popular *Sueños (Visions)*. But the similarity between his dream vision and Quevedo's *Visions* ends there. Whereas Quevedo's grotesque, macabre visions were designed to scourge and to scare his readers out of their licentious ways, Hamilton's is designed to appraise the literary virtues and vices of his contemporaries. Like most dream visions, Quevedo's tales are inhabited by personifications of virtue and vice; Hamilton's, however, is inhabited by the actual authors (under the pseudonyms they used) who wrote for the *Maryland Gazette*. And whereas many dream visions—Quevedo's especially—take place in an unfamiliar, frightening world (typically hell), Hamilton's occurs in a social hall, where all the contributors to the *Gazette* have unwittingly assembled to have their virtues and vices appraised by Hamilton and Green. The hall is a hell of sorts, but it is not particularly hellish; it is, instead, one of the easiest rooms in the literary hell of colonial letters where good authors are few and inept authors are legion.[11]

Hamilton presents his dream vision as a letter to Jonas Green and stages it as a dialogue between Green and himself. Having been lulled to sleep one evening by an "important and *ponderous Performance*" in the *Gazette*, Hamilton finds himself in a room full of "several strange Persons, who, by their Gesture and Discourse,

---

11. Donald W. Bleznick, *Quevedo* (New York, 1972), 41–69. A good discussion of the dream vision conventions employed during the early eighteenth century is Donald Kay's chapter, "The Dream Vision-Cum-Allegory," in *Short Fiction in "The Spectator"* (University, Ala., 1975), 61–77. Addison published numerous dream visions, but only *Spectator* No. 83 (where he imagines himself in an art gallery criticizing living and dead artists) bears any resemblance to Hamilton's vision.

appeared to be *Poets, Politicians,* and *Philosophers*.... While I admired this strange *Medley,*" he says,

> you [Green] enter'd the Hall: Immediately I made up to you, bluntly asking, who these odd Fellows were, and what they were about? I am not surprized, you replied, that you do not know them; for I cannot say any of them are the *Minions of Fame,* tho' they aim at being thought so with all their Might: In short, they are *my Authors,* who oblige me with their *Compositions* in *Prose* and *Verse,* to fill up [the] Gap[s] in my *Gazette.*

Such a "Multitude" has assembled that Green offers to help Hamilton become better acquainted with only "the most remarkable of them." Taking along "a small *Nipperkin of Punch,*" Hamilton and his friendly guide sit at one end of the hall apart from this pandemonium of performers and, while passing the bowl back and forth, comment upon their literary virtues and vices. It is hardly the same as Dante talking to Virgil, but Hamilton's whole point is that he and his Maryland Virgil do not have as much to work with.

In his running dialogue with Green, Hamilton satirizes the majority of the contributors to the *Gazette* for their ineptness. "Who is that queer Fellow," he wonders, "stuck up in yonder dark Corner, or Nitch?" "His Name suits his Place," Green replies;

> 'tis one *Mr. Q in the Corner,* a paltry Linguist and pitiful Logician: I durst publish but one Specimen of his Wit; for it was so universally laughed at, that I chose not to risque the Character of my Paper by putting out any more of his Stuff.——That *grotesque Figure,* who smiles so sarcastically upon him, is his *Cousin P on a Pinnacle.* However, since it has been the Fate of many better *Authors* to die as soon

as born, from which sudden Exit, I fear, few of *my Authors* are exempted, ——here's to their *good Repose,* with all my Heart.¹²

And so Hamilton and Green drink to the departure of Q and P and to most of the other authors who contributed to the *Gazette* in its first three years under Green's editorship. These include a "devilish Clan of *Poets*" and a slew of "*moral* or *ethical Writers*" who, Green says, "patch together some Scraps for my Paper, which they think may be worth reading; but they are mistaken, for these trite Subjects have already been much better handled, . . . and so they may be called a Set of *Plagiaries.*" And even "the *splenetic Writer* of WHAT NEWS?" makes a cameo appearance, ingloriously accompanied by "a few others of less Note."

Hamilton satirizes Green, too, for his penchant to print anything for profit. Aware that one particularly lengthy debate in his paper centers less around the "specious" question of liberty versus authority than around the private interests of the contending parties, Green nonetheless prints these articles because, he says, "they pay me for it, and I'll publish any Thing for Money, if it is not impious or treasonable."¹³ When the personification of Public

---

12. "Q. in the Corner" attacked the proposed tobacco inspection law in the *Maryland Gazette,* Apr. 28, 1747; "P. on a Pinnacle" sarcastically responded in the May 5, 1747, issue.

13. From January to May, 1748, Green carried a political dispute from Prince George's County in the *Gazette*. On one side of the debate was the "Freeholder" and "Americano Britannus"; on the other, "Philanthropos," "Anonymous," and a "Native of Maryland," whose "tedious Prolixity" lulled Hamilton to sleep at the beginning of his dream vision. "The Pretence upon one Side," Green says, "is *the Liberty of the Subject,* and the *Security of every Man's Purse and Property.* That on the other is the Cause of *injur'd Magistracy,* and to chastise the daring and *insolent Contempt of Authority;* both specious and plausible Subjects of Debate, to cover over something else that is meant, to wit, whether a *Court-House* shall be built in *this Place* or in *that*

Opinion appears at the end of the vision and "sneeringly" asks Green why he "trouble[s] the Public" with "such a Rabble of *Authors*" and their valueless productions, he again responds,

> As for their *Works*, ... I never gave my self the Trouble to weigh the Value of any of them, my *Types* are always in Readiness for them, when they send me a *Piece of Money*, and instead of reading the *Author's Piece*, to find the value of it, I read the *Money Bill* he sends along with it, and according as that is more or less in Value, so I put a greater or less Value upon the *Author* and his Performance.

Hamilton's satire of Green's editorial policies actually functions as a blatant advertisement that Green will print just about anything for the right price. That Green would publish such a satire upon himself demonstrates not only his exceptional good humor but the extent to which colonial printers would go to make ends meet.

Hamilton singles out for praise three of the *Gazette*'s contributors, the first of which is "A. B.," the persuasive advocate for the tobacco inspection law. "He has done well," Hamilton says, "in serving his Country with such a true and commendable Zeal" and is "the only one among our *Authors* who deserves to live." No doubt Daniel Dulany, the "A. B." of the *Gazette*, appreciated his new son-in-law's judicious compliment.[14] Only Dulany, however, receives Hamilton's unmixed blessing. The other two writers he

---

Place, agreeable to the Interest, not of the Public, but of either contending Party." Hamilton and Green discuss at length the difference between hereditary right and a "*Right in Trust*, committed to [a king] upon certain Conditions by the *People*, which Conditions, if he observes not, he forfeits this Right." They end up granting Philanthropos "a *hereditary Right* to be *King of the Blunderers*" and drinking a toast to the Freeholder and "all true *Whigs*."

14. Hamilton married Margaret Dulany on May 29, 1747; it was with genuine admiration and, no doubt, remarkable shrewdness that he placed his wife's father at the head of the *Gazette*'s contributors. Hamilton's marriage and Dulany's influence upon him is discussed in ch. 1.

praises—both poets, the Reverend James Sterling and his former medical school classmate, Dr. Adam Thomson—are also ridiculed for their foibles. A "young dapper Gentleman," Thomson is a bit too "precise and affected in his Carriage" and a bit too dogmatic and "prolix in his Discourse," and there is a little too much "Fire mixt with his Phlegm." Green points out, however, that in his *"Satyrical Epistle to his Friend"* Thomson has sensibly "ridicul[ed] the Vice and Ignorance that prevail in this *Infant Province,* which Vice and Ignorance, he seems to say, arise from the Want of good Education, *Universities,* and *Seminaries of Learning.*——There he is right," Hamilton replies, "but I think he should also have brought in bad and indifferent *Poets,* and all wretched Authors, among his other *Fops.*" Less precise in his behavior, Sterling enters the visionary stage gesticulating and ranting "in a furious Manner, expanding his Arms, and stamping with his Foot.—— 'Ha, ye Gods! ye immortal Essences!' What a noble Conception was there! Stop, stop the gaudy fugitive Thought, lest it outfly my *Pegasus.*" "Is this Person," Hamilton asks Green,

> a *Pindaric Poet,* or a *religious Zealot?* Methinks his Behaviour somewhat resembles Madness.——That there Gentleman [Green replies] is the *first Rate Poet* in our *Province;* a most thundering and verbose *Son of the Nine Muses;* he has a Fancy like lightning; and not only in his *Compositions,* but in his common *Discourse,* he darts out Notions and Conceptions which no Mortal but himself ever thought of. He deals much in *ideal Beings, figurative Personages,* and antient *Pagan Mythology;* and is desirous to be understood by none but *People of Taste.*—
> —But his must be a strange *Taste* [Hamilton says], which makes the relishing of what is romantic and obscure to almost all your *Readers,* an essential *Criterion of Taste.*

Despite Sterling's "strange volatile Humour," Green reminds Hamilton that he possesses "a good Measure of Sense and Learning.... He is one of my prime *Authors*," Green concludes, "and I wish he would write oftner." "I'm sorry to find him then in the Company of these *Fops*," Hamilton replies, "but here's to his good Success, and may he be crowned *Poet Laureat* of *Maryland*."[15]

For contributing to his paper, Green informs Hamilton that he has "the Honour to be classed among [his] *Authors*" and pins to his coat "their *Badge of Distinction*, ... the Device of *a Monkey riding a winged Ass,* and in the *Offskip, Mount Parnassus reversed, with its double Top wrapt in a thick black Cloud*." "Thank you kindly, *Jonas*," Hamilton replies, "but I hope some Time or other to be in better Company." According to Hamilton, aside from the regular contributors he praises and one or two others who occasionally published in the *Gazette* (including "Ned Type," Benjamin Franklin),[16] the remaining authors assembled in the hall have only served "the *drowsy god*" with their tedious performances. His vision concludes when, just as Green is drinking to Public Opinion and to their "better Acquaintance," Hamilton hears a loud clamor in the next hall, where a group of Quakers are engaged in a hot dispute. But before he has a chance to enter the

---

15. Sterling and Thomson had both visited the Tuesday Club by this time, and Sterling was welcomed again in 1753. For his "volatile Humour" and rodomontade expressions, Hamilton labeled him "Reverend Rodomanthus" in *The History of the Tuesday Club*. Hamilton apparently considered Thomson a better doctor than poet, for he vigorously defended him in a dispute about smallpox inoculation (see ch. 1). For further discussion of Sterling's contributions to Maryland culture, see Lemay, *Men of Letters*, 257–312.

16. Green reprinted Gov. William Gooch's speech upon the fire that consumed the capitol at Williamsburg in the Apr. 14, 1747, issue of the *Gazette*. In the June 16, 1747, issue Franklin burlesqued Gooch's speech and, Hamilton says in his vision, "metamorphosed his *lame Prose* into *hobbling Verse*." Gooch appears "in *Effigie*" in Hamilton's vision since his speech was borrowed from another paper. Franklin's burlesque appears in *The Papers of Benjamin Franklin*, ed. Leonard W. Labaree et al. (New Haven, 1961), 3:135–40.

"A Few Crude Thoughts"

Pennsylvania chamber of their literary hell, he is "bit in the Leg by a curs'd *Musketo*," and so, he says, "the whole Vision vanishing, I left off dreaming and fell to scratching." Thus the plague of these diminutive performances is replaced by another diminutive pest that most colonists found even more troublesome than bad prose and verse.

Before he had barely finished scratching his critical itch, Hamilton entered another literary dispute by publishing a satiric tall tale in the August 31, 1748, issue of *Maryland Gazette*. Thomson's satiric "Epistle to a Friend," published in the February 24, 1748, issue of the *Gazette*, had provoked a response in the March 30 issue by the Reverend Theophilus Swift, who accused Thomson of being a plagiarist and "a stupid Rhymester." Thomson answered by publishing a witty epigram in the May 4 issue but apparently was more upset by Swift's attack than the epigram indicated. Hamilton's attitude toward both figures is clear from his dream vision. He considered Thomson a competent and perceptive poet but a bit too headstrong and vain about his abilities; and he labeled Swift "the obscurest and most abusive" of all the contributors to the *Gazette*. "Pray what does he rail at honest *Philo* [Thomson] for?" Hamilton asks Green in his vision; "Because," Green replies, "he imagines he has classed him among his *Dunces*, seeing he has not given him a Place among the *Worthies* in his *Satyrical Epistle*." By not being praised, Hamilton suggests, Swift felt he had been indirectly insulted.

In his prefatory letter to the editor, Hamilton indicates that his satiric tale is directed not only against Thomson and Swift but against all those who have taken part in this trifling dispute:

As Affectation of Wit and Humour very commonly leads Men into many Absurdities and Disgraces, . . . by a Misapplication of other Mens Works, by hot Disputes about dull and trifling Matters; by playing upon

> Words, or the Ambiguity of their Sense; or, what is most usual, by acute Nonsense: They do not appear in the most advantageous Light, to Men of common Sense; and if they chance to gratify the Curiosity of any of that Class, 'tis but as Monsters do, not for their Beauty.
>
> 'Tis for the Use of such Dealers in Trash in this Infant Country ... that I have sent you the following Relation; which, as it is written in the facetious Way, generally allowed a proper Way of Writing on some Occasions, it is hoped may be suitable to such as it is intended for.

The insinuation is clear: Hamilton's story is intended not for people of taste, who pursue sense in discourse and Beauty in Nature, but for the "Dealers in Trash" who seek to "gratify [their] Curiosity" by becoming embroiled in such nonsense.

Like any good tall tale, the story is framed by a straight man, who, having heard that the "poor *Laureat* was no more, ... had the Curiosity" to go to his lodgings and discover the truth for himself. His prying curiosity, the trait Hamilton detested, is rewarded when he becomes the butt of one of the finest whoppers in colonial literature. Upon his "being particular in enquiring" of the poet's servant, Mrs. ———, "in what Manner the Disorder appeared," she relates the following story:

> About the latter End of *March* last, this Gentleman ... took a very sudden melancholy Turn; the Occasion of which was a Gazette then come to hand, that had something in it that touched the poor Man so, that he has never held up his Head since: ... I reason with him sometimes, and tell him the Author of those few Lines is only making himself merry with your Poetry, and the more angry you are with him, the better pleased he will be with you: But he will not believe it to be so, and goes on scribbling in hopes of saving his Credit.
>
> But to make short of my Story, the poor Man growing worse and worse, I thought fit to send for his Friend Dr. *Cacofogus*.... Well,—

"A Few Crude Thoughts"

the Doctor comes, and taking a View of his Patient, he stood with his Arms folded across, his Head reclined on the left Shoulder, as in a musing Posture; and in five or six Minutes, raising his Head and balancing his Hands, broke out in these Words: Oh Madness! Oh Madness! Then after a little Pause, turning short to me; Do you know, Mrs. ———, if he has been costive for any Time? Puh, says I, to my Knowledge he has not had a Stool these three Months and upwards, tho' straining seven or eight Hours every Day. The Doctor shaking his Head, That was enough to make any Man in the Universe mad— We must get a Glyster immediately: And so he prepares one of the strongest Ingredients we could find, and proceeds to his Business; ... But unluckily for poor *Cacofogus,* his medicine proved so powerful, that before he had Time to withdraw to a convenient Distance, ... the Patient lets drive slap in his Face,—upon the Receipt of which Salutation the Doctor being a little startled, reclines his Head backwards, as before to the left, and jumping up and retreating as quick as Thought, stumbles over a Stool that stood behind him with so much Force, that he could not stop himself 'til he got to the farthest Corner in the Room, where he did me some little Damage. Well,—getting upon his Legs again,——I have got a random shot you see, Mrs. ———: I see you have, Sir, says I; but you should have duck'd— —The Shot came so thick, he replies, there was no Possibility of avoiding it:——Then taking a View of himself in the Glass; Is not this fine, is not this very fine, Mrs. ———? and falls into a great Passion, cursing the poor mad Man, and calling him such Names as I am ashamed to repeat. But away he runs out of the Room, calling for Water; the Children, and some others, in the next Room, instead of answering his Demand, ran out of the House as if the D—— was in them all, the Dogs barking, the whole House to be sure in an Uproar. ——To mend the Matter, the Doctor runs after one of the Curs, and makes a Kick at him, but elevating his Heel too high, misses his Aim, and down he tumbles upon his Back: To be sure, how angry he was. Well,—we got him all the Help we could, holding our Noses, and he making such Grimaces as I shall never forget. ...

Well,—the Doctor, after he had got out of the Suds, had a Mind to see his Patient again, and stepping softly to the Room Door, peeps in,—thrusting in his Head farther and farther by Degrees. But the mad Man was ready for him, for no sooner had the Doctor got his Head in, than he empties his Jordan full-butt in his Face, in a most plentiful Manner.——The Doctor comes running back to us in an Instant, calling out, More Water here!——His sudden Return was a little surprizing to us, but we soon smelt out the Cause;—if he was chagrin'd before, he was ten times more so now: Oh! I am blinded, I am blinded, says he, with his Hands on his Eyes, and stamping his Feet, in a most sad Condition.

We had the same Tune over again with the Doctor, but no sooner had we done, than out comes the mad Man again, with a large Pan full of what I don't like to name, the Consequence of the Glyster, and drives it among us all;—but unfortunately for the poor Doctor, the largest Share fell to him, which disfigur'd him, if possible, more than ever;—and washing his Mouth at that Time, which happened to be wide open, as he gargled the Water in his Throat, he received such a Meal as had like to have been his last: I am sure he was a Quarter of an Hour before he could speak, swallowing some, and out with the rest: so that I believe he digested about one half, and with much Difficulty came to himself.

After we had got the Doctor clean once more, he was in great Haste to be gone; and his Horse being brought to the Door, just as he had mounted and was setting off, out comes another Jug full of that same, from the mad Man's Window, and takes him on the Back; but it never retarded his Course, tho we would have him to take the other Lather, but he would not be prevailed on to alight; and so he proceeded on his Journey in great Order.

"This is the Fruit of Infant Poetry," the narrator concludes, "which is published for a Warning to nasty Scribblers, whose Fate is generally bad."

Hamilton's satiric tale is more than just a warning to "nasty Scribblers." It does, of course, satirize Thomson for overreacting

"A Few Crude Thoughts"

to the criticism he had received from Swift and Swift for overreacting to the "random shot" he had received from Thomson. But it also satirizes all those who poke their noses into such nasty business, including the meddlesome well-wisher who only makes matters worse and the prying narrator whose patently smug moral suggests that he, too, has swallowed an outrageous load of——. And surely Hamilton is also satirizing his own previous involvement in that equally trifling affair with the Baltimore Bards. It hardly seems coincidental that Cacofogus applies the same methods to cure the poor distracted poet that Polypharmacus used to cure Bard Bavius of his frenzy. Only this time the good doctor suffers the repercussions of his meddlesome cure.

As he devoted more and more of his energy to recording the adventures of the Tuesday Club, Hamilton contributed fewer and fewer pieces to the *Maryland Gazette*. Out of commiseration for Jonas Green, however, who was constantly "under the cruel Necessity" as editor of the *Gazette* of "making Sense out of Nonsense," Hamilton published in the April 12, 1749, issue an advertisement satirizing the "odd Sort of Grammar and Orthography, in Use among our *Underlings of the Theatre*," taken, he claims, "from an authentic Original of the Author's own Hand-Writing" and intended to illustrate the "vexatious and puzzling Labour" of Green's office. The advertisement is one long misspelled, miscapitalized, unpunctuated sentence. It satirizes not only unintelligible theatrical advertisements and the general state of illiteracy in colonial America but, most of all, Hamilton's fellow physicians. Though the *"itinerant Virtuosi"* who write these unintelligible advertisements "may be a Degree or two below the Learning and Erudition of our Professors of *Physic* . . . or our *Stage-Doctors;* yet it must be observed," Hamilton says, "that tho' the latter may sometimes write more correctly, yet the Performances of the former come nigher to what they promise."

Hamilton's final contribution to the *Maryland Gazette,* published January 24, 1750, and signed "Nic. Turntype," parodies Masonic ceremonies and satirizes popular misconceptions about the mysterious rites of Freemasonry. Along with other members of the Tuesday Club, Hamilton had recently formed a Freemason's lodge in Annapolis and had been appointed Grand Master.[17] His satiric sketch, written as a letter to Jonas Green (also a member of the Annapolis lodge) and ostensibly "in Praise of *Printers,* and their noble Art," is actually a covert account of the mysteries of Freemasonry, which would have been particularly on the minds of all enquiring Annapolitans at this time. Having "made it [his] Business diligently to search the Writings of the Learned," Hamilton has discovered that, because the first printing house was located in Westminster Abbey, all subsequent printing houses have been called chapels, and whenever a new printing house is established "that Part of the House where the *Press* is erected is *consecrated;* which Ceremony is performed, at the Master's Command, by the *senior Freeman,* or *Father of the Chapel:* It is performed by drinking Success to the Master, sprinkling the Walls with Strong-Beer, and singing the *Cuz's Anthem.*" The workers in the printing house, or the "*Chapelonians,*" are required to follow "certain wise Laws, framed for the Good of the Company, and for regularly carrying on the Master's Work." Those who transgress these laws are fined and, if they refuse to pay, excommunicated, which prevents them from participating in "the *grand anniversary Solemnity,* commonly called the *Way-Goose Feast,*" and from being able to redress "any waggish Trick, or Mischief" played upon

---

17. The foundation of the Annapolis lodge and Hamilton's role at Master of the lodge is discussed in ch. 1.

them. These two great deprivations make all chapelonians pay their fines promptly.

Any apprentice to the printer must undergo an extraordinary rite of passage, during which the chapelonians

> walk thrice round the Room, with their Right Arms under the Lappets of their Coats, the Boy who is to be made a *Cux* carrying a wooden Sword before them; then the Boy kneels, and the *Father of the Chapel* exhorts him to be mindful of his Business, and not to discover the Secrets and *Mysteries* of the Trade, squeezes a Spunge of Strong Beer on his Head, and gives him the noble Title of... *Duke of the Dunghill,* of the *Hog-Stye,*... or in case he lives nigh any *Lane, Alley,* or *Dock,*... he is stiled *Duke of Thieving-Lane, Pissing Alley,* or *Puddle Dock.*

While the young apprentice is still kneeling before them, the chapelonians walk around him singing the Cuz's Anthem,

> BA, Ba,
> Be, Ba-be,
> Bi, Bi, Ba be bi,
> Bo, Bo, Ba-be-bi bo,
> Bu, Bu, Ba-be bi bo-bu,

and so on through all the consonants of the alphabet.

These solemnities, Hamilton concludes, demonstrate "the Sacredness of a *Printing Office*" and the reverence that should be paid to "a Place consecrated in so awful a Manner." Although "the Ignorant and Profane" may view these ceremonies as "trifling and puerile," they are "every whit as significant," he claims, "as those exhibited in other Consecrations and Installments." Yet how often, he laments, have the Walls of these sacred *Chapels* been profaned, and their Immunities been violated with Impunity, by a Parcel of Ruffians, who have made no Scruple to break open the *Sanctum Sanctorum* by mere Force and Violence, and to destroy the sacred Utensils; to drag away the very *Priests* officiating at the *Altars,* even with Pistols cock'd at their Heads, pretending to accuse them of Treason, Sedition, Infidelity, Atheism, and such like sham Charges.

Hamilton punningly concludes that this "is Sacrilege of the deepest Dye, and ought to be punished in the highest Manner; but alas! we live in a profane Age, when every Thing sacred is turned into Mockery and Ridicule, and trod under Foot; and the *Mysteries of Printing* . . . are become the Objects of Derision and Contempt."

Like Hamilton, I have tried to provide a maximum amount of entertainment and a minimum amount of instruction in this chapter. Several instructive strains do, however, emerge from these periodical pieces. The most apparent is Hamilton's obvious contempt for the general state of letters in colonial Maryland. The majority of items in the *Gazette,* he repeats again and again, are dull, dull, dull, and as he remarks in his dream vision, the general state of literacy and education is equally poor. His periodical pieces are therefore meant not only to inject entertainment into a dull literary climate but to instruct writers and readers in the art of good, lively prose.

Hamilton also repeatedly attacks inquisitiveness in these selections. In the *Itinerarium* he identifies inquisitiveness as a particularly American trait, but in these pieces he views it more generally as symptomatic of the times. When Addison and Steele spoke of curiosity as Mr. Spectator's "prevailing Passion," they were speaking of the prevailing passion of an inquisitive, empirical age. Hamilton welcomed the inquisitiveness after scientific information, but again and again in his works he emphasizes the extent to which

"A Few Crude Thoughts"

curiosity could obliterate sensible communication when it entered the realm of private affairs. His attacks against curiosity carry an implicit attack against his generation's lust for information.

But the most interesting strain that emerges from these selections is Hamilton's constant derogation of poetry. Poetasters have always been ridiculed, but Hamilton goes beyond ridiculing incompetent poets. He considered Sterling and Thomson competent poets, yet he ridicules them both in his dream vision and in his tall tale. Writing poetry is, to say the least, an unseemly occupation in Hamilton's periodical pieces. In "WHAT NEWS?" he complains about the "*monstrous Births of Poetry*" that have appeared in the *Gazette;* in the battle between the Baltimore Bards and the Annapolis Wits he talks about the "fits of Rhiming" occasioned by an "epidemical distemper" or "poetical Contagion" and treats Bard Bavius as a lunatic whose ravings require "copious Injections of Warm Glysters"; in his dream vision he states that Sterling's ranting "somewhat resembles Madness," even while praising him as the best poet in Maryland; and in his tall tale he again depicts a competent poet as a madman and again subjects him to glyster therapy; indeed, in that piece everyone—the narrator, the doctor, and the poet's servant—repeatedly emphasizes that the poet is a madman.

Hamilton was clearly helping to create a bias not just against bad poets but against writing poetry. Why? Most likely because he equated being a poet with being a romantic. Sterling, the best poet his culture has to offer, appears in Hamilton's dream vision seeking to appeal to people of taste, but by focusing upon "ideal Beings" and "romantic and obscure" allusions he is, Hamilton stresses, sadly out of touch with the taste of the times. Hamilton himself wrote a poem once every five years or so; not surprisingly, his only surviving poem is romantic in content and tone and his comments accompanying the poem indicate that he viewed the act of writing poetry as a romantic indulgence.[18] In an age that increasingly viewed factual observation and the common occurences of daily life as the substance of good literature, the traditionally elevated status of poetry was being supplanted by history, the travel narrative, biography, and other prose forms, including, slowly but surely, the novel. For Hamilton, the poet was fast becoming a comic romantic anachronism—a sort of literary madman—incongruously out of touch with the emerging literary tastes of the times. His excrementitious exorcisms were designed not only to purge poetic nonsense but to usher out the old and usher in an intellectual climate more receptive to prose and to the new boy in town, something that looked a bit more like *The History of the Tuesday Club*.

---

18. In a letter to his brother-in-law, the Reverend David Smith ([fall] 1743), Hamilton included a poem, "To Philosophy, a Hymn," written in blank verse. "I shall Imagine myself now near your Ruinous Tower, that stands within view of your house," he wrote Smith, "sitting by the brook Side, surrounded with thickets and Romantic objects, and thus could I break out, addressing myself to Philosophy." The poem expresses thoughts that arise from contemplating nature in solitude. A letter by Dr. Upton Scott indicates that Hamilton wrote at least one other poem, "Man," also in blank verse (Howard Family Papers, MS 469).

CHAPTER FOUR

"*The Sempiternal Comedy*"
The History of the Tuesday Club

The History of the Tuesday Club is, to use one of Hamilton's favorite words, a "puzzlementationful" book. As James Carroll observed in 1824 upon delivering his copy of the "Record of the Tuesday Club" to a member of the Baltimore Library Company,

> it is all designed for humour, how far successful in this, you must judge for yourself. It is a sort of farcical Drama of Mock Majesty played off for a length of time, many years ago, by a sett of Annapolitan Wits on an elderly Gentleman of considerable wealth & good standing in Society; he their Lord or King with his Chancellor, Secretary, Attorney General, poet laureate, Champion, &ct—and the good old Man all along unconscious of being thus a Subject of their Merriment. The Production is unique and about as much connected one part with another as a dictionary, when you take it in hand begin in the middle of the Book & read backwards, then forwards & skip about, I think now & then you will find something that will set you a roaring.[1]

---

1. Carroll's letter appears at the front of the "Record of the Tuesday Club," Maryland Historical Society, MS 854.

The Comic Genius of Dr. Alexander Hamilton

Carroll's remarks about the "Record" apply equally well to the tone and spirit of the *History*, and so does his perplexity about what to call the "Record." Hamilton employs and burlesques so many literary and non-literary forms in the *History* that it ends up looking like a sort of amorphous literary oddity. In each of its fourteen books, he typically begins with an opening essay on some grand or trivial topic—it hardly matters which, since the grand becomes trivial and the trivial becomes grand—then continues his narrative of the club's misadventures, introducing letters, speeches, trials, indictments, commissions, set dramatic pieces, poetry, music, and drawings—anything he can to embellish his narrative. It is an extraordinary attempt to merge various literary, rhetorical, and artistic modes into one narrative—but what, finally, is it?

Although Hamilton would have been the last to admit it, *The History of the Tuesday Club* is a comic novel. Written between the publication dates of the two great comic novels of the eighteenth century—Fielding's *Tom Jones* (which Hamilton read and admired) and Sterne's *Tristram Shandy* (which was published after Hamilton's death)—*The History of the Tuesday Club* in many ways resembles both. Two of its most prominent features—the introductory essays to each of its fourteen books, and the dominant voice of its witty, self-dramatizing narrator—owe much to the example Fielding set in *Joseph Andrews* and *Tom Jones*.[2] But Hamilton's narrative is, by design, far more experimental and discursive

---

2. Fielding was not the first, of course, to use introductory essays or self-dramatizing narrators, but he was responsible more than any other author for popularizing them. A good discussion of these and related issues is William Park, "What Was New about the 'New Species of Writing'?" *Studies in the Novel*, 2 (1970), 112–30. As J. A. Leo Lemay observes, "In imitation of Fielding, Hamilton writes a rambling seemingly extraneous, but invari-

than the "architectonic" *Tom Jones*.³ More often than not, the *History*'s loose plot—concerning the rise of the Ancient and Honorable Tuesday Club to its peak of clubific felicity, and its fall as the insidious forces of luxury, ambition, and pride infest its members—is lost behind a maze of digressions. In the end, the plot hardly matters; structurally and thematically, digression is everything. In its structural and thematic discursiveness and in the variety of verbal high jinks Hamilton incorporates into his narrative *The History of the Tuesday Club* anticipates *Tristram Shandy* as much as it imitates *Tom Jones*.

Like *Tristram Shandy*, *The History of the Tuesday Club* is a comic novel that borrows heavily from the "anatomy," a genre particularly popular during the eighteenth century.⁴ As Northrop Frye has argued, the "anatomist"—Swift, for instance, in *Gulliver's*

---

ably fascinating first chapter for each of the [fourteen] books.... Each is an essay, complete in itself—but each also forwards the unified design—an attempt to record a complete philosophy of life" (*Men of Letters in Colonial Maryland*, 250).

3. The symmetrical structure of *Tom Jones* is the focus of Robert Alter's chapter "The Architectonic Novel" in *Fielding and the Nature of the Novel* (Cambridge, Mass., 1968).

4. Throughout this paragraph, I use "anatomy" as Northrop Frye defines it in *Anatomy of Criticism* (Princeton, 1957), 308–14. In Hamilton's day, it would have been used more typically to describe a treatise such as Robert Burton's *Anatomy of Melancholy* (which Hamilton parodies in book 2, ch. 1, of the *History*) rather than a narrative prose work. Anticipating his critics, Hamilton also refers to the *History* as a "prolix Rhapsody" (1:v), a word that by the eighteenth century had come to imply a literary work of miscellaneous or disconnected pieces. At one point Loquacious Scribble mentions in a letter that the Tuesday Club has yet to appoint an "able Historiographer, to connect and form [the club's affairs] into an uniform Rhapsody" (1:535), a notion that would have been recognized as a ludicrous contradiction in terms. Although the *History* resembles—and indeed burlesques—the rhapsody, Hamilton was clearly poking fun at those who might perceive his narrative as nothing more than that.

Travels or Voltaire in *Candide*—is primarily concerned with "intellectual themes and attitudes" and with "piling up an enormous mass of erudition about his theme or . . . overwhelming his pedantic targets with an avalanche of their own jargon." The novel and the anatomy are not, however, mutually exclusive; indeed, particularly during the eighteenth century they frequently converged in the same work. "It was Sterne," Frye says, "who combined them with greatest success. *Tristram Shandy* may be . . . a novel, but the digressing narrative, the catalogues, the stylizing of character along 'humor' lines, . . . the symposium discussions, and the constant ridicule of philosophers and pedantic critics are all features that belong to the anatomy."[5] Much the same can be said of *The History of the Tuesday Club*. It is a comic novel whose narrative centers around the social behavior of a humorous cast of characters, but at the same time one whose narrator provides a comic anatomy of eighteenth-century society and ideas.

Like other eighteenth-century novelists, Hamilton chose to call his narrative neither a novel nor an anatomy but a "history." He would not have been flattered had anyone in his day called *The History of the Tuesday Club* a novel any more than Fielding would have been flattered had anyone called *The History of Tom Jones* a novel. The reason is clear from their remarks concerning "novels" and "romances" throughout their works. Modern critics have often pointed out that the word "novel" came to mean many things during the eighteenth century; what we have not stressed enough, however, is how frequently "novel" and "romance" were used almost in the same breath by mid-century writers such as Hamilton and Fielding. Lennard J. Davis argues that there was "a

---

5. *Anatomy of Criticism*, 311, 312.

profound rupture, a discursive chasm between these two forms" in eighteenth-century England, and so "the romance is not usefully seen as a forbear of, a relative of, or an influence on the novel."[6] Davis's observation is at once insightful and misleading. There *was* a sharp break between romance and what we *now perceive* as the novel as it was emerging in the works of Richardson and Fielding by mid century. But at the time they were writing their novels, "novel" and "romance" were virtually synonymous and equally pejorative terms: both were perceived as being overly concerned with the past, with impossible situations, and with idealized characters. During an empirical age that valued factual observation and expected writers to focus their narratives on daily life, most authors consciously avoided associating their narratives with either genre.[7]

Writers such as Hamilton and Fielding therefore turned not toward the "novel" or "romance" in defining their narratives but toward "history," the most respected prose genre in the eigh-

---

6. *Factual Fictions: The Origins of the English Novel* (New York, 1983), 25. Davis presents a strong argument for the influence of contemporary news and journalism, rather than popular romances, upon eighteenth-century fiction, but he overstates his case, I think, when he claims that by mid century most English writers clearly distinguished romances from novels (pp. 103–104).

7. The best study of the movement toward historicity in narrative during the early eighteenth century is Michael McKeon, *The Origins of the English Novel, 1600–1740*. McKeon nicely summarizes the early eighteenth-century perception of romance and of particular romances that Hamilton attacks (see esp. pp. 26–28, 52–64). Two good studies of Fielding's attitude toward romance are James J. Lynch, *Henry Fielding and the Heliodorian Novel: Romance, Epic, and Fielding's New Province of Writing* (Rutherford, N.J., 1986), and Henry Knight Miller, *Henry Fielding's Tom Jones and the Romance Tradition* (Victoria, British Columbia, 1976).

teenth century.[8] By the end of the seventeenth century the conception of "history" as a genre had become blurred by European writers who called their romances "histories" simply because their narratives were based on real characters. "In those enlightened times," Hamilton facetiously observes, history

> received additions and Improvements which it never before had, and was dressed up in very fine and Gaudy trappings, to the Immortal Geniuses of that age, we owe, the new and rare Invention of Romance writing, a kind of History, altogether Novel, (hence some kinds of Romances are called *Novels*) and hitherto unknown, from these great Historians, came the Prodigious Histories of *Amadis De Gaul, Amadis de Grece, Don Bellianis, Esplandian, Palmerin,* and a hundred other voluminous pieces, equally witty amusing and Instructive. These were the Heroical Histories of the times. There were also the amorous Histories of *Cassandra, Cleopatra, Clelia,* & *Almahyde,* all adapted to excite amorous and tender passions, particularly among the readers of the fair Sex. (2:26)

---

8. As H. Trevor Colbourn observes, by mid century "the testimonial on history's behalf was overwhelming." Hume called it "the greatest mistress of wisdom," and other of the century's most influential writers from Locke to Franklin similarly praised its value (*The Lamp of Experience,* 5–6; for further discussion of the prominence of history during this period, see John Butt, *The Mid-Eighteenth Century,* 191–243). History was so respected that, as Jerry C. Beasley points out, the 1740s witnessed "the elevation of private experience to the status of public history," and private experience accordingly became the substance of narrative "histories" during this period (*Novels of the 1740s,* [Athens, Ga., 1982], 43; Beasley discusses the "fictionalization" of history by mid century on pp. 74–84). Hamilton also plays upon what his contemporaries would have perceived as the double meaning of "history" and "historian": as not only a narrative of daily life but also a narrated story or *histoire* told by a *histor* who shapes and interprets its details, whether it be Fielding's *History of Tom Jones* or Gibbon's *History of the Decline and Fall of the Roman Empire.* (Leopold Damrosch, Jr., argues this point well in *God's Plot and Man's Stories: Studies in the Fictional Imagination from Milton to Fielding* [Chicago, 1985], 273.)

"The Sempiternal Comedy"

Hamilton's complaints about "Romantic Historians" who have "palm[ed] upon the world, a hideous collection of fables" (2:4) are typical of the eighteenth-century attempt to restore the factuality of history and to establish factuality as the foundation of any good prose narrative.

Rather than associate himself with these romantic historians, Hamilton, like Fielding in *Joseph Andrews*, defines his narrative as a "true history."[9] By doing so he meant not only to indicate that his narrative was rooted in fact but also, like Fielding, to distinguish between "a naively empiricist and a more 'imaginative' species of belief."[10] Some historians, Hamilton felt, were "too strictly attached to what they call truth and demonstration," and others were "only dry drivelling narraters of Incidents and facts" (1:2). For Hamilton, as for Fielding, the "true historian" sought not simply to present facts accurately but to frame those facts with "the proper and decent seasoning of apposite remarks and observations" (1:2); to create characters who were combinations of "light" and "shade" (1:vii) rather than one-dimensional; and most of all to copy Nature in all its fullness (1:4). What both authors were attempting to define as "true histories" we now call novels.

As much as Richardson or Fielding, Hamilton was creating a "new species of writing."[11] His opening chapter "Of History and

---

9. Hamilton's conception of "true history" and the distinctions he draws between history and romance are very similar to Fielding's remarks in *Joseph Andrews*, book 3, ch. 1, book 9, ch. 1, and *Tom Jones*, book 4, ch.1.
10. McKeon, *The Origins of the English Novel*, 404.
11. This phrase has been attributed to Richardson (see *The Correspondence of Samuel Richardson*, ed. Anna Laetitia Barbauld [London, 1804], 1:lxxiii, and *Samuel Richardson, Clarissa: Prefaces, Hints of Prefaces, and Postscript*, Augustan Reprint Society, No. 103 [Los Angeles, 1964], 7–8). Fielding similarly claimed that he was creating a "new province of writing" in his preface to *Joseph Andrews*.

Historians," like Fielding's "Bill of Fare to the Feast" in *Tom Jones*, invites the judicious reader to partake of his historical feast and to keep in mind the distinction between his narrative and the more dubious narratives of romance writers or novelists: "Histories founded upon truth, and wrote in a plain, easie and natural Stile," he says,

> are Sirloins of beef plainly dressed, wholesome, hearty and nourishing to a robust and healthy Stomach, but those erected upon fiction, and stuffed with Bombast and fustian phrazes, are vapid, windy, unwholsom and adulterated with your damn'd sauces and pickles, fitted only for crazy and luxurious apetites, which require a Spur to excite them to a proper pitch, and are apt to breed worms, maggots and monstruous Crudities, in the brains and Intelects of such students as feed upon them. Such are Romances, novels, fairy tales, Love adventures, ... and other such verbose trumpery, with which the french Artists have crouded our Libraries, as their Cooks have confounded our kitchens and loaded our tables, with Devilish Ragoos, fricassies, ... amulets, Solomongundies, and the like. The first kind of Cookery breeds as many crudities in the Intellect of the readers, as the other does in the Stomachs and habits of the eaters. (1:3–4)

"The History which I am now about to present to [the reader]," Hamilton asserts, "is none of your vamped up Frenchified pieces of Cookery, it is a Solid and Serious performance, plain and homely, and withal true, every article thereof, being copied exactly from nature and the life" (1:4).

Hamilton's feast metaphor not only introduces a new narrative dish to the literary menu, it invites reader participation, identifying the forthcoming narrative as a public performance meant to be consumed by a community of discriminating readers, and it introduces the reader to the ironic voice of the narrator.[12] The judicious reader immediately suspects that Hamilton's remarks, like Fielding's, contain "a core of serious truth qualified by irony; the reader is offered excellent guidance which he must follow with caution because of a lurking suspicion that the deft hand of the narrator, in the midst of explanatory gestures, is somehow pulling his leg."[13] Hamilton's narrative follows Nature and is indeed "founded upon truth." But it is hardly a "serious performance," and it clearly exaggerates rather than exactly copies the events that transpired in the life of the Tuesday Club. In the "Record of the Tuesday Club" Hamilton merely states, for instance, that on July 16, 1745, "Collonel Edward Lloyd was admitted this night an honorary member of this Club, and took his place accordingly";[14] on that night in the *History*, however, Colonel Courtly Phraze

> made his appearance so suddenly, that none present could certainly tell, in what manner he came into the Room, tho' many affirmed, that he seemed to them to enter back foremost; and turning his face to the Company, made a most profound bow, passed some polite compliments, and sitting down gravely, told the members that he had Just now left the Company of the Ladies, those dear angelical creatures!... The Collonels discourse concerning the Ladies, put the members of the Club into an amorous vein, and there was not one there excepting Mr Jole, but resolved to have his Girl that very night; Drawlum Quaint Esqr... seemed to be more agitated by this amorous enthusiasm, than any of the other members, for, he went out of

---

12. Hamilton died before publishing *The History of the Tuesday Club*; it is evident from his frequent remarks to his "readers" throughout his narrative, however, that he expected to publish his manuscript. When I speak of his "readers," I am therefore talking about the audience he anticipated.
13. Alter, *Fielding and the Nature of the Novel*, 30–31.
14. *Records of the Tuesday Club of Annapolis, 1745–56*, ed. Breslaw, 10.

Club... and was resolved not to return, till he had blunted the edge of his desires, with some Gentle and kind Nymph, but, his resolution did not carry him thro' thick and thin, for, he was so terrified, at the Sight of a Superannuated female, who... opened her door to him, that all his tender Ideas vanished like Smoke, and taking to his heels, as if the Devil had been after him, he run faster back than he went forth, and took his Seat again in Club, quite out of breath. (1:173–74)

"It was not so," however, "with Laconic Comas Esqr, and [Prattle] Motely, two Stanch Longstanding members, but what their adventures and exploits were," Hamilton says, "we shall not relate here, as having nothing to do with the History of the Club, which is of too grave and Solid a nature, to admit of the detail and relation of amours, these triffles, properly belonging to Romances and Novels, and therefore cannot be any credit to True histories such as this" (1:174). According to Hamilton's understanding of narrative genres, *The History of the Tuesday Club* is a "true history," but his ironic tone at the same time begs us to question whether it is a true "true history."

Hamilton's "historical" stance is therefore in part a serious attempt to distinguish his narrative from previous narratives and in part an ironic pose designed to fool only the most literal-minded or naively empirical reader. As he well knew, he was embellishing, exaggerating, and sometimes completely inventing events in the club's history to transform fact into fiction. Each of the characters in the *History* is similarly exaggerated to play a particular role in their comic struggle for power. Although Loquacious Scribble, for instance, was clearly patterned after Hamilton himself, he is hardly the same secretary who was the heart of the Tuesday Club and the spirit of conviviality that sustained it for eleven years;[15] rather, he is a

"The Sempiternal Comedy"

> Sly, cunning, Insinuating, deceitful, mischief making member, the continual Author and promoter of Brawls, wrangles, Jealousies, Grumblings, heartburnings, hubbubs and hurly burlys, ... generally carried on, under pretence of doing honor to the President, and for the advantage of the Club, yet, for the most part, terminat[ing] in mischievous purposes and attempts, either to make tools of the Longstanding members, or to derogate from the honor and prerogative of the honorable Chair. (1:243)

Ambitious, conniving, envious, and self-aggrandizing, Scribble perpetually seeks to usurp the positions of the more powerful club officers and to "set his honor the president and the Club together by the Ears" (1:498–99). But despite all his schemes to foment dissension in the club, he actually proves to be "a cunning, Sly and conceal'd operator, for advancing the Authority of the Chair, ... [since] all his actions, designs and plots (under a mistaken policy to advance himself) had a tendency to establish a tyrannical power in the Club" (1:279). He is a "dark and

---

15. Early in his narrative Hamilton identifies himself as secretary of the Tuesday Club: "I shall not here Characterize myself," he writes, "but defer that, till the time, when I shall appear in ... the ancient and honorable Tuesday Club, In the Quality of their Orator and Secretary" (1:126). A few chapters later, he again identifies himself as a member of the club, stating that President Jole "had his particular foibles, which I ... am obliged faithfully to recount, out of the great Regard I have for truth, and I shall promise, to be as little sparing to the other Longstanding members, and even to myself, in that way, as to his honor" (1:228). But when he characterizes Secretary Scribble just a few pages later, he avoids using the first person; indeed, he always refers to Scribble in the third person, as if to distinguish Scribble's voice from his own first-person narrative voice. Had he the time to go back and edit the *History* before dying, I suspect Hamilton would have omitted the references to himself as secretary to avoid confusion; nevertheless, it soon becomes clear to the reader that the narrator and Scribble are two distinct characters with distinct voices.

Mysterious" character is this Scribble (1:191).

The final ingredient in Hamilton's fictional feast is a voice that never appears in the "Record"—the first-person narrator who comments upon the preposterous behavior of Scribble and the other club members. This narrator—clearly Hamilton himself[16]—carefully frames each incident in *The History of the Tuesday Club*. Hamilton's narrative voice, like Fielding's in *Tom Jones*, creates "a curious interplay between the vigorous life of the action and a certain urbane reassurance that reality, however vivid or coarse, will not get out of hand."[17] The events he narrates are interesting in their own right, but the main event is his comic commentary on those events. Had anyone told Hamilton that he was an intrusive narrator he would hardly have known what to say other than, perhaps, what else should I be? Like Fielding, Hamilton's "whole literary method works on the tacit assumption of a community of values, both moral and aesthetic, between writer and reader, ... [so] it is logical that he should reinforce this shared outlook by speaking through a witty, humane [narrator] with whom we can feel a sort of urbane camaraderie of like intelligences."[18] In an age whose social ethic permeated all walks of life and all disciplines, it was only natural that Hamilton, like

---

16. Robert C. Elliott has rightly stressed the importance of personae in eighteenth-century writers such as Swift (*The Literary Persona* [Chicago, 1982]). The narrator of the *History*, however, is a persona in only a very loose sense, and a good case in point that we need to beware of "multiplying entities [too] liberally" (Irvin Ehrenpreis, "Personae," in *Restoration and Eighteenth-Century Literature: Essays in Honor of Alan Dugald McKillop*, ed. Charles Carroll Camden [Chicago, 1963], 36).

17. Claude Rawson, *Order from Confusion Sprung: Studies in Eighteenth-Century Literature from Swift to Cowper* (London, 1985), 270.

18. Alter, *Fielding and the Nature of the Novel*, 44.

"The Sempiternal Comedy"

Fielding, would invite his readers to sit down and partake of his "historical" feast, just as it was only natural for him to sit at the dinner table and talk with them. In their day self-dramatizing narrators were essential, not intrusive, for what was dinner without the host?

Hamilton presents himself primarily as the defender of laughter in a world of carping critics and censors who do not appreciate the value of laughter. After circuitously haranguing the reader on the importance of not wasting time in the opening paragraph of his preface, he writes that

> Some people, who may find time enough to throw away in reading of this, will undoubtedly exclaim, Well! and what the Deuce is the meaning of these grave observations? . . . Many, I am satisfied, will either be mightily astonished, or pretend to be so, that any Mortal Wight, could waste, as they Call it, so much precious time, besides paper and ink, in compiling and Collecting, the History of, (as it may seem to them) a Ridiculous Club, whose chief pastime (they'll say) appears from the face of the History it self, and from the Grotesque Stile of its Idle Author, to have been the carrying on, a Silly, Stupid and unmeaning farce. Very well, my good friends, what if I should grant you all this, . . . the Subject of this History is a farce, and a very Silly one too, . . . I will not Indeed so easily grant you that it is an unmeaning one, since it bears an exact resemblance to many other farces in human life, esteemed (tho they are not really so) of a more Serious nature, I will grant you too, that I the Compiler, am more Silly if possible in collecting the history of this arrant farce, than any of the members of that ridiculous and foolish Club, (as you esteem it,) in acting it, and I have squandered a deal of precious time, Ink and paper, besides fire and Candle, in the Compiling of it. (1:x–xi)

Hamilton concedes that he might have spent his time more profitably than by compiling this silly—though not unmeaning—

farce; he cannot concede, however, that he has spent his time any more foolishly than the critic who would take him to task for his foolishness. "If I have laid out much time in writing of these triffles, as you call them, pray," he argues,

> have not you and many others as wise as either you or I, that is, in their own Conceit, laid out an equivalent of time, upon equivalent, if not greater triffles, only with this difference, that this triffling Scribble of mine, required some thought and application, and your triffling Occupations require no thought at all.... Have I not been poring reading studying and turning over Ancient Authors, and modern wits, in the composition of this History, to the great Solace and Improvement of my Rational, Intellectual and Gelastic faculties, when you, and twenty other such Loggerheads as you, who pretend to call me to account for it, have been exercising the keenest acumen of your obtuse thoughts upon a game at whist, ... bawling at a boxing match or Cock pit, ... fumbling and tumbling a whore in a bagnio, ... or taking an afternoons nap, after having spent two hours more than what was necessary in beastly cramming.... Now, I would Seriously ask you, which of us have been employed to the best purpose, you, in these triffling pastimes, ... or I, in writing this (as you call it) Silly history. (1:xi–xi[a])

According to Hamilton, life is a comedy full of trifles—great and small, to be sure, but, regardless of the size, still trifles—and the most trifling figure of all is the critic who cannot enjoy the human comedy. "All that passes in this ... petty scantling of time," he says, "which we have allotted us to peregrinate thro' this absurd worldly wilderness, and to rant our Comical ... parts out upon this terrestrial Stage, is but of a triffling nature" (1:297–98). Why, then,

> should any ... finical coxcomb of a Clubical Critic, ... pretend to say, that this our famous History, is more triffling than any other history,

> or this our ancient and honorable Club more triffling in it's constitution, ... than any other Society whatsoever, great or small.... Has not the Tuesday club, it's president, State officers, officers of the Commons, Longstanding members, honorary members, and an Empire or kingdom, it's Emperor or king, prime ministers, rulers, nobles, commons &ct: and wherein I pray do they differ but in bulk.... Pray does not an Emperor eat, drink and sleep as much as a [club] president; does he not stink at times as hideously as a president? ... may he not be poxed as well as a president? may he not have the plague, ... the Ripples, the whiffles, nay the Itch as well as a president? nay, may he not play the fool as much as a president? What then is the difference between an Emperor and a president, ... a triffle, believe me, a very triffle, and not worth Contending for. (1:298, 301–302)

"I question not," Hamilton says, that

> I shall be asked, why I should fall into this odd Rhapsody, ... but let me tell you my grave, Serious friends, ... that your ridiculous, Silly, and Idle remarks, uttered with a grave tho unmeaning face, ... against the Lawful recreations of Innocent mirth, and Inoffensive drollery, has been the occasion of all this rant, so, if I have Committed any mortal Sin, at your doors I lay it, ye Impertinent, precise, Stiff, Starch'd up, Cynical Logerheads. (1:303)

"Oh how I pity you," he concludes his tirade against these "Incorrigible Anticlubarians,"

> for your want of that blessed humor, which set Democritus a Laughing, and Heraclitus a crying, ... for, ye dry withered Stocks of human Society, ... you can neither laugh nor Cry in earnest, ... [but] like a flitch of Smoked bacon, whose Salt is soaked out, you go out of [the world], dry, dead, musty, Insipid and Sapless, having never in your lives enjoyed the Sweets and delights of clubical humors and recreations, without which life is not worth enjoying, but is a *tabula rasa* ... in which nothing of Sense or Significancy can be read or discerned. (1:309–10)

These sparring sessions between Hamilton and his unappreciatively dull straw critics are as much a part of the narrative conflict in *The History of the Tuesday Club* as the conflict that develops in the narrative itself. Hamilton's favorite corner man during these sessions is Democritus, "a profound philosopher" who was considered mad in his day because of his "often breaking into violent fits of Laughter, when no body knew for what, little dreaming that he laughed at the Sempiternal Comedy, which he saw acted from day to day on this great earthly stage" (1:464). Who can observe "this medley of absurdity," Hamilton wonders, "without Laughing Immoderatly, either with Democritus, or any other Gelastic Philosopher; and who can blame the members of the... Tuesday Club, for Laughing at all the world, as well as at themselves, and furnishing a fund of Laughter to all those who have a turn for the Gelastic humor" (3:351).

The Tuesday Club, in all its mock heroic grandeur and inflated sense of self-importance, emerges as the prime exhibit in this "medley of absurdity," and Hamilton emerges as a prime example of what Anthony Ashley Cooper, the third Earl of Shaftesbury, called "the comic genius." Traditional Greek comedy, Shaftesbury stated,

> was of admirable use to explode the false sublime.... Everything which might be imposing by a false gravity or solemnity was forced to endure the trial of this touchstone.... The comic genius was applied as a kind of caustic to those exuberances and funguses of the swollen dialect and magnificent manner of speech.... Manners and characters, as well as speech and writings, were discussed with the greatest freedom. Nothing could be better fitted than this genius of wit to unmask the face of things and remove those larvae naturally formed from the tragic manner and pompous style which had preceded.[19]

---

19. "Soliloquy: Or Advice to an Author" (London, 1710), in *Eighteenth-Century Critical Essays*, ed. Scott Elledge (Ithaca, N.Y., 1961), 1:191.

"The Sempiternal Comedy"

In our time, Elder Olson has similarly identified this "minimization of the claim of some particular thing to be taken seriously" as the central element of the comic.[20] Through satire, burlesque, wit, humor, farce, irony, and other forms of the comic, Hamilton achieves that end perhaps better than any writer of his generation.

Exploring the comic in *The History of the Tuesday Club* is much like exploring the comic in *Tom Jones*. Richard Keller Simon has suggested that Fielding created *Tom Jones* as a "comic labyrinth." "It does not simply reflect the kinds of comic alternatives that Fielding inherited from the traditions of satire and humor," Simon argues,

> it makes them into a comic labyrinth of intricate shape and proportions, a novel that is simultaneously comic and about the comic, that raises questions about ridicule, humor, laughter and the comic in discussion and in demonstration, contrasting and combining practice and theory, events and concepts, offering a series of tentative answers for the reader whose only guide is... the confused and confusing narrator.

Fielding's narrator, Simon states, demonstrates that

> consciousness itself [is] comic, comic because of its incongruous nature. This is an important moment in the history of laughter, for thereby... the comic is neither an unpleasant characteristic of men and women, which reminds us of our baseness, nor an incredibly rosy characteristic, which attempts to convince us of our loving kindness. It is, however, a fundamental quality shared by everyone, an essential attribute of our consciousness, of the patterns of human thought.[21]

---

20. *The Theory of Comedy* (Bloomington, Ind., 1968), 23.
21. *The Labyrinth of the Comic: Theory and Practice from Fielding to Freud*, 23–24, 17.

The reader follows Hamilton through a similar comic labyrinth in *The History of the Tuesday Club*. Hamilton examines in theory and illustrates in practice many forms of the comic, often in incongruous ways. He places himself at the center of the eighteenth-century dispute between "true" and "false" satire, for instance, stating that "The true Character and Spirit of Satyr, always ought to be generally placed, and rather seem to laugh in a pleasant manner, than grin with a Sneer"; if so, it "will never fail to please, with such as have any humor at all" (1:462).[22] Loquacious Scribble accordingly advises the club's members to observe this "General Rule":

> let your Laughing or Gelastication, be accompanied with good humor, a pleasant open, and Candid Countenance quite stript of Satyr, Sarcasm or Sneer, . . . for, by Laughing in this manner, we shall be always Safe, and always in a pleasant vein; the other methods of Laughing, to say, the Cynical and Sarcastical methods, are sometimes, nay, many times, followed with weeping and wailing, and, if we do not at least, draw the laugh upon ourselves, by Laughing Sarcastically, we may perchance do *worser*, that is, pull an old house about our ears. (3:518)

Despite Scribble's sage advice, however, the club repeatedly slips into the sort of satire marked by its severity, "accrimination," "sharp railing," and "invective" (1:272, 146, 246). Even their normally temperate president is "at times very sharp and satirical . . . against those who offended him, . . . and the Secretary in particular, felt the poignancy of his Satyr upon many occasions, which

---

22. Hamilton's definition of true satire echoes the distinction Addison and Steele established earlier in the eighteenth century between true and false satire (see *Spectator*, Nos. 23, 35, 355, 451, and *Tatler*, No. 242; I further discuss the influence of those distinctions in the Introduction).

"The Sempiternal Comedy"

made him often scratch, where he did not itch" (1:229). On one momentous occasion Quirpum Comic, the high steward for the evening, sends a "satyrical letter" to President Jole, mocking his honor's peculiar living arrangements (Jole is a bachelor who lives with a bevy of cats) by informing him that he has "taken care to whip out all *Cats* and dogs [from the meeting room], Cats especially, as being a vermin mighty apt to breed fleas, and to piss about, and excite a very disagreeable perfume" (1:512). The club nearly loses their president as a result of this satirical sneer. On another occasion Solo Neverout delivers a satirical speech in club, proving that one of its most respected longstanding members, Drawlum Quaint, is actually a "dead member"; the offended member returns the favor by writing a satirical poem upon the amorous adventures of a certain "Littlebreeches," mortifying poor Neverout (1:248). And when Philo Dogmaticus, the club's chancellor and leading reactionary, abdicates his position and delivers a satirical farewell poem to the club, Neverout retorts with a satirical poem against

> This Chancellor so Diabolic,
> Whose Rhimes would give a man the Colic,
> Whose Speeches at a single look,
> Would make a man both —— & puke. (3:392)

"Thus was this great officer, the Chancellor," Hamilton remarks at the close of Neverout's poem,

> who had been so Signally Serviceable to the Club, in Contending for its liberties and privileges, against the arbitrary proceedings and tyranny of the Chair, treated with burlesque poems and Satyrs, . . . an Instance of the great depravity and degenerate State of the Club, at this time, and a Shoking example of the Corruption and Ingratitude of the times, when true Patriotism and worth, become the Subjects of Satyr and ridicule. (3:398)

The wealth of examples of "false" satire in the *History*, the exaggerated moral commentary that frequently accompanies them, and the pot shots that Hamilton himself takes at figures such as the Reverend George Whitefield and Horace Walpole all illustrate the obvious delight he took in this sort of satire.[23] To be sure, in a general manner *The History of the Tuesday Club* also satirizes all the "passions Incident to human Nature, and their effects" (1:xiv). Most chapters follow a common pattern: Hamilton normally begins with the wise sayings of celebrated authors—such as Addison's "ye Gods! what havoc does ambition make among your works!" (1:233)—or with his own sage observations—on such things as vanity, caprice, assurance, pride, or enthusiasm; he then uses the Tuesday Club to illustrate the effect of these vices upon society; and he ends by reaffirming the moral of the chapter. Yet the comic disparity between the solemn observations that frame each chapter and the preposterous incidents that illustrate them constantly undercuts the sober moral. The distinction Hamilton poses between true and false satire is a clear and simple one to the reader—and, we suppose, to Hamilton—but the true becomes false as Hamilton undercuts the true and presents the false in a far more diverting light. The only thing that keeps the reader from becoming thoroughly confused by these apparent contradictions is an awareness of the basic premise of Hamilton's comic stance: that anything that has been solemnly discussed by critics or by himself—even something he so solemnly endorses as "true" satire—will be comically undercut. That is the only way out of his comic labyrinth.

---

23. The sharp satire in several of Hamilton's periodical pieces also supports this claim (see ch. 3).

"The Sempiternal Comedy"

Hamilton's discussion and application of satire is only one of several ways in which he undercuts his authority as narrator and moral commentator. His pose as a model of eighteenth-century decorum and good sense is frequently undercut by his tirades against those "perverse anticlubarians" (1:307) and by his inability to talk about even the simplest topic without digressing. Try as he might to be the model eighteenth-century man, Hamilton plays the fool as much as any of the characters in his *History* and idles away his time in a medley of trifles. A true clubbist, he places himself at the center of the folly he satirizes, not above it. His self-awareness of the absurdity of his pose and of the solemn observations that accompany his pose makes us all the more willing to believe in his philosophy of laughter because we witness its humanizing effect not only upon the members of the club but upon the narrator himself.

By intrusively commenting upon his narrative and by employing assorted means of editorial tinkering, Hamilton also comically undercuts the authority of his own text. He repeatedly disparages his narrative throughout the *History* and at one point compares it to a volume of state trials, "The Reading of which ponderous book, like this Club history, Is, in General, as little amusing as Instructive" (2:92). As editor of his own work, he informs the reader of instances where he has "with some difficulty procured" (2:417) original copies of letters or poems not existing in the "Record," even though in some cases they *do* appear in the "Record." In other instances he leaves rows of asterisks in the *History* where there is "a most miserable defect in the record" (2:444). Is it just coincidence, one wonders, that the most "horrible Gap or hiatus" (2:435) in his narrative occurs on the night when women ruled the club? For the curious phrase "the Gentleman being in his boots" he provides the even more curious footnote: "What the historian [meaning himself] can Intend by this Circumstance of the boots, cannot be Conjectured, unless he means to Imitate that remarkable passage in the apocrypha, *and Tobit went forth, and the dog went also*" (3:526). But perhaps his most interesting editorial maneuvers are when he *creates* mistakes in his narrative just so he can correct them as editor. He changes a letter dated Feb. 28, 1748, in the "Record," for instance, to March 28, 1748, in the *History* just so he can provide the editorial footnote: "a mistake of the month, which ought to have been february" (1:397–98).

The end result of Hamilton's playful labyrinthine scheme is a truly innovative narrative, not just by eighteenth-century but by any century's standards. The only way to demonstrate its innovativeness would be to print entire chapters of the *History*, but, as Hamilton would say, I will avoid doing so "for fear this [work] should exceed the Size of a portable volume" (1:93). Readers will find echoes and imitations of Fielding, Burton, Swift, Butler, Pope, and other authors running throughout the *History*, but finally it is like nothing any of those authors produced. It is, as James Carroll first suggested, unique.

But *The History of the Tuesday Club* is more than just a unique narrative. It is, above all, a smorgasbord of eighteenth-century wit, loaded with pseudo-learned essays and digressions, surprising metaphors and allusions, raillery and repartee, bombastic letters and speeches, doggerel verses and mock trials, brain-teasing riddles and conundrums, delicate and often indelicate puns, even nonsensical hieroglyphics and missing passages—and, of course, a generous dose of scatological humor and "polite smutt" (*Itin.*, 177). The basic prerequisite to reading *The History of the Tuesday Club* is a love of eighteenth-century wit, along with a cultivated taste for the dry stretch, for it contains numerous dry stretches, usually intentionally dry but sometimes, Hamilton would be the first to admit, unintentionally so. The more clubically inclined reader endowed with these sensibilities will find the *History* a comedic dish matched, perhaps, but unsurpassed in eighteenth-century literature.

Hamilton was familiar with the writings of all the major British authors involved in the critical debate concerning wit, especially with the four—Dryden, Locke, Pope, and Addison—who set the terms of the debate in the late seventeenth and early eighteenth centuries. Locke established the distinction between wit and judgment that lasted well into the eighteenth century: "men who have a great deal of wit, and prompt Memories," he wrote,

> have not always the clearest Judgment, or deepest Reason. For *Wit* lying most in the assemblage of *Ideas,* and putting those together with quickness and variety, wherein can be found any resemblance or congruity, thereby to make up pleasant Pictures, and agreeable Visions in the Fancy: *Judgment,* on the contrary, lies quite on the other side, in separating carefully, one from another, *Ideas,* wherein can be found the least difference.... This is a way of proceeding quite contrary to metaphor and allusion, wherein, for the most part, lies that entertainment and pleasantry of wit which strikes so lively on the fancy, and is therefore so acceptable to all people.[24]

Like Dryden, who loosely defined wit as "a propriety of thoughts and words ... elegantly adapted to the subject," Pope stated that true wit was "*Nature* to Advantage drest, / What oft was *Thought,* but ne'er so well *Exprest.*"[25] But according to Pope, since true wit

---

24. *An Essay Concerning Human Understanding,* ed. Peter H. Nidditch (Oxford, 1975), 156.
25. Preface to *The State of Innocence* (1677), in *The Works of John Dryden,* ed. George Saintsbury (Edinburgh, 1883), 5:124; *An Essay on Criticism* (1711), in *The Poems of Alexander Pope,* ed. E. Audra and Aubrey Williams (London, 1961), 1:273.

followed Nature, the true wit possessed not simply a quickness of perception displayed in sudden flashes of the fancy but the judgment necessary to discriminate between proper and improper topics of wit and the imagination necessary to integrate wit into the overall design of a literary work.[26] Other critics more nearly aligned themselves with Locke, including Addison, who essentially agreed with Locke's distinction between wit and judgment but added that "every Resemblance of Ideas is not that which we call Wit, unless it... gives *Delight* and *Surprize* to the Reader." He further distinguished between "true" and "false" wit: "*true Wit*," he argued, "generally consists in [the] Resemblance and Congruity of Ideas," and "*false Wit* chiefly consists in the Resemblance and Congruity sometimes of single Letters, as in Anagrams... and Acrosticks: Sometimes of Syllables, as in Ecchos and Doggerel Rhymes: Sometimes of Words, as in Punns and Quibbles; and sometimes of whole Sentences or Poems, cast into the Figures of *Eggs, Axes,* or *Altars.*"[27]

Not to be left out of this critical debate, Hamilton provides not only his own definition of wit in *The History of the Tuesday Club* but his own history of wit. "An accurate history of wit," he writes at the opening of volume two of the *History,* "is what has been much wanted in the republic of letters, for, after Indefatigable

---

26. Pope's defense of wit is best discussed by Edward Niles Hooker, "Pope on Wit: The *Essay on Criticism,*" *Essential Articles for the Study of Alexander Pope,* ed. Maynard Mack (rev. ed.; Hamden, Conn. 1968), 185–207.

27. *Spectator,* No. 62. Hamilton was probably also familiar with the most precise attempt to define comic terms at mid century, Corbyn Morris's *An Essay Towards Fixing the True Standards of Wit, Humour, Raillery, Satire, and Ridicule* (London, 1744). In his essay Morris reviews previous definitions of wit and states that "Wit is the Lustre resulting from the quick Elucidation of one Subject, by a just and unexpected Arrangement of it with another Subject" (p. 1).

Searches, ... I cannot find any single author of our Clubical Class, that has treated this Subject in an historical manner" (2:2). He acknowledges that several authors, including Addison and Sir Richard Blackmore, have touched upon the subject and that numerous Grubstreet hacks have compiled "collections of witty Sayings and Jests," but, he concludes, "not one of all these famous Grubeans, ... has designed to give us a detail historical and critical, of that distinguishing faculty of human Nature. I therefore, tho altogether unqualified, for so arduous an undertaking, and only a Star of the Second or third magnitude, among these Illustrious sons of Hesperus, shall humbly presume to lead the way, and open a door for abler heads, and Sharper pens, to treat this curious and new Subject" (2:2–3).

After indulging himself in over thirty pages of examples of ancient and modern wit, Hamilton decides that the time has come to define his subject: "The Species of wit, which is my proper Subject," he says, "is what I call true Sheer wit, and, as it is usual for Learned authors to define their Subject, before they enter fairly upon it, I shall here take some pains, to define that Sort of wit which is here treated of":

> Mr. Locke, Mr Dryden, and Sir Richard Blackmore, have all of them defined wit differently, and, as it is common for wits to differ, ... I (tho a puny wit) shall beg leave to differ from them all. . . .[28]
>
> Wit then, is a certain faculty, actuated by the fancy, which can out of Chaos bring order, and again reduce order to a Chaos, the mate-

---

28. Hamilton here provides Locke's, Dryden's, as Blackmore's definitions: "Sir Richard Blackmore," he says, "Informs us very Gravely, [in *An Essay on Wit* (London, 1716)] ... That 'Wit proceeds from a Concurrence of regular and exalted ferments, and an affluence of animal Spirits, rectified and refined to a degree of purity'" (2:35).

rials it works upon, being the brain furniture of a poet or Critic of the Celebrated academy of Grubstreet, which Chamber and furniture exactly resembles a Lumber Garret, and its Miscellaneous contents, The operator *Fancy,* putting the broken pieces together, consistently or Inconsistently as she pleases, by which she always excites Gelastic motions in the Landlord of the said Garret or the wit himself, and sometimes in others, but more frequently in these others produces furious contorsions of the countenance, scornful frowns, and contemptuous grins and Sneers, this garret lumber being often full of spikes Snags, and crooked rusty nails, which being hursled about in a violent manner by the fantastical operator Fancy, are apt to gall, prick, fret and wound whenever they touch tender parts. (2:34–36)

This "sheer" definition, which continues for another page, mocks what Hamilton felt was a witlessly tedious concern among his contemporaries to establish the parameters of "true wit."[29] At the same time, however, his definition itself demonstrates what wit implied to Hamilton. Like Locke and Addison, Hamilton in part perceived wit as the ability to connect apparently discordant ideas in a surprising manner, as he does in his garret metaphor. But the most striking aspect of Hamilton's definition is his suggestion that wit is not only a means of creating similitude from discord; it is a means of "reduc[ing] order to chaos." Unlike Dryden or Pope, Hamilton viewed wit as the ability to say in many words, through elaborate metaphors, twists and turns of phrases, irony, digression, and bombast, what one could say more plainly in few. For Hamilton, wit was finally less a matter of appropriate expression than the rhetorical art of indirection, circumlocution, and obfuscation.

---

29. Hamilton's contemporaries meant the same thing by "true" or "sheer" (pure) wit. Hamilton facetiously links them both together and puns on the alternate meaning of sheer (plain or unadorned) by creating such an elaborate definition.

"The Sempiternal Comedy"

The principal means of indirection and circumlocution in *The History of the Tuesday Club* is digression. Hamilton's use of digression is as central to his narrative structurally and thematically as it is in the works of Swift, whom he refers to more than once in the *History*. Chapter two, on "Antiquity, It's dignity and Importance," sets the standard for the digressive style of writing that permeates the *History*. In this chapter Hamilton begins by soberly observing that of all things we revere "Antiquity holds the foremost Rank" (1:7) and then embarks upon one irreverent account after another of the antiquity of ancient nations, cities, families, and even horses. "Much might [also] be said of the antiquity of the families of monkeys, parrots, cats, dogs, hawks, and other tameable and domestic animals," he remarks, "but this I shall wave, having no purpose or design to swell these my observations into a bulky Volume" (1:19). Then he discusses the antiquity of inanimate objects, and as he becomes sidetracked into talking about the deference paid to the owners of those objects, he realizes it is time "to evade digressions and come to the point" (1:21). So he turns to discussing the antiquity of "old rotten rags, worm eaten Chips and pieces of wood, rusty nails, Jaw bones and Shank bones, perhaps honeycombed by the pox, teeth, beards, whiskers, [and] parings of nails" (1:21). By the time he is through, Hamilton has taken a grand and glorious topic and digressively whittled it down to a trifle.

Hamilton's use of digression, then, is central to his perception of the world as a medley of inflated trifles. His history of wit is itself one huge digression, designed to deflate a topic that he felt had been too soberly and too narrowly discussed. "Upon my entry into the Second Volume of this most prodigious History," Hamilton states, "methinks I am like one embarked, and ready to lose himself in a vast and Boundless Ocean, where I shall be tumbled about and carried to and fro, over restless and rolling waves, and scarce find any landing place, or the least prospect of *terra firma,* or land mark, whereon to fix my roving view" (2:1). He lights upon wit as a suitable topic to start the second volume and announces, "I am now to engage in a very Intricate and difficult task, That is, to give a short and summary History of wit and Humor, short and summary, I say, because I shall only skim the Surface, and take the Cream as I go along" (2:1). Fifty pages later, after discussing such things as the "admirable Charm" of abracadabra (2:22), he caps off his chapter with an enlightening discussion of the history of garter posies and ring posies. "And now having finished this Important Chapter," he concludes, "whose length I suppose, will less Chagrin the reader, when he considers that this extensive Subject has been discussed in so small a Compass, I have nothing now to do, but to proceed with our History" (2:51). Hamilton probably enjoyed writing that chapter more than any other in the *History.* It says nothing important; rather, it is purposely designed simply to be an exercise in wit for wit's sake—and where better than in a history of wit.

Another means of indirection and circumlocution in the *The History of the Tuesday Club* is bombast. Despite Hamilton's ironic claims to the contrary at the opening of volume one, the *History* is chock full of "bombast and fustian phrases" (1:4). Sometimes entire chapters, such as his "Learned Dissertation in the Stile and Manner of the Ingenious Mr. Robert Burton," become elaborate exercises in bombastic rhetoric. Moreover, there is hardly a more bombastic, fustianic character in eighteenth-century literature than the character Hamilton created to play his role as secretary, Loquacious Scribble. "Such a Surprize and astonishment as possessed the old hoary and Squalid anarch Chaos," Scribble announces to President Jole at the start of one of his several anniversary speeches,

"The Sempiternal Comedy"

"Mr Secretary Scribble Delivering a Speech in Club."
Hamilton's Drawing in *The History of the Tuesday Club*.
(John Work Garrett Library, Milton S. Eisenhower Library,
The Johns Hopkins University)

when he was waked out of his eternal Slumbers, by the elucidation of the Celestial lights, when Creation first sprung, such a Surprize, I say, Honorable Sir, must at this Instant possess my Sensorium when I behold the members of this here ancient Club, Incumbent over those capacious bowls, replete with precious punch, most Splendidly elucescent, with those Glittering and Lumeniferous badges, like so many oriental and bright planets, Rising upon the watery deep, and adorning the azure Expance with their Immortal Irradiations! whilst you, Great Sir! like the Solar Center of this grand Clubicular System, dispence Inexhaustible Lustre to all, and, from your fountain undeminished, the whole emanation of light proceeds, the Splendor of our Longstanding members being nothing else, but the reflected glory of your honor, our most honorable president. (2:136)

Scribble continues in this vein, similarly praising the club's champion, Sir John, when Jole interrupts him, saying "I think we have [had] enough of this Stuff" (2:137). And if it's not Jole interrupting him, it's Sir John saying "Hoh! why so much Fiddle come farts about nothing?" (2:304), or "Phogh! damn the fustian" (3:212). Following Scribble's lead, other of the club's members indulge in this sort of bombastic, mock heroic rhetoric in numerous club speeches and letters. As arch defendants of the plain style and plain truth, President Jole, Sir John, and Laconic Comas try their best to rid the club of this contagion, but their witless cries fall on deaf ears.

What finally replaces this bombastic wit are the numerous trials in volume three of the *History*, which, like the legal proceedings they are designed to mock, are full of "such triffling distinctions, such minute punctillios and forms, far fetched definitions, distorted reasonings, and prolix tautologies, as would make any reasonable man ... split his midriff with Laughter" (3:531). On one occasion, poor Solo Neverout, recently appointed attorney gen-

"The Sempiternal Comedy"

eral in place of Jealous Spyplot, tries his best to prosecute the insurgent chancellor, Philo Dogmaticus:

> Attorney General: I must own, may it please your honor, that it grieves me—I say Sir, it grieves me, to think, that our Chancellor, a person, who, on account of his eminent degree,—I say Sir, his eminent degree in this here Club, ought to have behaved himself in a manner more agreeable, to his Supposed wisdom and dignified Station,—I say Sir, his Supposed wisdom and dignified Station—I grieve much, may it please your honor, I say, to think that this here Chancellor,—I say Sir this here Chancellor, should have so deviated from his duty, especially against your honor—I say Sir against your honor, a person Remarkable for mildness and Clemency, . . . so, that may it please your honor, it may be said of your honor, . . . as the Celebrated Gil Blas says, in his Greek annotations, *Tois, nois*—hoh!—hoh!—[here an Interruption]
> Jonathan Grog: He, he, hi, hi, hi, hih.
> Attorney General: *Nois, Presidentois,*—chi, chi, chuck!
> Quirpum Comic: Ha, ha, he, hi, hi.
> Attorney General: *Is te Cox-Comboy*—pugh—Pho—
> Jonathan Grog: Comeboy! aha, aha, ahi, ahi. The attorney Calls the horses, aha, aha, ha, hi.
> Attorney General: *Kay Clodepateon, nidjotton, hoi fooleroi asinos-s-s-s-soi,* hoh,—hoh. [here the attorney seemed to hesitate much]
> Sir John: Hoh, hoh, hoi, hoh, ho, hoi, hoh, ho, hoi, lancets! lancets!—hoh,—I must be Immediatly blooded, hoh,—else I shall die—hoh, hoh,—the laughing at this Stuff—hoh—has given me a damn'd Stich in my Side—hoh, hoh—o. (3:258–59)

The dutiful Neverout struggles on with his introductory remarks for another three pages; as he finally prepares to examine the evidence, the club quashes the indictment because of a minor slip he made in calling the chancellor the *late* chancellor. If not for that one word, his indictment would have been perfectly sensible.

At the other extreme from these forms of rhetorical inflation, Hamilton further avoids clarity by deleting words or phrases, reproducing strange hierogylphics, and speaking in invented tongues. He leaves curious gaps of asterisks in sentences, and sometimes he reproduces mangled pieces of prose or verse, such as the fragment of a satirical piece by Giddy Thoughtless upon Bard Bavius's remarks concerning a lady's neck:

> *** me ***** Lord.
> ******* one single Turd
> **** for ***** flat
> ******** a nine taild cat.
> A Ladie's neck no more is like a Swan,
> Than you ye monster's like an apish man. (1:189)

"The above fragment," Hamilton reports, "was snatched out of the hands of an Ignorant Clown, who was Lighting his pipe with the only remaining copy of this excellent piece, and the words wrote down, are what remained unburnt" (1:190). Hamilton also imitates Swift's curious way of writing in "Clubical latin," then goes Swift one better and produces some clubical Dutch too (3:108–10, 543). He also writes in "law Latin" on more than one occasion, invents maxims in mysterious languages—such as the "Golden Maxim" of Arnoldus Merdologus, "*Prigma pragma Padanarum, pujolas, pish, Panjoulteras*"—and leaves facetious footnotes directing "Critics of future times to Interpret" these foreign tongues (3:444). But only the most "Ingenious Club Linguist" can ever hope to unravel these passages (3:110).

These forms of wit satirize the eighteenth century's preoccupation with cryptic languages; equally important, like bombast and digression, they are designed not to enhance but to obstruct clarity. Little wonder that in his history of wit Hamilton repeatedly associates wit with artifice, trickery, alchemy, and deception, and directly links "wit and Subtilty," "wit and Ingenious finesse" (2:6). The grand original of wit, he says, was the devil, "who outwitted mother Eve" with "certain quibbling Speeches" (2:4). Like the devil, true wits possess more than just quick metaphorical minds; they are rhetorical con-artists. Rather than speak directly and plainly, they indulge in various rhetorical forms of indirection. This kind of wit is the central device in Hamilton's comic labyrinth. Sympathetic wits, however, will not get lost in Hamilton's rhetorical maze or even seek to find a way out; they will enjoy wandering in a rhetorical land of indeterminate meaning.

This dimension of wit as rhetorical subterfuge, although essential to writers such as Hamilton, Swift, and, later, Sterne, was generally ignored in the eighteenth century by the definers and redefiners of wit, who for the most part were preoccupied with either defending true wit or deploring the extent to which wit had been abused. Stuart M. Tave argues that the effort made by critics such as Addison to distinguish true from false wit indicates that by the turn of the century the word "wit" "was sinking into common, trifling, and narrow usages—mere quickness and sharpness in the making of similitudes, the odd metaphor, the lucky simile, the wild fetch, epigrammatic turns and points, quibble, conceit."[30] In *The History of the Tuesday Club*, however, these forms of wit contribute to a larger rhetorical scheme of wit and are considered no less important because of their "trifling" nature. The club's poet laureate, Jonathan Grog, is acknowledged the reigning wit of the Tuesday Club because he is "as well stocked with Jests, quaint Stories, puns, conundrums, and other such conceits, as any wit, either ancient or moderen, that ever was heard of" (1:480). Indeed, it is clear from reading the *History* that, despite the objections of Addison and others, the average eighteenth-century gentleman absolutely delighted in this type of

---

30. *The Amiable Humorist*, 58.

wit, and that Hamilton in particular considered it one of the most amusing of a medley of trifles.

The Tuesday Club especially delighted in puns, conundrums, and "other such conceits," and the bawdier the better. Probably the longest-running joke in eighteenth-century literature is the joke of the "longstanding members" of the Tuesday Club. Literally, the longstanding members were the club's regular members, but throughout the *History* Hamilton reminds us of the phrase's alternate meaning. The first of the favorite maxims of that "celebrated Club wit," Jonathan Grog, states "that if one would gain a Ladie's affections, he ought to persevere, and stand stiffly to it without shrinking." "This was a good Standing Joke," Hamilton adds, "and fit for a Longstanding member" (1:483). Two of the club's longstanding members, however, are recalcitrant members: "one of these gentlemen, loved a piece of old hat very well (as the Saying is) but his humor led him to partake of it in a hugger mugger way, as for the other, he was a Sort of apathy, [and] had not the least Inclination for that Sort of amusement" (1:146). For his failure to maintain his membership in good standing, the first of these longstanding members is ignominiously dubbed "Littlebreeches" (1:248). The second—the "Sort of apathy"—is the club's president, Nasifer Jole, whom Loquacious Scribble ironically hails as the chief longstanding member—the "*Mento, mentula et Naso Longissimus*"—of the club (3:27). After the astonishing night when women officers presided over the longstanding members, Jealous Spyplot, considering "such Innovations to be dangerous to the constitution" of the club, requests that Jole "issue his warrant, *de ventre Inspiciendo,* for searching and Inspecting these females, in order to discover, whether or not they were Effectual, and true Longstanding members," and Philo Dogmaticus, the president's arch antagonist, further moves that, "since his

"The Sempiternal Comedy"

Lordship has given no proofs of his virility,... it may be Scrutinized, whether we have not now, a Pope Joan, in the Chair" (2:448, 449). His lordship was not amused at having his membership questioned.

But perhaps the most memborable joke concerning the longstanding members occurs one evening when Electro Vitrifrice, a stranger invited to the club, adds the finishing stroke to the dispute over whether one of the club's members, Quirpum Comic, had the right to put up for public auction the presidential chair, which, according to his testimony, would not sell because its seat "smelled of a fox" (3:297). For offending the chair, Secretary Scribble proposes that Quirpum Comic be degraded from a longstanding member to an honorary member. "Why Mr Secretary," Jonathan Grog interjects, "you would not have us to dock the Gentleman, I suppose the member, however he may stand now at this Juncture is as long as ever." "Ha, ha, ha," chuckles Crinkum Crankum, "the longstanding members methinks are waggish." "Longstanding members, I think Gentlemen, with Submission," Electro Vitrifrice replies, "are not so properly waggish, because if they stand they cannot wag" (3:299). It should surprise no one that "Electro Vitrifrice" is Benjamin Franklin.

The History of the Tuesday Club abounds with numerous examples of this sort of smutty wit. In his learned analysis "Of Club Stile, and Clubical terms," for instance, Hamilton discusses the derivation of *conundrum:*

> Every one, who understands the french Language, knows what is meant by the word *Con*, which, for fear of offence to modest ears, I shall not translate into English, it is derived then, ... from this french word *con*, and two english words added to it, vizt: the words *under* and *him*, but the two last words for the ease of our polite pronouncers and writers have been contracted thus, *und'r'um*, and the whole

Joined together make *Conund'r'um,* which without the break and apostrophaes, make the plain word *Conundrum.* (1:218–19)

Not surprisingly, several of the club's sixty-four conundrums are unabashedly bawdy: "Why is a wanton Lass in bed," Jonathan Grog asks the club's pensive members one evening, "like a book Just printed?—because," he replies to the befuddled members, "she is in *sheets* & wants *Stitching*" (2:96). On another evening, "to raise again the flagging Spirits of the Longstanding members," the club drinks toasts to the ladies, providing epithets that rhyme with the ladies' names: "This is an exercise of wit," Hamilton says, "much used in polite Companies, for Example, suppose one should drink miss Smart, has gained my heart." After several of these toasts, a certain Miss Hunt is proposed to the members, at which Laconic Comas says "bluntly, in his dry manner, Who? Miss Hunt? it will be no difficult matter to find a rhyme to fit her name—and was Just going to say more, when an universal Laugh broke out among the members, . . . but Laconic Comas Esqr, looked very much amazed and said once or twice, Well! damn it!—what then?—what then?" (2:85–86).

Most of the bawdy in *The History of the Tuesday Club* is, in keeping with another of the club's maxims, "cleanly wrapt up" (3:143), and the majority of the wordplay that passes between the club's members requires no wrapping at all. To honor the club's president, for instance, Jonathan Grog composes an acrostic "To Mr President Jole," which "very much pleased his honor the President, who was not for the most part a great admirer of that Sort of wit" (2:99–100). Most of the club's conundrums, moreover, belie the word's supposedly bawdy etymology. "Why is a well stoped bottle of Claret," Jonathan Grog asks, "like the Island of Ireland?"—to which Slyboots Pleasant rightly answers, "because there is *Cork* in it" (2:204). "If Jonathan Grog Esqr, had the most happy Genius in framing those exquisite pieces of wit called Conundrums," Hamilton writes, "it must also be allowed that Slyboots Pleasant Esqr, had the luckiest and Clearest apprehension, in the Solution of these knotty Involutions" (2:205). Once again, the least responsive of the longstanding members is President Jole, "but even granting that his honor never possessed that ready talent of resolving knotty Conundrums, yet, with him, as with other men . . . the observation will hold true, that the less a man's Stock of wit is, the Stronger and deeper is his Judgment, and depth of Judgment all will allow is a talent more necessary in a president than Quickness of wit" (2:206). Locke probably would have applauded the sentiment but questioned the application.

Eventually the conundrums fall into disrepute as a result of a satirical sneer. "Why is L—— C——'s mouth like a puppet Show?" (2:114), Philo Dogmaticus asks the club one evening; since no one else will dare to answer for fear of offending Laconic Comas, Philo Dogmaticus answers it himself: "Because there is always *Punch* in it" (2:115). Gravelled by this personal insult, Laconic Comas cannot find the words to reply. President Jole tells him that "he Surely had less brains than tongue, which was next to none at all, to let this Scurvy Joke pass upon him unanswered; this Sharp Rebuke," Hamilton says, "made Mr Comas's heart Rise to his mouth, and it was said that the tears gushed out at his eyes" (2:116). Shortly thereafter, the club decides to abolish the conundrums from future proceedings, "as a Species of low wit altogether unworthy of the dignity of the Club. . . . These pieces of Ingenuity," Hamilton concludes, were bound to cause dissension after awhile, "since all men are not of an equal acuteness and genius, in exercises of wit, [and] those who are more dull and slow of apprehension, Generally have a Jealousy of, or rather picque at such as set up for being wits" (2:238). But since "human wit... will always be nibbling" (1:286), the club's members find various other means of exercising their wit, until even the conundrums return when Spatterdash Wouldbe unleashes his "Surprizing wit" (3:190).

Hamilton's remark that the conundrums were expelled "as a Species of low wit" is tongue-in-cheekishly directed against those "finical fellows [who] distinguish mirth into two Sorts, vizt: high mirth and low mirth" (3:517). For Hamilton, "wit" implied the full range of wordplay during the eighteenth century. Rather than narrowly define wit, he sought to celebrate it in all its manifestations, from the gastro-intestinal to the mock heroic, from the simplest pun or acrostic to more sophisticated forms of rhetorical artifice. It was his broad rather than finical nature that allowed him to integrate the entire spectrum of eighteenth-century wit into his narrative in a way equalled by few other authors in his time.

The History of the Tuesday Club is wondrously innovative and wondrously witty, but what, finally, is it all about? As I suggested earlier in this chapter, it is a broad satire of human folly. But it is also concerned with the most central social issues in Hamilton's day. Like most eighteenth-century writers, Hamilton believed that "man [was] a Sociable animal" (1:164) and that sociability was the root of happiness. He humorously observes that, as Newton would have it, "there exists a certain attraction or fellow feeling, between all bodies in nature, by which they have a strong tendency... to Join, and even to Incorporate, and... a perfect antipathy is never, a partial one seldom to be met with" (1:25). This power of attraction, Hamilton says, explains "that great propensity in human nature, to unite and form into Clubs" (1:25). Exactly how this works—"whether this is done by the perpetual flying off of thin Surfaces from one member to another,... or by the communication of some Imperceptible Sympathetic qualities"—he does not know, that "being a more Intricate and difficult enquiry" than he is capable of resolving (1:26). But he is "certain that the fact is so, that there is a particular Sympathetic Social quality in Mankind, that makes them fond of Clubbing, whether they be adapted for conversation or not" (1:26).

Our natural failings, however, sometimes create havoc in even the best regulated societies, rendering "those who were before, good Club companions and friends, bitter enemies to one another, to the great hurt and Dammage, of that Social Clubical disposition, which nature has been so careful to Implant in mankind" (1:151). A well-regulated society, Hamilton suggests, operates much like a well-regulated body:

> The natural body is nourished by the taking in of various Substances at the mouth, these, mixed in the Stomach, and concocted... in the Intestines, are Convey'd by proper conduits into the mass of Blood; This mass is the Strength and Support of the natural body, and the Chief mechanical Cause of life and Motion...; according then, to the nature of the Substances taken in to Compound, and Supply this mass, the mass it self must become more or less fit for answering the purposes for which nature designed it; if the Substances taken in, are of a mild and balsamic texture, and easily reduced to that smooth and equable Consistence, necessary to constitute wholesome blood, the animal and vital functions are Carried on in an equable uninterrupted Course, and, tho sometimes a tumultuous circulation may happen from a plethoric habit, yet the constitution is free from fevers, convulsions, palsies, Lethargies, and distempers of the like terrible aspect; whereas, if acrid and Stimulating Substances are taken in, or what are called by people of a modish and refined taste, rich food, the miserable frame often sinks under all these distempers. (2:477–78)

Similarly, when acrid substances produced by the excesses of luxurious living infiltrate the body politic, society reels from these distempers and sometimes suffers irreparable convulsions (2:478).

Hamilton's extended metaphor about the distempers caused by luxurious living is central to *The History of the Tuesday Club* and to the eighteenth century. According to John Sekora, the outcry against luxury was probably "the greatest single social issue" in eighteenth-century England, particularly during the 1750s and early 1760s.[31] Numerous allusions in the *History* indicate that Hamilton knew the works of many British authors who had argued on both sides of the controversy over luxury. His references to Addison, Henry St. John, Viscount Bolingbroke, William Pulteney, and Fielding show that he was familiar with the *Spectator* essays protesting the harmful effects of luxury (see nos. 55, 260, 294, 331, 478, and 574); with Bolingbroke's and Pulteney's denunciations of luxury, which became the buzzword in the Opposition's frequent attacks against the Walpole government; and perhaps even with Fielding's claim that "the fury after licentious and luxurious pleasures is grown to so great a height, that it may be called the characteristic of the present age."[32] Likewise, he had surely read the most influential essays defending luxury, especially

---

31. *Luxury: The Concept in Western Thought, Eden to Smollett* (Baltimore, 1977), 75, 66. Sekora's book is the best study on this topic. Other useful discussions of the luxury debate in England and Europe include E.A.J. Johnson, *Predecessors of Adam Smith: The Growth of British Economic Thought* (New York, 1937), 281–97; Simeon Monroe Wade, Jr., "The Idea of Luxury in Eighteenth-Century England" (diss., Harvard University, 1969); Elizabeth Rawson, *The Spartan Tradition in European Thought* (Oxford, 1969), 344–67; and Ellen Ross, "Mandeville, Melon, and Voltaire: The Origins of the Luxury Controversy in France," *Studies on Voltaire and the Eighteenth Century*, 155 (1976), 1897–1912. A good study of the influence of the luxury controversy on American thought toward the end of the eighteenth century is Drew R. McCoy, *The Elusive Republic: Political Economy in Jeffersonian America* (Chapel Hill, 1980), 21–100.

32. *A Charge Delivered to the Grand Jury . . . of Westminster . . .* (London, 1749), quoted in Sekora, *Luxury,* 89–90.

"The Sempiternal Comedy"

Bernard Mandeville's *Fable of the Bees,* which advocated the pursuit of luxury and self-interest and, perhaps more than any other single work, provoked the laments against luxury and degeneracy that lasted well into the second half of the eighteenth century.[33]

The controversy over luxury was even more pronounced in the colonies than in Britain. As Jack P. Greene asserts, "the force of the idealized model of the founders that colonials always had immediately before them" left writers throughout the colonies, especially during the 1740s and 1750s, bewailing the "alarming . . . increase in extravagance, dissipation, and addiction to pleasure." Particularly in the South there existed "a widespread conviction that the present generation was inferior in industry, enterprise, frugality, . . . and virtue to the groups who had performed the Herculean task of wrestling plantations out of the wilderness."[34] In Virginia, for instance, Commissary James Blair admonished his parishioners against extravagant "Gratifications of their Luxury, . . . plentiful Tables, Mirth, Musick, and Drinking."[35] These extravagances provoked Benjamin Whitaker to exhort the people of South Carolina

---

33. After the Tuesday Club abandons its frugal one-dish law, Hamilton snidely observes that this was "not the first time, that good Laws, ordained for the establishment of frugality and temperance, have been annulled . . . and Luxury and Epicurism, have met with strenuous advocats to support their cause, and vindicate the practice of these effeminate vices; whoever doubts of this, needs only read, the Learned and Ingenious Doctor Mandeville, his *Fable of the bees,* where . . . it is seemingly made out, beyond all dispute, if you will take the Doctor's own word for it, that private vice is public emolument" (1:172).

34. Greene, "Search for Identity: An Interpretation of the Meaning of Selected Patterns of Social Response in Eighteenth-Century America," *Journal of Social History,* 3 (1970), 204, 201, 193–94.

35. *Our Saviour's Divine Sermon on the Mount* . . . 2nd ed. (London, 1740), 1:127.

[181]

to abstain from that Luxury and Excess, which within a few Years... has pour'd in upon us like a Torrent,... [and] to stop the further Progress of an Evil, which has so greatly contributed to enervate and soften our Minds, and to sink us, into Indolence and Inactivity; if we were to return to our former Frugality, Temperance and moderate Enjoyments,... we should soon resume our Spirits, and recover that Firmness of Mind, which enabled our Predecessors to make a Stand and to struggle with the many Difficulties they had to contend with.... But if Liberty shall degenerate into Licentiousness,... if Luxury, Vice, and Iniquity prevail, Society must be dissolved, and all Things fall into a State of Anarchy and Confusion.[36]

Hamilton's hometown newspaper, the *Maryland Gazette,* also published many pieces promoting industry and disparaging luxury during the eleven years the Tuesday Club met. Most of these items were reprinted from British newspapers, such as one from the *Remembrancer* entitled "Epicurism ruinous to the State," whose author claimed that "a life of frolick and extravagance... is a life of infamy" and concluded that *"the chains of Luxury are the easiest borne, and the hardest to break, of any in the world."*[37] Perhaps

---

36. *The Chief Justice's Charge to the Grand Jury for the Body of This Province* (Charles-town, S.C., 1741), 10–11.

37. *Maryland Gazette,* Dec. 14, 1748. Particularly during the early 1750s, the *Maryland Gazette* reprinted several other essays concerning luxury that had appeared in British newspapers, including essays on contentment and industry (May 30, Oct. 10, 1750); "On Frugality" (Feb. 13, 1752); "A Letter from a Dying Libertine to His Friend" (Sept. 14, 1752); "Of Health, Temperance, and Sobriety" (Dec. 28, 1752); "An Essay on Contentment in Prosperity" and "An Essay on Contentment in Adversity" (Feb. 22, 1753); a serious defense of pleasure on moral grounds (Aug. 2, 1753); "Of Happiness" (Apr. 25, 1754; cf. July 11, Aug. 15, 1754); and an essay on gravity (Jan. 8, 1756). One of the more interesting local essays, a piece on sloth, appeared in the Mar. 25, 1756, issue, even as Hamilton was completing the third volume of the *History* shortly before his death. Numerous other essays and poems

the most widely read of the American selections in the *Gazette* was "The Prevalence of Luxury; with a Burgo-Master's excellent Admonition against it," reprinted in the March 9, 1748, issue after having appeared in several other colonial newspapers. Its author maintained that many colonists had "prostituted [their] noble Talents to vile and sordid Purposes" by indulging in all sorts of excesses. Whereas "All other Nations have each their favorite Luxury," he claimed, in America "our Taste is universal," encompassing all of the other countries' extravagances put together.

As these and numerous other passages suggest, the eighteenth-century conception of luxury drew mainly upon two traditions: upon the Old Testament notion of luxury as "anything unneeded," an immoral violation of Jehovah's law, and, more important, upon the classical notion of *luxus* (sensuality, splendor, pomp) or *luxuria* (riot, excess, extravagance), which replaced subordination to Jehovah's law with subordination to a sense of propriety and hierarchy.[38] Luxury still implied immorality, especially as preached up by eighteenth-century divines, but for most writers it implied immorality not because it violated Jehovah's law, but because it violated any reasonable person's sense of good conduct. It was considered both a domestic and a political evil: a domestic evil because any kind of extravagant personal behavior, such as excessive drinking, eating, whoring, or even snuff-taking, violated the basic sense of moderation that served as the rational person's moral barometer; a political evil because any kind of riotous, insubordinate behavior threatened to undermine the social

---

addressing more restricted issues, such as immoderate drinking, gaming, or even "painting," also appeared in the *Maryland Gazette* (see, for example, Jan. 4, Aug. 2, 1749, and Aug. 23, 1753).

38. The definition provided in this paragraph encapsulates Sekora's observations in *Luxury*, 23–131.

and political fabric of eighteenth-century England and violated the rational person's sense of hierarchy. "Luxury" therefore implied not only the domestic vices of drunkenness, gluttony, lust, avarice, ceremony, vanity, effeminacy, and affectation, but also the political vices of ambition, pride, enervation, bribery, corruption, and subjection. The first set of vices, many feared, inevitably led to the second. That is precisely what happens in *The History of the Tuesday Club*, where Hamilton mocks the Jeremiahs of his generation by posing as one himself and inverts what Northrup Frye identifies as the central theme of the comic, "the integration of society,"[39] by comically depicting the disintegration of society as a result of the harmful effects of luxury.

In the opening chapters of the *History* Hamilton recalls the golden age of the Tuesday Club, when the natural body and the body politic were equally well regulated. At the first meeting of the Tuesday Club, on the memorable 14th of May, 1745, the club's members passed the following laws "with great wisdom and Sagacity":

> Law I. That the meeting of the Club be weekly, at the members houses, by turns, thro' out the year, upon Tuesday evening.
> Law II. The Steward for the time being, shall provide a gammon of bacon, or any other one dish of dressed vittles and no more.
> Law III. No Liquor shall be made, prepared or produced after eleven o clock at night, and every Member shall be at liberty to retire at pleasure.
> Law IV. No members shall be admitted without the concurring consent, of the whole Club, and after such admission, the member shall serve as Steward next meeting. (1:142–43)

---

39. *Anatomy of Criticism*, 43.

These laws exemplified the singular "frugality and moderation" (1:148) that sustained the club during its earliest days. "How charming, how regular, and how much like the Simple frugality of the Golden age was this," Hamilton recalls, "and how different from that luxury and profuseness that prevails in most of our moderen Clubs" (1:148). These were the glorious days of the one-dish law when men were men.

But these days were short-lived. "Happy, O happy had it been for this ancient and honorable Club," Hamilton moans, "had they always kept to this golden mean of frugality and temperance, but the mode soon Changed, and Luxury crept in by degrees" (1:143). In place of the "heroic frugality" that governed the club's first meetings,

> Luxury began to peep from behind the Scene, and prepare for her pompous entry upon this Clubical Stage, . . . this bold actress took one great Stride at her first advance, and proceeded afterwards, with a *grand pas,* to expell Simplicity and plainness from the Club, and to Introduce, pomp show and extravagance, her constant pages and attendants, while [Ceremony], her companion and coactor, with the like buskined pride, . . . so disguised and poisoned the manners and behavior of the longstanding members, . . . that they did in no manner seem to be the same persons they were at their first Institution. (1:170–71)

Once this bold actress enters the scene, the club's members gradually display all the vices associated with it during the eighteenth century.

Given the eighteenth-century conception of luxury, we should immediately sense that the Tuesday Club is headed for disaster when Hamilton introduces the club's president, Nasifer Jole, who, excepting his disinclination for the ladies, embodies all the domestic vices associated with luxury in the eighteenth century. As a money-grubbing merchant, he humorously exemplifies the Opposition's belief that, unlike the landed gentry, those who gained their fortunes in the workaday world were motivated by avarice rather than by a desire to promote the public good. To the dismay of his ignorant customers, Jole insists that "300 per cent [profit], tended more to the public good, ... than 50 per cent, because ... 300 per cent, is a living price, and enables the merchant to carry on trade and commerce, with vigor and life, whereas, any thing under that is a pitiful peddling price, and occasions trade ... to languish and decay" (1:154). A colonial Scrooge, Jole even sells the toys in his shop to children at a "living price."

Jole likewise promotes drunkenness, gluttony, ceremony, vanity, and affectation, but his outstanding attribute is effeminacy. While aboard a man-of-war, he acquired "many useful arts, particularly that of Cookery, and he was such a proficient in that noble Science, that he understood as well as any notable husiff, how to stew a frecassee ... or raise a pasty" (1:155). "He had a curious and elegant taste," moreover, "in cutting out patterns of work for Sempstresses," and he "understood perfectly well ... how to paper candlesticks and adorn glass Sconces, ... and how in the most charming and elegant taste to dress up a nosegay" (1:157, 156). Indeed, whenever he went to church he wore a nosegay "in his buttonhole, ... while he kept twirling a charming pink Iris, Jonquille, or Aenemonie betwixt his finger and thumb" (1:156–57). Some of the members of the congregation suspected that Jole "intended thus to lay traps" to ensnare the ladies, and for that same reason "he often used perfumes, such as musk, ambergrise, Civet, Bergamot, and the like" (1:157). But he preferred instead "a Society of Cats for his friends, fellows and playmates, both at bed and board, and so far did his extraordinary charity and benevolence extend to those Cats, that ... he would stroke down their soft

"The Sempiternal Comedy"

Skins, apply their mouths to his," and when any of his favorites died, he would "shut himself up, and grieve for some time, as a tender mother does for her babes" (1:164–65).

Jole initiates the degenerate trend toward luxury by encouraging extravagance in eating and drinking. When Jole abandons the wise frugality of the one-dish law, Hamilton sadly observes that "here madam Luxury first pop'd her head from behind the curtain, ... and slap dash, there followed a whole troop of frecassees, ragous, hashes, ... dumplings, tarts, Gellies and Syllabubs" (1:171–72). During the course of the *History,* several members facetiously move for the revival of the one-dish law, but, following the lead of their illustrious president, no one ever again paid serious attention to "that frugal Law" (1:437). Instead, the dinners become so extravagant and costly that the club, which previously met once a week, is obliged to meet only once a fortnight, causing Hamilton to bewail "the effects of Luxury and unnecessary expence" (1:197). Hamilton gloomily predicts that we shall "find more of [Luxury's] pernicious effects presently taking place" by paving the way for "arbitrary and despotic power in the Club" (1:197–98), but first he returns to the domestic excesses that precipitate the political excesses. Not the least of these is the club's increasing vanity in apparel, an extravagance again inspired by President Jole. All might have gone on "tollerably well," Hamilton allows, had Jole stopped after introducing "Luxury in matters of eating and drinking," but on December 10, 1745, he appeared in club

> in a flamming Suit of Scarlet, a magnificent hat, bound round with massy Scolloped Silver lace, a fine large and full fair wig, white kid Gloves, ... a Silver hilted Sword, with a beautiful Sword knot of Ribbons, white Silk Stockings rolld, large Shining Silver Shoe buckles, his coat and vest edged round with gold twist, ... the button

holes trimmed with gold and several brilliant rings upon his fingers, ... in this luxury of dress did he ascend the chair of state, and looked like a flaming comet in his perihelion. (1:223–24)

And as Jole goes so goes the club. At their first anniversary even so unaffected a member as Sir John appears "dizened up in a fine Spencer wig, and a wastcoat with massy gold lace, ... an Instance of the Luxury of the times" (1:295). "O Luxury! O excess!" Hamilton balefully cries out, "whether wilt thou arive at last, wilt thou not, now thou hast begun, go on in an unwearied round, 'till thou hast utterly ruined and anihilated this ancient and honorable Club?" (1:225).

Hamilton's fears nearly come true, as the contagion of luxury rapidly spreads from the club's eating, drinking, and dressing habits to their speaking and writing habits. Nearly all the members develop a "pestilent itch of speech making" (1:242), but the most grandiloquent of all is, of course, Loquacious Scribble himself. Then ensues a whole invasion of ceremony and pomp as the members introduce into their proceedings club seals, club badges, club medals, chairs of state, canopies of state, caps of state, anniversary odes, anniversary speeches, and even anniversary processions. Already smitten by ceremony by the time of their first anniversary, the members parade through the streets of Annapolis in full club regalia, being "Sufficiently stared at ... by persons of all Ranks and degrees, who seemed to be as much astonished, as the mob is at a coronation procession, or any such Idle pageantry" (1:293). But "in this luxurious and effeminate age," Hamilton explains, ceremony has become a necessary evil, serving to hold the public in awe and to "keep the great Leviathan of Civil Society under proper discipline and order" (3:174, 172). Effectively employed, ceremony acts as a potent hypnotic, tranquilizing the rabble and neutralizing sedition.

"The Sempiternal Comedy"

"The Second Grand Anniversary Procession."
Hamilton's Drawing in *The History of the Tuesday Club*.
(John Work Garrett Library, Milton S. Eisenhower Library,
The Johns Hopkins University)

"The Honorable Nasifer Jole Esqr, Wears the Cap of State."
Hamilton's Drawing in *The History of the Tuesday Club*.
(John Work Garrett Library, Milton S. Eisenhower Library,
The Johns Hopkins University)

"The Sempiternal Comedy"

Hypnotized to the point of enervation, the Tuesday Club now falls easy prey to the political consequences of their domestic extravagances. By continually flattering Jole and sanctioning "his turn for Luxury" (1:251), the members, like the ancient Spartans, who "bartered their plainness and humility for Luxury and pride, and... became at last Illustrious slaves to Philip of Macedon" (1:10–11), gradually become subservient to the whim of their president. Having allowed Jole to introduce "Luxury in eating, drinking and dress," they now permit him, "without the least resistance, to create two great and powerful officers [a club Champion and a Master of Ceremonies] in one night" (1:268). Shortly thereafter, they again sit idly by, "too much benumned and stupified, to feel the twinge that was given them, and instead of exerting themselves to put a Stop to these proceedings, they allowed another state officer, and another officer of the Commons [a club Speaker and Musician] to be palmed upon them" (1:277). "Such a State of Supineness and Stupidity was this ancient Club now fallen into," Hamilton says, "that their constitution was as it were paralytic, and they did not in the least feel where the Shoe pinched, their whole attention being fixed upon magnificence and Show, and the aggrandizing of their Lord president" (2:417). When they finally sanction Jole's arbitrary powers by approving the debasing Frontinbrassian Articles, Hamilton knells, "Thus we see into what a Slavish and Contemptible State this Club had brought themselves into by their Luxury, and overstrained Complaisance" (2:318).

Their complaisance also makes the members susceptible to "that monster *Party*" (2:163). "When the Ancient and honorable Tuesday Club, kept within decent bounds, as to expence, pageantry, Show, and presidential power," Hamilton remarks, "they flourished,... but when the power of the Chair was stretched to an extraordinary extent, and the longstanding members strove one among another... [for] favor and Influence with the honorable Chair, then the glory power and Character of the Club began to decline" (1:420). During its glory days the club cordially gathered simply to share a friendly evening together; now, some of the more ambitious members, especially Loquacious Scribble and Philo Dogmaticus, their scheming secretary and overweening chancellor, have taken to "barefacedly Walpolizing it in this here Club, that is promoting... bribery and corruption" (1:433) to advance their own self-interest. And "when pimps in office, are flattered and cajoled, by worse pimps out of office,... and all Sort of Luxury and extravagance encouraged and countenanced," then, Hamilton laments, "the Clubical State may for a little time make a great noise and Show, but suddenly... all its pride and Glory tumbles to the Ground" (1:389; cf. 2:478).

The club's glory receives a crippling blow when its members revolt against the president and force him to abdicate his throne during the infamous Chancellor's Rebellion. By this time the club had arrived "to that degree of Luxury, as to be in danger of falling precipitatly Into Civil Combustions" (2:481), and with the chancellor and secretary goading them on, they ignominiously besiege the presidential chair. Incensed by the president's refusal to give up the club seal, the chancellor urges his compatriots "to fight like Lions for their liberty and property," while the sergeant at arms, Prim Timorous, after shamefully cowering behind the presidential chair, "was thrown into such a terrible panic that he swore several times over *God—bless the king,* and run and hid himself in some private Corner" (2:493–94). But his lordship, undaunted by this fierce attack, still refuses to give up seat or seal. Realizing that a frontal assault upon such a formidable foe is hopeless, Quirpum Comic finally unseats Jole by applying several unkind thumps to the rump of his chair, lending "such a Strong concussion and repercussion, to his Lordship's buttocks, that he rebounded at least half a foot from his Seat at each blow, and was obliged to quit his Chair of State" (2:494), and inspiring the chancellor, secretary, and all the clamorous rout to let out a victory yell. This unseemly rebellion, Hamilton soberly observes, should serve as "a woeful example to all, who suffer themselves to be misguided by flattery, and Immerged in the soft allurements of Luxury, which mislead them into ambitious and aspiring designs," for the ancient and honorable Tuesday Club hereafter was "perpetually upon the declining hand, [which] ought to be a warning to other Clubs, how they follow these dangerous paths of Luxury, vain pomp and excess" (2:499).

Jole obstinately refuses to rejoin the club following his decathedration, obliging the members to send several deputations soliciting his return. To aid their efforts, the club's poet laureate, Jonathan Grog, pens "The Clubs Lamentation for the Loss of their President," which contains this lamentable stanza:

> The Birds Lament the General loss,
> The beasts in Concert groan,
> The little fish pop up their heads
> And Cry, alas! he's gone.
> Oft when with beating breasts we Cry,
> O Jole, where art thou, where,
> Eccho, from each resounding hill
> Replies he is not here. (2:511)

Grog's sublime warblings and the club's obsequious cries eventually lure Jole back to the presidential chair. Jole wisely insists, however, that the club stop flattering him with pompous titles and speeches, and with his restoration the club returns to a semblance of its former simplicity and sociability.

But that baleful monster luxury is just one step behind. Shortly after his return, Jole tours the town with Coney Pimp Frontinbrass "in his triumphal Carr, being dressed in Red, with a large full flaxen wig." To flatter Jole and to gratify the "many Spectators" who are standing at their windows to get a view of him, Frontinbrass obligingly "stopped his Chariot at several public places in the City, ... to give the curious Spectators a better opportunity of seeing his honor as he rode in State" (3:73–74). The implication is clear: history is about to repeat itself.

The effects of luxury and the "distempers of the body politic" (2:480) it produces are so far reaching that, even though Jole's return initially restored order and simplicity, ultimately the members find themselves in a more subservient position than ever. Of the forty-two club maxims established on December 19, 1752, the following three typify the unprecedented power yielded to President Jole after his restoration:

> 11 That his honor the President must not be thwarted or contradicted, in any Scheme or project whatsoever, ... his Station raising him above all arguefication. ...
>
> 12 That his honor the President's powers are Conveyd to him by a Supernatural power, and his authority is *jure divino,* and that he has in himself, an absolute Indefeasible right, to rule and domineer as he pleases in the Club.
>
> 13 That nonresistance and Passive obedience are absolutely necessary, in the Longstanding members towards the President, for the preservation of our Clubical Constitution. (3:144)

Unable to stomach this miserable servility, Loquacious Scribble bludgeons the club at their ninth anniversary with the lengthiest speech against luxury in the *History*. Lamenting the "great decline and falling away, of the wonted Glory and magnificence of this here Club," Scribble contends that

> Luxury has in a great measure got footing in this here ancient and honorable Club, Luxury, in the opinion of all wise men has been the bane and ruin of States and nations, and therefore must at last be the ruin of Clubs, where it has been admitted, are there not longstanding members here present who have seen ... an end to that virtuous and heroic frugality, that prevailed in [the club] at its first Institution, have they not seen Luxury, peeping from behind the Scene, and preparing for her pompous entry upon this Clubical Stage, have they not seen this bold actress, take one Great Stride at her first advance, and then proceed afterwards, with a *grand pas,* to expell Simplicity and plainness from the Club, and Introduce pomp, Show, and extravagance, her Constant pages and attendants, while [Ceremony], her Companion and Coactor, with the like buskined pride, ... has so disguised and Intoxicated the behaviour and manners, of the Longstanding members ... that they now seem not to be the same persons that they were at their first Institution.
>
> Happy, thrice happy, in those heroic times of Innocence & Simplicity, were the Longstanding members of this here ancient and honorable Club, for then, without molestation, ... they might rise up, go to the Side board, & after having taken their Sliver of Gammon or Slice of Cheese standing, Return again to their Compotation, Jocosity or Clubical Conversation, ... how like the Simple frugality of the Golden age was this, and how different from the present Luxury, and profuseness that prevails in most Clubs....
>
> In fine, ... I have presumed to lay all those matters before you, that you may have a Clear view of the present deplorable State of this here ancient and honorable Club, and the ruin that threatens it, if proper means are not used to prevent it, therefore, you will Remain without excuse if you do not ... reinstate the Club in its ancient Simple constitution.... (3:355–57, 364)

Scribble's excessive harangue spans thirteen manuscript pages and itself illustrates the effects of luxury upon the club even as he chastizes the club's members for their luxurious ways. As Hamilton's notes to the speech indicate, the loquacious secretary has previously delivered most of it at various other times. The club's members have heard it all before, and those who have endured the harangue without dozing off merely pass it off as Scribble's lament. Rather than heed his advice, they slip deeper and deeper into subjection, and rather than vent their frustration on the president, they spend much of their time conducting trials and prosecuting one another. From drunkenness, gluttony, ceremony, vanity, and affectation to ambition, pride, enervation, bribery, corruption, subjection, and finally self-persecution, the paths of luxury lead to depravity.

Through laughter Hamilton thus diffuses what was probably his generation's greatest fear—that society would be destroyed by the effects of luxury. The central incongruity between his baleful moralizing and the ludicrous incidents that provoke his moral commentary—and our awareness that he, too, recognizes that incongruity—makes *The History of the Tuesday Club* one of the most delightfully comic novels in eighteenth-century literature and one whose comic moral stance is precociously modern. As Ronald Paulson observes, "the early novel was created in an age when moral justification was still necessary and the description of everyday life for its own sake was considered frivolous."[40] Whereas Fielding's ironic tone helps to reinforce the serious moral strain in his works, Hamilton's ironic tone and facetious moralizing undercut the moral baggage that the novel had inherited and point toward laughter—indeed, laughter at a "medley of absurdity"—as the only sensible moral stance for modern men and women.

There is, to be sure, a core of serious truth behind his comments about the consequences of luxury. Hamilton was well aware of the extent to which luxury had crippled previous civili-

---

40. *Satire and the Novel in Eighteenth-Century England*, 18.

"The Sempiternal Comedy"

zations. But his comic perspective of human folly enabled him to see that reports of his own civilization's demise had been greatly exaggerated and to recognize that a "perfectly well governed" society, "exact in their morals, ... unblameable in their behavior, wise, just, innocent, simple and divested of Luxury and vice," never existed "but in the whimsical fancies" of romantic authors (2:476). Without shame, he and the other members of the Tuesday Club gladly welcomed whatever luxuries they could muster in provincial Maryland. For Hamilton and his club companions, the bane of society was not luxury but those "solitary, moaping, morose, humdrum fellows" (1:69) who stifled merriment and moaned about degeneracy, not only because they spoiled a good time but because they failed to see how necessary a little luxury was, especially in colonial America. As his ironic tone reassures his judicious readers throughout *The History of the Tuesday Club,* their world was not coming to an end because of the disastrous effects of luxury; it was just playing out another scene in the sempiternal comedy.

Epilogue

Hamilton died before completing the third volume of *The History of the Tuesday Club;* had he lived, he probably would have continued writing as long as the Tuesday Club gave him something to write about. There could well have been a fourth, maybe even a fifth volume, again left unfinished at his death. That will chagrin critics who expect a sense of closure from any literary work, but as Mikhail Bakhtin and Michael McKeon have both argued, the evolving sense of contemporary reality and the unending consumption of languages and genres is what the novel—and, in Hamilton's case, *a* novel—is all about. Novels are "more free and flexible" than other literary genres, Bakhtin asserts, because "their language renews itself by incorporating extraliterary heteroglossia.... They become dialogized, permeated with laughter, irony, humor, elements of self-parody,... [creating] an indeterminacy, a certain semantic openendedness, a living contact with unfinished, still evolving contemporary reality."[1] Or, as McKeon writes, the novel is a "newcomer that arrives upon a

---

1. *The Dialogic Imagination: Four Essays,* ed. Michael Holquist, trans. Caryl Emerson and Michael Holquist (Austin, Tex., 1981), 7.

scene already articulated into conventional generic categories and that proceeds to cannibalize and incorporate bits of other forms—the traditional and canonic genres as well as aberrant, 'nonliterary' writings."[2] Bakhtin and McKeon were hardly thinking of *The History of the Tuesday Club* when they wrote those passages, yet it illustrates their claims particularly well. It incorporates various literary and nonliterary languages and genres into one narrative, producing an internalization of dialogic discourse, a self-reflexive sense of play and self-parody, and an evolving sense of reality to a degree equalled by few other eighteenth-century novels.

Like Bakhtin, Morris Dickstein states that the novel "embodies the spirit of modernity that resists the closure of genre and recreates the open weave of life itself."[3] Hamilton's *History* is just that—an *open* weave. Various strands form patterns to the weave of *The History of the Tuesday Club,* but there is no formal closure to the weave. It grows by incorporating more strands, more languages, more genres, and by creating more patterns, but it is finally open-ended. As Eric Rothstein argues, eighteenth-century authors such as Sterne "depend upon the reader's mental mechanics to create transitions, pull narrative and thematic elements into episodes, and shape rhythms from repetition."[4] Hamilton depends upon the same sort of mental gymnastics from his readers. His comic world is a "medley of absurdity," but not an absurd world. Even the most absurd routines that the Tuesday Club enacts become part of the patterns in the weave; their absurd, ritualized

---

2. *The Origins of the English Novel,* 1600–1740, 11.
3. "Popular Fiction and Critical Values: The Novel as a Challenge to Literary History," *Reconstructing American Literary History,* ed. Sacvan Bercovitch (Cambridge, Mass., 1986), 45.
4. *Systems of Order and Inquiry in Later Eighteenth-Century Fiction* (Berkeley, 1975), 252.

Epilogue

behavior becomes part of a weave of sociability and laughter that makes sense of absurdity.

Given his temperament and the temper of the times, it was inevitable that Hamilton, like so many others of his generation, would turn to the novel. Donald Green put it best, I think, when he wrote that the eighteenth-century was above all an age of exuberance and experience, an age characterized by its "immense intellectual diversity" and an "apparently inexhaustible fund of sheer energy."[5] Hamilton typifies that exuberance, which found its most natural literary outlet in the novel. Despite his naggingly poor health, he possessed a social, intellectual, and literary energy that placed him at the center of his culture. In his daily life, an ethic of liberality and sociability led him to devote an enormous amount of energy to others through his work as a physician, his public service, and his serving as the guiding genius of colonial Maryland's foremost gentleman's club for over a decade. In his writing, he embraced all forms of the comic in numerous genres, particularly the expansive genres of the travel narrative and the novel, with their seemingly endless cast of characters, incidents, and ideas. In his life and literature, he represents the best of the spirit of his age.

---

5. *The Age of Exuberance: Backgrounds to Eighteenth-Century English Literature* (New York, 1970), 101, 92, v.

Bibliography

Primary Works

TRAVEL DIARY

"The Itinerarium of Dr. Alexander Hamilton," Huntington Library, MS 922.

PERIODICAL PIECES

(all in the *Maryland Gazette*)

An essay on the impertinent question, "What News?" signed "KLMN PQRST" (Jan. 7, 1746).

A cure for distempered authors, signed "Theophilus Polypharmacus" (Feb. 4, 1746).

A mock advertisement for a runaway wit, signed "Jehoiakim Jerkum" (Mar. 18, 1746).

An essay on curiosity, signed "O.O." (Jan. 27, 1747).

A dream vision on the contributors to the *Maryland Gazette,* signed "Don Francisco de Quevedo Villegas" (June 29, 1748).

A tale for melancholic authors, unsigned (Aug. 31, 1748).

A notice on odd orthography, signed "Philotypographus" (Apr. 12, 1749).

A parody of Masonic ceremonies, signed "Nic. Turntype" (Jan. 24, 1750).

TUESDAY CLUB PAPERS

Minutes of the Tuesday Club, vol. I (May 14, 1745, to Feb. 25 1755), John Work Garret Collections, Milton S. Eisenhower Library, Johns Hopkins University; vol. II (May 27, 1755, to Feb. 11, 1756), Library of Congress, Peter Force Collection, Series 8D, Item 170.

"Record of the Tuesday Club" (a revision of the minutes from May 14, 1745, to Apr. 22, 1755). Maryland Historical Society, MS 854.

"The History of the Ancient and Honorable Tuesday Club," vols. I-III, John Work Garrett Collections. (A portion of Hamilton's draft of the "History" is appended to vol. III; for the table of contents, dedication, and preface of the draft, see Maryland Historical Society, MSS 854 and 1265.)

LETTERS

Hamilton Letter Book. Maryland Historical Society, Dulany Papers, MS 1265. "Copie Letters to Baillie Hamilton Concerning the Battle in America," National Library of Scotland. Microfilm copy at Maryland Historical Society, MS 2018.

OTHER WORKS

Specimen medicum inaugurale, de morbis ossium ipsam substantiam afficientibus, ex causis internis oriundis. M.D. thesis, Edinburgh, 1737.

A Defence of Dr. Thomson's Discourse on the Preparation of the Body for the Small Pox, and the Manner of Receiving the Infection. Philadelphia, 1751.

"A Discourse Delivered from the Chair, in the Lodge-Room at *Annapolis*, by the Right Worshipful the Master, to the Brethren of the Ancient and Honourable Society of *Free and Accepted* Masons in *Maryland*." In John Gordon, *Brotherly Love Explained and Enforc'd* (Annapolis, 1750), 23–27.

Editions of Hamilton's Works

Breslaw, Elaine G., ed. *Records of the Tuesday Club of Annapolis, 1745–56.* Urbana and Chicago: Univ. of Illinois Press, 1988.

Bridenbaugh, Carl, ed. *Gentleman's Progress: The Itinerarium of Dr. Alexander Hamilton, 1744.* Chapel Hill: Univ. of North Carolina Press, 1948; repr. Westport, Conn.: Greenwood Press, 1973.

Hart, Albert Bushnell, ed. *Hamilton's Itinerarium: Being a Narrative of a Journey from Annapolis, Maryland, through Delaware, Pennsylvania, New York, New Jersey, Connecticut, Rhode Island, Massachusetts and New*

Hampshire, from May to September, 1744. St. Louis: William K. Bixby, 1907; repr. New York: Arno Press, 1971.

Micklus, Robert, ed. *The History of the Tuesday Club.* 3 vols. Chapel Hill: Univ. of North Carolina Press, 1990.

Publications on Hamilton and the Tuesday Club

Breslaw, Elaine G. "The Chronicle as Satire: Dr. Hamilton's 'History of the Tuesday Club.'" *Maryland Historical Magazine,* 70 (1975), 129–48.

———. "A Dismal Tragedy: Drs. Alexander and John Hamilton Comment on Braddock's Defeat." *Maryland Historical Magazine,* 75 (1980), 118–44.

———. "Dr. Alexander Hamilton and the Enlightenment in Maryland." Diss., Univ. of Maryland, 1973.

———. "The Tuesday Club of Annapolis." *Maryland Heritage News,* 1 (1983), 12–14.

———. "Wit, Whimsy, and Politics: The Uses of Satire by the Tuesday Club of Annapolis, 1744 to 1756." *William and Mary Quarterly,* 3rd Ser., 32 (1975), 295–306.

Freeman, Sarah Elizabeth. "The Tuesday Club Medal." *The Numismatist,* 58 (1945), 1313–22.

Hare, Robert R. "Electro Vitrifrico in Annapolis: Mr. Franklin Visits the Tuesday Club." *Maryland Historical Magazine,* 58 (1963), 62–66.

Lemay, J. A. Leo. "Dr. Alexander Hamilton: Wit." In *Men of Letters in Colonial Maryland.* Knoxville: Univ. of Tennessee Press, 1972, pp. 213–256.

———. "Hamilton's Literary History of the *Maryland Gazette.*" *William and Mary Quarterly,* 3rd Ser., 23 (1966), 273–85.

Micklus, Robert. "The Delightful Instruction of Dr. Alexander Hamilton's *Itinerarium.*" *American Literature,* 60 (1988), 359–84.

———. "Dr. Alexander Hamilton's 'Modest Proposal.'" *Early American Literature,* 16 (1981), 107–32.

———. "'The History of the Tuesday Club': A Mock-Jeremiad of the Colonial South." *William and Mary Quarterly,* 3rd Ser., 40 (1983), 42–61.

———. "The Secret Fall of Freemasonry in Dr. Alexander Hamilton's *The History of the Tuesday Club.*" In *Deism, Masonry, and the Enlight-*

enment: *Essays Honoring Alfred Owen Aldridge.* Ed. J. A. Leo Lemay. Newark: Univ. of Delaware Press, 1987, pp. 127–36.

Needler, Geoffrey D. "Linguistic Evidence from [Dr.] Alexander Hamilton's 'Itinerarium.'" *American Speech,* 42 (1967), 211–18.

Rutledge, Anna Wells. "A Humorous Artist in Colonial Maryland." *American Collector,* 16 (1947), 8–9, 14–15.

Talley, John Barry. *Secular Music in Colonial Annapolis: The Tuesday Club, 1745–56.* Urbana and Chicago: Univ. of Illinois Press, 1988.

Other Secondary Works Cited

Adams, Percy G. "Perception and the Eighteenth-Century Traveler." *The Eighteenth Century: Theory and Interpretation,* 26 (1985), 139–57.

———. *Travelers and Travel Liars, 1660–1800.* Berkeley: Univ. of California Press, 1962.

———. *Travel Literature and the Evolution of the Novel.* Lexington: Univ. Press of Kentucky, 1983.

Alter, Robert. *Fielding and the Nature of the Novel.* Cambridge: Harvard Univ. Press, 1968.

———. *Partial Magic: The Novel as a Self-Conscious Genre.* Berkeley: Univ. of California Press, 1975.

Arner, Robert D. "Literature in the Eighteenth-Century Colonial South." In *The History of Southern Literature.* Ed. Louis D. Rubin, Jr. Baton Rouge: Louisiana State Univ. Press, 1985, pp. 34–47.

Baker, Nancy T. "Annapolis, Maryland, 1695–1730." *Maryland Historical Magazine,* 81 (1986), 191–209.

Bakhtin, Mikhail M. *The Dialogic Imagination: Four Essays.* Ed. Michael Holquist; trans. Caryl Emerson and Michael Holquist. Austin: Univ. of Texas Press, 1981.

Barker, Charles Albro. *The Background of the Revolution in Maryland.* New Haven: Yale Univ. Press, 1940.

Batten, Charles L., Jr. *Pleasurable Instruction: Form and Convention in Eighteenth-Century Travel Literature.* Berkeley: Univ. of California Press, 1978.

Beasley, Jerry C. *Novels of the 1740s.* Athens: Univ. of Georgia Press, 1982.

Beirne, Rosamond Randall. "The Reverend Thomas Chase: Pugnacious Parson." *Maryland Historical Magazine,* 59 (1964), 1–14.

Bibliography

Bell, Whitefield J., Jr. "Medical Practice in Colonial America." *Bulletin of the History of Medicine*, 31 (1957), 442–53.

———. "A Portrait of the Colonial Physician." *Bulletin of the History of Medicine*, 44 (1970), 497–517.

Bercovitch, Sacvan. "America as Canon and Context: Literary History in a Time of Dissensus." *American Literature*, 58 (1986), 99–107.

———. "The Problem of Ideology in American Literary History." *Critical Inquiry*, 12 (1986), 631–53.

Beveridge, Craig. "Childhood and Society in Eighteenth-Century Scotland." In *New Perspectives on the Politics and Culture of Early Modern Scotland*. Ed. John Dwyer, Roger A. Mason, and Alexander Murdoch. Edinburgh: John Donald, 1980, pp. 265–90.

Brock, William R. and C. Helen Brock. *Scotus Americanus: A Survey of the Sources for Links between Scotland and America in the Eighteenth Century*. Edinburgh: Edinburgh Univ. Press, 1982.

Bryson, Gladys. *Man and Society: The Scottish Inquiry of the Eighteenth Century*. Princeton: Princeton Univ. Press, 1945.

Burleigh, J.H.S. *A Church History of Scotland*. London: Oxford Univ. Press, 1960.

Bushman, Richard L. "American High-Style and Vernacular Cultures." In *Colonial British America: Essays in the New History of the Early Modern Era*. Ed. Jack P. Greene and J. R. Pole. Baltimore: Johns Hopkins Univ. Press, 1984, pp. 345–83.

Butler, Jon. "Enthusiasm Described and Decried: The Great Awakening as Interpretative Fiction." *Journal of American History*, 69 (1982), 305–25.

Butt, John. *The Mid-Eighteenth Century*. Edited and completed by Geoffrey Carnall. Oxford: Clarendon Press, 1979.

Camic, Charles. *Experience and Enlightenment: Socialization for Cultural Change in Eighteenth-Century Scotland*. Chicago: Univ. of Chicago Press, 1983.

Carroll, Douglas Gordon, Jr. *Medicine in Maryland, 1634–1900*. Baltimore: Library of the Medical and Chirurgical Faculty of the State of Maryland, 1984.

Chitnis, Anand C. "Provost Drummond and the Origins of Edinburgh Medicine." In *The Origins and Nature of the Scottish Enlightenment*. Ed. R. H. Campbell and Andrew S. Skinner. Edinburgh: John Donald, 1982, pp. 86–97.

Clark, Michael. "The Subject of the Text in Early American Literature." *Early American Literature,* 20 (1985), 120–30.
Cohen, I. Bernard. *The Newtonian Revolution.* Cambridge: Cambridge Univ. Press, 1980.
Colacurcio, Michael J. "Does American Literature Have a History?" *Early American Literature,* 13 (1978), 110–32.
Colbourn, H. Trevor. *The Lamp of Experience: Whig History and the Intellectual Origins of the American Revolution.* Chapel Hill: Univ. of North Carolina Press, 1965.
Cox, Richard J. "Stephen Bordley, George Whitefield, and the Great Awakening in Maryland." *Historical Magazine of the Protestant Episcopal Church,* 46 (1977), 297–307.
Crowley, J. E. *This Sheba, Self: The Conceptualization of Economic Life in Eighteenth-Century America.* Baltimore: Johns Hopkins Univ. Press, 1974.
Damrosch, Leopold, Jr. *God's Plot and Man's Stories: Studies in the Fictional Imagination from Milton to Fielding.* Chicago: Univ. of Chicago Press, 1985.
Davie, George Elder. *The Democratic Intellect: Scotland and Her Universities in the Nineteenth Century.* Edinburgh: Edinburgh Univ. Press, 1961.
Davis, David Brion. *The Problem of Slavery in Western Culture.* Ithaca: Cornell Univ. Press, 1966.
Davis, Lennard J. *Factual Fictions: The Origins of the English Novel.* New York: Columbia Univ. Press, 1983.
Davis, Richard Beale. *Intellectual Life in the Colonial South, 1585–1763.* 3 vols. Knoxville: Univ. of Tennessee Press, 1978.
Deibert, William E. "Thomas Bacon, Maryland Clergyman." *Maryland Historical Magazine,* 73 (1978), 79–86.
Dickstein, Morris. "Popular Fiction and Critical Values: the Novel as a Challenge to Literary History." In *Reconstructing American Literary History.* Ed. Sacvan Bercovitch. Cambridge: Harvard Univ. Press, 1986, pp. 29–66.
Dinkin, Robert J. "Elections in Proprietary Maryland." *Maryland Historical Magazine,* 73 (1978), 129–36.
Donovan, A. L. *Philosophical Chemistry in the Scottish Enlightenment: The Doctrines and Discoveries of William Cullen and Joseph Black.* Edinburgh: Edinburgh Univ. Press, 1975.

Bibliography

Ehrenpreis, Irvin. "Personae." In *Restoration and Eighteenth-Century Literature: Essays in Honor of Alan Dugald McKillop*. Ed. Charles Carroll Camden. Chicago: Univ. of Chicago Press, 1963, pp. 25–37.

Elkin, P. K. *The Augustan Defence of Satire*. Oxford: Clarendon Press, 1973.

Elliott, Robert C. *The Literary Persona*. Chicago: Univ. of Chicago Press, 1982.

Fischer, David Hackett. "John Beale Bordley, Daniel Boorstin, and the American Enlightenment." *Journal of Southern History*, 28 (1962), 327–42.

Foucault, Michel. *The Birth of the Clinic: An Archaeology of Medical Perception*. New York: Pantheon Books, 1973.

Franklin, Wayne. *Discoverers, Explorers, Settlers: The Diligent Writers of Early America*. Chicago: Univ. of Chicago Press, 1979.

Frantz, R. W. *The English Traveller and the Movement of Ideas, 1660–1732*. 1934; rpt. Lincoln: Univ. of Nebraska Press, 1967.

Frye, Northrop. *The Anatomy of Criticism*. Princeton: Princeton Univ. Press, 1957.

Fussell, Paul, Jr. "Patrick Brydone: The Eighteenth-Century Traveler as Representative Man." In *Literature as a Mode of Travel: Five Essays and a Postscript*. Intro. Warner G. Rice. New York: New York Public Library, 1963, pp. 53–67.

Gambrill, Olive Moore. "John Beale Bordley and the Early Years of the Philadelphia Agricultural Society." *Pennsylvania Magazine of History and Biography*, 66 (1942), 410–39.

Gray, James. *History of the Royal Medical Society, 1737–1937*. Edinburgh: Edinburgh Univ. Press, 1952.

Greene, Donald. *The Age of Exuberance: Backgrounds to Eighteenth-Century English Literature*. New York: Random House, 1970.

Greene, Jack P. *The Quest for Power: The Lower Houses of Assembly in the Southern Royal Colonies, 1689–1776*. Chapel Hill: Univ. of North Carolina Press, 1963.

———. "Search for Identity: An Interpretation of the Meaning of Selected Patterns of Social Response in Eighteenth-Century America." *Journal of Social History*, 3 (1970), 189–220.

Guilhamet, Leon. *Satire and the Transformation of Genre*. Philadelphia: Univ. of Pennsylvania Press, 1987.

Gura, Philip F. "The Study of Colonial American Literature, 1966–1987: A Vade Mecum." *William and Mary Quarterly*, 3rd Ser., 45 (1988), 305–41.

Gurewitch, Morton. *Comedy: The Irrational Vision*. Ithaca: Cornell Univ. Press, 1975.
Hamilton, David. *The Healers: A History of Medicine in Scotland*. Edinburgh: Canongate, 1981.
Hartdagen, Gerald E. "The Anglican Vestry in Colonial Maryland: A Study in Corporate Responsibility." *Historical Magazine of the Protestant Episcopal Church*, 40 (1971), 315–35, 461–79.
———. "The Vestry as a Unit of Local Government in Colonial Maryland." *Maryland Historical Magazine*, 67 (1972), 363–88.
Hatfield, Glenn W. *Henry Fielding and the Language of Irony*. Chicago: Univ. of Chicago Press, 1968.
Heintze, James R. "Alexander Malcolm: Musician, Clergyman, and Schoolmaster." *Maryland Historical Magazine*, 73 (1978), 226–35.
Hindle, Brooke. *Pursuit of Science in Revolutionary America, 1735–1789*. Chapel Hill: Univ. of North Carolina Press, 1956.
Hoffman, Ronald. *A Spirit of Dissension: Economics, Politics, and the Revolution in Maryland*. Baltimore: Johns Hopkins Univ. Press, 1973.
Holmes, J. D. "Early Years of the Medical Society of Edinburgh." *University of Edinburgh Journal*, 5 (1968), 333–40.
Hook, Andrew. *Scotland and America: A Study of Cultural Relations, 1750–1835*. Glasgow and London: Blackie, 1975.
Hooker, Edward Niles. "Pope on Wit: The *Essay on Criticism*." In *Essential Articles for the Study of Alexander Pope*. Ed. Maynard Mack. Rev. ed.; Hamden Court: Archon Books, 1968, pp. 185–207.
Hunter, J. Paul. *Occasional Form: Henry Fielding and the Chains of Circumstance*. Baltimore: Johns Hopkins Univ. Press, 1975.
Isaac, Rhys. *The Transformation of Virginia, 1740–1790*. Chapel Hill: Univ. of North Carolina Press, 1982.
Jacob, Kathryn Allamong. "The Woman's Lot in Baltimore Town: 1729–97." *Maryland Historical Magazine*, 71 (1976), 283–95.
———. "The Women of Baltimore Town: A Social History, 1729–1797." M. A. Thesis, Georgetown Univ., 1975.
Jacob, Margaret. "Newtoniansim and the Origin of the Enlightenment." *Eighteenth-Century Studies*, 11 (1977), 1–25.
———. *The Radical Enlightenment: Pantheists, Freemasons and Republicans*. London and Boston: Allen and Unwin, 1981.

Bibliography

Johnson, E. A. J. *Predecessors of Adam Smith: The Growth of British Economic Thought.* New York: Prentice-Hall, 1937.

Kagle, Steven E. *American Diary Literature, 1620–1799.* Boston: G. K. Hall, 1979.

——— . "The Diary as Art: A New Assessment." *Genre,* 6 (1973), 416–27.

Kamei, Shunsuke. "Cultural Clubs in Colonial America, 1720–1750." *Studies in English Literature* (English Literary Society of Japan), English Number (1963), 37–70.

Kay, Donald. *Short Fiction in "The Spectator,"* University: Univ. of Alabama Press, 1975.

Kolodny, Annette. "The Integrity of Memory: Creating a New Literary History of the United States." *American Literature,* 57 (1985), 291–307.

Kropf, Carl R. "The Nationalistic Criticism of Early American Literature." *Early American Literature,* 18 (1983), 17–30.

Land, Aubrey C. *Colonial Maryland: A History.* Millwood, N.Y.: KTO Press, 1981.

——— . *The Dulanys of Maryland: A Biographical Study of Daniel Dulany, the Elder (1685–1753) and Daniel Dulany, the Younger (1722–1797).* 1955; rpt. Baltimore: Johns Hopkins Univ. Press, 1968.

Law, Alexander. *Education in Edinburgh in the Eighteenth Century.* London: Univ. of London Press, 1965.

Lindeboom, G. A. *Herman Boerhaave: The Man and His Work.* London: Methuen, 1968.

Lockwood, Thomas. "The Augustan Author-Audience Relationship: Satiric vs. Comic Forms." *English Literary History,* 36 (1969), 648–58.

Lovejoy, David S. *Religious Enthusiasm in the New World: Heresy to Revolution.* Cambridge: Harvard Univ. Press, 1985.

Lynch, James J. *Henry Fielding and the Heliodorian Novel: Romance, Epic, and Fielding's New Province of Writing.* Rutherford, N.J.: Fairleigh Dickinson Univ. Press, 1986.

May, Henry F. *The Enlightenment in America.* New York: Oxford Univ. Press, 1976.

McCoy, Drew R. *The Elusive Republic: Political Economy in Jeffersonian America.* Chapel Hill: Univ. of North Carolina Press, 1980.

McDougall, Warren. "Gavin Hamilton, Bookseller in Edinburgh." *British Journal for Eighteenth-Century Studies,* 1 (1978), 1–19.

———. "Gavin Hamilton, John Balfour and Patrick Neill: A Study of Publishing in Edinburgh in the Eighteenth Century." Diss., Edinburgh University, 1974.
McElroy, Davis Dunbar. *A Century of Scottish Clubs*. Edinburgh: Edinburgh Public Library, 1969.
———. "The Literary Clubs and Societies of Eighteenth-Century Scotland." Diss., Univ. of Edinburgh, 1952.
———. *Scotland's Age of Improvement: A Survey of Eighteenth-Century Literary Clubs and Societies*. Pullman: Washington State Univ. Press, 1969.
McFadden, George. *Discovering the Comic*. Princeton: Princeton Univ. Press, 1982.
McKeon, Michael. *The Origins of the English Novel, 1600–1740*. Baltimore: Johns Hopkins Univ. Press, 1987.
Menard, Russell R. "Population, Economy, and Society in Seventeenth-Century Maryland." *Maryland Historical Magazine*, 79 (1984), 71–92.
Merritt, Richard L. *Symbols of American Community, 1735–1775*. New Haven: Yale Univ. Press, 1966.
Micklus, Robert. "Colonial Humor: Beginning with the Butt." In *Critical Essays on American Humor*. Ed. William Bedford Clark and W. Craig Turner. Boston: G. K. Hall, 1984, pp. 139–54.
Miller, Henry Knight. *Henry Fielding's Tom Jones and the Romance Tradition*. Victoria, British Columbia: Univ. of Victoria, 1976.
Morais, Herbert M. *Deism in Eighteenth-Century America*. 1934; rpt. New York: Russell and Russell, 1960.
Nash, Gary B. *The Urban Crucible: Social Change, Political Consciousness, and the Origins of the American Revolution*. Cambridge: Harvard Univ. Press, 1979.
Olson, Elder. *The Theory of Comedy*. Bloomington: Indiana Univ. Press, 1968.
Park, William. "What Was New about the 'New Species of Writing'?" *Studies in the Novel*, 2 (1970), 112–30.
Parks, George B. "The Turn to the Romantic in the Travel Literature of the Eighteenth Century, *Modern Language Quarterly*, 25 (1964), 22–33.
Paulson, Ronald. *The Fictions of Satire*. Baltimore: Johns Hopkins Univ. Press, 1967.

Bibliography

———. *Satire and the Novel in Eighteenth-Century England.* New Haven: Yale Univ. Press, 1967.

Phillipson, Nicholas T. "Culture and Society in the 18th-Century Province: The Case of Edinburgh and the Scottish Enlightenment." In *The University in Society: Europe, Scotland, and the United States from the 16th to the 20th Century.* Ed. Lawrence Stone. Princeton: Princeton Univ. Press, 1974, pp. 407–48.

———. "The Scottish Enlightenment." In *The Enlightenment in National Context.* Ed. Roy Porter and Mikulas Teich. Cambridge: Cambridge Univ. Press, 1981, pp. 125–47.

Popkin, Richard H. "Divine Causality: Newton, the Newtonians, and Hume." In *Greene Centennial Studies: Essays Presented to Donald Greene in the Centennial Year of the University of Southern California.* Ed. Paul J. Korshin and Robert R. Allen. Charlottesville: Univ. Press of Virginia, 1984, pp. 40–56.

Rawson, Claude. *Order from Confusion Sprung: Studies in Eighteenth-Century Literature from Swift to Cowper.* London and Boston: Allen and Unwin, 1985.

Rawson, Elizabeth. *The Spartan Tradition in European Thought.* Oxford: Clarendon Press, 1969.

Reps, John W. *Tidewater Towns: City Planning in Colonial Virginia and Maryland.* Williamsburg, Va.: The Colonial Williamsburg Foundation, 1972.

Roger, Jacques. "The Living World." In *The Ferment of Knowledge: Studies in the Historiography of Eighteenth-Century Science.* Ed. G. S. Rousseau and Roy Porter. Cambridge: Cambridge Univ. Press, 1980, pp. 55–91.

Ross, Ellen. "Mandeville, Melon, and Voltaire: The Origins of the Luxury Controversy in France." *Studies on Voltaire and the Eighteenth Century,* 155 (1976), 1897–1912.

Rothstein, Eric. *Systems of Order and Inquiry in Later Eighteenth-Century Fiction.* Berkeley: Univ. of California Press, 1975.

Schaffer, Simon. "Natural Philosophy." In *The Ferment of Knowledge: Studies in the Historiography of Eighteenth-Century Science.* Ed. G. S. Rousseau and Roy Porter. Cambridge: Cambridge Univ. Press, 1980, pp. 55–91.

Scott, Anne Firor. *Making the Invisible Woman Visible*. Urbana: Univ. of Illinois Press, 1984.
Sekora, John. *Luxury: The Concept in Western Thought, Eden to Smollett*. Baltimore: Johns Hopkins Univ. Press, 1977.
Shields, David S. "Happiness in Society: The Development of an Eighteenth-Century American Poetic Ideal." *American Literature*, 55 (1983), 541–59.
Shryock, Richard Harrison. *Medicine and Society in America, 1660–1860*. New York: New York Univ. Press, 1960.
Simon, Richard Keller. *The Labyrinth of the Comic: Theory and Practice from Fielding to Freud*. Tallahassee: Florida State Univ. Press, 1985.
Skaggs, David Curtis. *Roots of Maryland Democracy, 1753–1776*. Westport, Conn.: Greenwood Press, 1973.
———. "Thomas Cradock and the Chesapeake Golden Age." *William and Mary Quarterly*, 3rd Ser., 30 (1973), 93–116.
Smith, Daniel Blake. *Inside the Great House: Planter Family Life in Eighteenth-Century Chesapeake Society*. Ithaca: Cornell Univ. Press, 1980.
Spengemann, William C. "American Literary History: Some Still Unanswered Questions." *Early American Literature*, 23 (1988), 90–100.
———. "American Things/Literary Things: The Problem of American Literary History." *American Literature*, 57 (1985), 456–81.
———. "American Writers and English Literature." *English Literary History*, 52 (1985), 209–38.
———. "Discovering the Literature of British America." *Early American Literature*, 18 (1983), 3–16.
———. "What Is American Literature?" *The Centennial Review*, 22 (1978), 119–38.
Spruill, Julia Cherry. *Women's Life and Work in the Southern Colonies*. 1938; rpt. New York: Russell and Russell, 1969.
Stafford, Barbara Maria. *Voyage into Substance: Art, Science, Nature, and the Illustrated Travel Account, 1760–1840*. Cambridge, Mass.: MIT Press, 1984.
Starin, Mary M. "The Reverend Doctor John Gordon, 1717–1790." *Maryland Historical Magazine*, 75 (1980), 167–91.
Sutherland, James. *English Satire*. 1958; rpt. Cambridge: Cambridge Univ. Press, 1967.

Bibliography

Tave, Stuart M. *The Amiable Humorist: A Study in the Comic Theory and Criticism of the Eighteenth and Early Nineteenth Centuries*. Chicago: Univ. of Chicago Press, 1960.

Torrance, Robert M. *The Comic Hero*. Cambridge: Harvard Univ. Press, 1978.

Trachtenberg, Alan. "The Writer as America." *Partisan Review*, 44 (1977), 466–75.

Trask, Kerry A. "Double Exposure: A Look at Southern Identity in the Eighteenth Century." *Southern Studies*, 22 (1983), 146–67.

Underwood, E. Ashworth. *Boerhaave's Men at Leyden and After*. Edinburgh: Edinburgh Univ. Press, 1977.

Vesey, Laurence. "The Autonomy of American History Reconsidered." *American Quarterly*, 31 (1979), 455–77.

Wade, Simeon Monroe, Jr. "The Idea of Luxury in Eighteenth-Century England." Diss., Harvard University, 1969.

Wheeler, Joseph Towne. "Reading and Other Recreations of Marylanders, 1700–1776." *Maryland Historical Magazine*, 38 (1943), 37–55, 167–80.

Wise, Gene. "'Paradigm Dramas' in American Studies." *American Quarterly*, 31, (1979), 293–337.

Wroth, Lawrence C. *A History of Printing in Colonial Maryland, 1686–1776*. Baltimore: Typothetae of Baltimore, 1922.

———. "A Maryland Merchant and His Friends in 1750." *Maryland Historical Magazine*, 6 (1911), 213–40.

Index

Addison, Joseph, 11n, 12, 13, 15, 16, 17, 113n, 122, 138, 160, 163–64, 165, 166, 173, 180
Annapolis: culture, 29; center of club life, 34; political climate, 37; Freemason's lodge, 62–63

Bacon, Rev. Thomas, 41–42, 49, 59, 63n
"Baltimore Bards," literary battle with "Annapolis Wits," 114–22
Blackmore, Richard, 165
Blacks, Hamilton's portrayal of, 98–99; *see also* Dromo
Blair, Hugh, 12
Blair, James, 181
Boerhaave, Hermann, 23, 27n, 68, 107
Bordley, John Beale (Quirpum Comic), 42, 43, 159, 171, 175, 192
Bordley, Stephen (Huffman Snap), 43, 48, 53–54
Braddock, Gen. Edward, 68–70
Brydone, Patrick, 77
Bullen, John (Bully Blunt, Sir John), 41, 43, 169, 171, 188

Burton, Robert, 162, 168
Butler, Samuel, 162

Callister, Henry, 31n
Carroll, Charles, 57
Carroll, James, 141
Chase, Rev. Thomas (Bard Bavius), 17, 115–22
Clubs and club life: in Scotland, 24; Whin-Bush Club (of Edinburgh), 25–27, 33; Easy Club (of Edinburgh), 27, 34; in Annapolis, 34–37; Red-House Club (of Annapolis), 36; Ugly Club (of Annapolis), 36–37
Cole, Charles (Nasifer Jole, President of Tuesday Club), 43, 47–48, 54, 55, 149, 159, 168–69, 174, 177, 185–88, 191–94
Colonial culture: and British culture, 5–6; crudeness of, 6, 100–1, 109–10; Hamilton's perception of, 6, 7, 29, 96–112; imitative, 7; emphasis on marriage, 54–56
Comic, the: and comedy, 8–9; and satire, 9–13; convergence of comic

Index

Comic, the: (*cont.*)
  forms in 18th century, 17–18; the "comic genius," 156–57; in *The History of the Tuesday Club,* 157–60; *see also* humor, laughter, ridicule, satire, wit
Congreve, William, 15
Cooper, Anthony Ashley, third Earl of Shaftesbury, 156
Cradock, Rev. Thomas (Mevius Pumpkin), 42, 46, 115, 120–21
Cumming, Thomas (Coney Pimp Frontinbrass), 194
Cumming, William, Sr. (Jealous Spyplot, Sr.), 41, 43, 48, 171, 174
Cumming, William, Jr. (Jealous Spyplot, Jr.), 43

Dennis, John, 12
Dorsey, Edward (Drawlum Quaint), 43, 149–50, 159
Dorsey, Richard (Tunbelly Bowzer), 43, 48
Douglass, Dr. William, 17, 107
Dromo (Hamilton's servant), 39, 94, 98
Drummond, George, 33, 108
Dryden, John, 163, 165, 166
Dulany, Daniel, 53, 61, 128
Dulany, Margaret, 53–54, 57
Dulany, Walter (Slyboots Pleasant), 43, 73n, 176–77

Easy Club, 27, 34
Empiricism, 18th-century attitudes toward, 21–22, 68, 79–80, 106–7, 145
"empiricks," Hamilton's disdain for, 22, 66–68, 106–7

Fielding, Henry, 16, 18, 75–76, 77, 142, 144, 147–49, 152, 157, 180, 196
Franklin, Benjamin (Electro Vitrifrice), 42, 130, 175
Freemasonry: in Annapolis, 62–63; Hamilton's discourse on, 63–65; Hamilton's parody of, 136–38

Golden age of Chesapeake culture, 7–8, 28
Gordon, Rev. John, 41, 63
Gordon, Robert, 41, 62
Green, Jonas (Jonathan Grog), 42, 43, 48, 72; club poet and wit, 49–52, 171, 173ff, 193; role as publisher of *Maryland Gazette,* 52, 113ff; Hamilton's literary guide, 125ff; satirized, 127–28

Halket, Peter, 68ff
Hamilton, Dr. Alexander (Loquacious Scribble)
—biography: birth, 19; parentage, 19–20; family, 19n; education, 20–24, 81–82; medical studies, 23–24; club life in Scotland, 24–27; emigration, 27–28; medical practice, 32; joins Ugly Club (of Annapolis), 36; poor health, 38–40; tour of northern colonies, 39–40; writes the *Itinerarium,* 40; contributes to *Maryland Gazette,* 52–53; participates in dispute with "Baltimore Bards," 114–20; helps to found Tuesday Club, 40; compiles records of Tuesday Club, 43–45; writes

The History of the Tuesday Club, 43–45; musical ability, 49; marries Margaret Dulany, 53; elected vestryman, 60; elected to Lower House, 61–62; freemason, 62–65; defends Thomson, 65–68; visits Braddock's army, 68; death, 70–73

—British sentiments, 1, 5–8; on colonial culture, 6–7, 96–112; early impressions of Maryland, 29–31; political views, 37–38, 61–62; religious views, 58–60, 108–9; comments on Braddock's defeat, 68–70; on nature, 85–86; on contributors to *Maryland Gazette*, 125–30; on poetry, 139–40; on critics, 153–56; on luxury, 196–97

—and Tuesday Club: founding member, 40; compiles records, 43–44; club orator, 49; club wit, 49–52

—prose style, 94, 113n

—writings: medical thesis, 23; minutes and "Record" of the Tuesday Club, 43, 141–42, 149, 161–62; discourse on freemasonry, 63–65; pamphlet on smallpox inoculation, 66–68; letter on Braddock's defeat, 68–70

—The *Itinerarium*, *75–112*: 6, 17; depiction of colonial culture, 6, 96–112; composition of, 40; plans for publication, 40n; "scientific gaze," 81–85; descriptions of landscape, 85–86; prose style, 94–95; colonial speech, 94–95, 98

—periodical pieces, *113–40*: literary nostrum to cure a *furor poeticus*, 116–17; mock advertisement to catch a runaway wit, 119–20; essays on curiosity and "What News?" 122–24; dream vision on contributors to *Maryland Gazette*, 124–31; tale for melancholic scribblers, 131–35; piece on odd orthography, 135; parody of Masonic ceremonies, 136–38

—*The History of the Tuesday Club*, *141–97*: imitative, 7; and the comic, 17–18, 156–60; composition of, 43–45; problems defining it, 142; narrative design, 142–43; rhetorical strategies, 142–43, 167–73; and the novel, 142–44, 199–200; and the anatomy, 143; and the "history," 144–50; narrative voice, 152–53, 161; collection of 18th-century wit, 162–78; and 18th-century dispute concerning luxury, 180–97

Hamiltons: Ann (sister), 19n; Gavin (brother), 19n, 30, 33, 38, 56, 69; Rev. Gilbert (brother), 19n, 27n; Janet (sister), 19n, 27n; Jean (sister), 19n; Dr. John (brother), 19n, 28, 68, 70–72, 116; Margaret (sister), 19n; Mary Robertson (mother), 19–20, 27n, 32, 33, 57n; Rev. Robert (brother), 19n, 21n;

Index

Hamiltons (*cont.*)
    Dr. Robert (cousin), 7n; William (father), 19–20; William (brother), 19n
Hawkesworth, John, 77–78, 90
History, and the novel, 144, 145–47
Humor, shift toward, 13–16

Imitation, 18th-century ideal, 7
Indians, Hamilton's portrayal of, 94, 99n
Inquisitiveness, attacked by Hamilton, 101–3, 122–24, 132, 138–39

Jennings, Thomas (Prim Timorous), 43, 192
Johnson, Samuel, 11n

Kearsley, Dr. John, 66, 68

Landscape, Hamilton's descriptions of, 85–86
Laughter, changing perception of, 13–15
Lewis, Richard, 5
Lloyd, Col. Edward (Col. Courtly Phraze), 149
Locke, John, 163–64, 165, 166, 177
Lomas, John (Laconic Comas), 41, 43, 150, 169, 176, 177
Lux, William, of Annapolis (Crinkum Crankum), 71, 175
Luxury: 18th-century controversy concerning, 180–84; its consequences in *The History of the Tuesday Club*, 184–96

Malcolm, Rev. Alexander (Philo Dogmaticus, Chancellor of Tuesday Club), 42, 43, 48, 49, 159, 171, 174, 177, 192
Mandeville, Bernard, 181
Marriage, emphasis on, 54–56
Marshe, Witham, 41, 53, 71
Maryland: culture, 28–29; politics, 37, 61; music, 49; religion, 59, 108; literature, 125–31
Maryland Gazette, 5; debate between "Native Marylander" and "Americano-Britannus," 5–6; essay on ridicule, 14; Hamilton's contributions, 113ff; essays on luxury, 182–83
Medicine: Scottish, 23–24; colonial, 32, 106; inoculation controversy, 66–67; *see also* "empiricks"
Monro, Dr. Alexander, 23
Morris, Corbyn, 11n
Music, in Annapolis, 49

Nationalism, in American studies, 1–2
Neilson, George, 34–36
Newton, Isaac, 21–23, 178
Novel, and romance, 144–45; and history, 145–47, 150, 199–200

Ogle, Samuel, 32

Quevedo Villegas, Don Francisco de, 125

Ramsay, Allan, 25, 26–27
Rapin, René, 12

Razolini, Onorio, 40
Red-House Club, 36
Richardson, Samuel, 145, 147
Ridicule, and satire, 9–12; proper objects of, 13–14; essay on, 14
Rogers, William, 41
Romanticism, in Hamilton, 85–86
Royal Medical Society of Edinburgh, 23–24

Satire, and comedy, 9–13; and ridicule, 9–12; "true" and "false," 16, 158; Hamilton's definition of, 17, 158–60
"Scientific gaze," and 18th-century perception, 81–85
Scott, Dr. Upton, 72
Scottish culture: educational ideal, 21; emphasis on sociability, 24; club life, 24–25; preoccupation with history, 26; religion, 58
Smith, Rev. David, 38, 60, 109, 140n
Sociability, ideal of, 13, 24, 33, 46, 78, 178
Southern studies, opportunities for research, 4–5; regionalism in, 7–8
St. John, Henry, Viscount Bolingbroke, 180
Steele, Richard, 16, 17, 122, 123, 138
Sterne, Laurence, 18, 142, 144, 173
Sterling, Rev. James, 5, 42, 129–30
Swift, Jonathan, 143, 162, 172, 173
Swift, Rev. Theophilus, 131ff

Thomson, Dr. Adam, 65–66, 129, 131ff
Thornton, William (Solo Neverout), 43, 47–48, 114–15, 159, 170–71
Tillotson, John, 11n
Travel literature: critical views of, 75–76; 18th-century views of, 76–78; criteria to evaluate it, 76n, 80, 84, 89–90, 94; reasons for its popularity, 78–80
Tuesday Club: founded, 40–41; membership, 41–43; its records, 43–44; proceedings of, 45–52; its laws, 47, 184–85; succumbs to luxury, 184–97

Ugly Club (of Annapolis), 36–37

Washington, George, 70
Whin-Bush Club, 25–27, 34, 61n
Whitaker, Benjamin, 181–82
Whitefield, Rev. George, 17, 93, 108–9, 115, 160
Wilkins, William (Spatterdash Wouldbe), 178
Wit, 18th-century debate concerning, 17, 163–64; Hamilton's definition of, 165–66; range of wit in *The History of the Tuesday Club*, 167–78
Women, in Maryland society, 54–57; Petticoat Club, 54–56; "Single Ladies of Annapolis," 55–56

v